A Guide to Interpreting NPScape Data and Analyses

Natural Resource Technical Report NPS/NRSS/NRTR—2012/578

William B. Monahan

National Park Service
Inventory and Monitoring Division
1201 Oakridge Drive, Suite 150
Fort Collins, Colorado 80525

John E. Gross

National Park Service
Inventory and Monitoring Division
1201 Oakridge Drive, Suite 150
Fort Collins, Colorado 80525

Leona K. Svancara

Idaho Department of Fish and Game and University of Idaho
121 Sweet Avenue, Suite 121
Moscow, Idaho 83844-4061

Tom Philippi

National Park Service
Inventory and Monitoring Division
c/o Cabrillo National Monument
1800 Cabrillo Memorial Drive
San Diego, California 92106

May 2012

U.S. Department of the Interior
National Park Service
Natural Resource Stewardship and Science
Fort Collins, Colorado

The National Park Service, Natural Resource Stewardship and Science office in Fort Collins, Colorado, publishes a range of reports that address natural resource topics of interest and applicability to a broad audience in the National Park Service and others in natural resource management, including scientists, conservation and environmental constituencies, and the public.

The Natural Resource Technical Report Series is used to disseminate results of scientific studies in the physical, biological, and social sciences for both the advancement of science and the achievement of the National Park Service mission. The series provides contributors with a forum for displaying comprehensive data that are often deleted from journals because of page limitations.

This report received formal peer review by subject-matter experts who were not directly involved in the collection, analysis, or reporting of the data, and whose background and expertise put them on par technically and scientifically with the authors of the information.

Views, statements, findings, conclusions, recommendations, and data in this report do not necessarily reflect views and policies of the National Park Service, U.S. Department of the Interior. Mention of trade names or commercial products does not constitute endorsement or recommendation for use by the U.S. Government.

This report is available from Your Network, region, division office and URL here, and the Natural Resource Publications Management Web site (http://www.nature.nps.gov/publications/nrpm/) on the Internet. This paragraph can be modified to meet your needs.

Please cite this publication as:

Monahan, W. B., J. E. Gross, L. K. Svancara, and T. Philippi. 2012. A guide to interpreting NPScape data and analyses. Natural Resource Technical Report NPS/NRSS/NRTR—2012/578. National Park Service, Fort Collins, Colorado.

NPS 909/114195, May 2012

Contents

Contents (continued)

Contents (continued)

Figures

Figures (continued)

Figures (continued)

Figures (continued)

Exhibits

Tables

Executive Summary

NPScape: Landscape Dynamics Monitoring of National Parks

NPScape is a NPS landscape dynamics monitoring project designed to help parks better understand the landscape-level opportunities and challenges they face in protecting park natural resources. To support these needs, NPScape produces and delivers landscape-level data, maps, analyses, and interpretations to inform natural resource management and planning at local, regional, and national scales.

Key NPScape objectives are to provide:

- A coherent conceptual and analytical framework for conducting landscape-scale analyses and evaluations that can inform decisions

- Useful Geographic Information System (GIS) data and maps at broad scales not typically available to individual parks

- Well-documented methods founded on strong science, and readily repeatable and extensible with local data

- Assistance to parks in interpreting results

The NPScape Interpretive Guide

This interpretive guide is intended to help NPS scientists and natural resource managers understand and evaluate landscape data and results from NPScape. In particular, the guide focuses on how the landscape-scale data and analyses provided by NPScape relate to past, current, and potential future conditions of park natural resources. Example questions that may be addressed using NPScape and are illustrated in this guide include:

- What types of human mediated landscape change are occurring around my park? How do these vary in intensity? How do they vary spatially in relation to park boundaries? What are the mechanisms by which human mediated drivers of landscape change might impact park resources?

- What are the major forms of land cover change occurring around my park, and how do these affect the amount, intactness, and connectivity of natural habitats? How much habitat loss is too much? What are some habitat thresholds that – when exceeded – lead to large ecological change?

- Who owns and manages lands around my park? To what extent do they manage their resources to meet the same goals and objectives? How much protected area around my park is sufficient for maintaining park natural resources?

- What are ecologically relevant areas of analysis? How does the selection of an appropriate analysis area vary according to the landscape-level question being asked? By extension, how should the spatiotemporal resolution of the source data affect my choice of analysis area?

Conceptual Ecological Foundation of NPScape

NPScape products are developed under a conceptual framework that links measurable attributes of landscapes to resources within parks. NPScape focuses on broad-scale factors and measures that are founded on consistent data available at a regional to national scale. Most NPScape data sources and products are best (or only) suited for analysis of areas that are hundreds to thousands of square kilometers. Information at these broad scales is increasingly needed to identify wildlife corridors, isolated habitats, and areas with important resources that may be at risk from projected land use changes around parks.

Consider by way of example a focal resource occurring inside a particular park. That resource is capable of persisting in part because of the ecological attributes of the larger natural system within which it exists. However, the value of the natural system with respect to the focal resource can be

> NPScape produces and delivers landscape-level data, maps, analyses, and interpretations to inform natural resource management and planning at local, regional, and national scales.

Broad categories of measures considered in this guide, and how they contribute to understanding the landscape context of parks and park resources.

Natural Systems
- Area of habitats
- Core areas
- Corridors
- Fragmentation

Human Footprint / Drivers
- Human population
- Housing
- Roads
- Impervious surface
- Hydrological impoundments

Status and value assessment

Threat assessment

Conservation Context
- Land ownership
- Land management
- Key patches

Vulnerability and opportunity

challenged by human-mediated drivers of landscape change. Precisely how these drivers interact with the natural system to impact the resource and, by extension, resource conservation vulnerability and opportunity, depends further on the stewardship of all management units within the natural system.

Together, these measures describe landscape condition at a range of scales of space and time. Historical information provides a context for change: how, and how fast, did we reach our present state or condition? Historical rates and magnitudes of change help determine the urgency of decisions, and they provide a social context important for understanding and relating to people who experienced these changes. Current information reflects status, and projections help identify trajectories in resource conditions or ecological drivers that are important for planning.

The historic, current, and future context provided by NPScape can help identify and evaluate opportunities to prevent resource damage or loss, assess actions for restoration, and identify key areas or threats to park resources. The relationships between park natural resources, nearby protected areas, and connecting corridors can determine opportunities for preserving resources.

NPScape Metrics for Landscape-scale Monitoring

NPScape products focus on a set of information-rich, landscape-scale measures and metrics that represent 'vital sign' indicators. Analyses summarize and deliver measures in six major categories (population, housing, roads, land cover, pattern, and conservation status) that broadly address the environmental drivers, natural attributes, and conservation context of NPS units.

Ecologically Informative Areas of Analysis

Landscape attributes important to park resources often vary with scale or spatial extent. Relevant scales or areas of analysis (AOAs) include the landscape within the park itself, the 'boundary' area immediately adjacent to the park (e.g., 1-3 km), the local area surrounding a park (e.g., within approximately 15-40 km of the park), watersheds upstream from the park, and the ecoregion. All of these AOAs are relevant for at least certain measures and metrics analyzed by NPScape. The park examples included in the guide provide basic guidance on when and how to select a particular AOA from this list. NPScape also provides standardized GIS data for all AOAs referenced above in an effort to streamline analysis and statistical reporting of NPScape metrics. In addition, NPScape enables users to consider other AOAs that may be more relevant to a

NPScape measures, metrics, and key data attributes (years of coverage, spatial resolution and park coverage by geographic area). Where possible, metrics and related GIS data are provided for Canada and Mexico for the benefit of parks located near these international boundaries.

Measure	Metric	Years	Resolution	Geographic coverage					
				Alaska	Lower 48	Pacific	Caribbean	Mexico	Canada
Population	Current: total and density	1990, 2000, 2010	Census block group	X	X	X	X		
	Historic: total and density	1790-1990, by decade	County		X				
	Projected: total and desnity	2010-2050, by decade	County	X	X				
Housing	Housing density	1970-2100, by decade	100 m cells		X				
Roads	Road density	varies, up to 2005	km/km²	X	X	X	X		X
	Distance from roads	varies, up to 2005	30 m cells	X	X	X	X		X
	Roadless area	varies, up to 2005	varies, down to 30 m	X	X	X	X		
Land cover	Natural vs. converted	varies, 1992-2006	30 or 250 m cells	X	X	X		X	X
	Anderson Level I & II	varies, 1992-2006	30 or 250 m cells	X	X	X		X	X
	Impervious surface	2001, 2006	30 m cells		X	X			
Pattern	Patch size	2001, 2005, 2006	30 or 250 m cells	X	X			X	X
	Morphology	2001, 2005, 2006	30 or 250 m cells	X	X			X	X
	Area density	2001, 2005, 2006	30 or 250 m cells	X	X			X	X
Conservation status	Area protected	varies	varies	X	X	X	X	X	X
	Ownership	varies	varies	X	X	X	X	X	X

particular park or question, such as AOAs established by 'protected area centered ecosystems', or PACEs, developed originally as part of the NASA-funded project, Park Analysis for Landscape Monitoring Support (PALMS). Parks may also wish to consider NPScape statistics within a local park planning region, or within the distributions of particular resources. In all such cases, NPScape users can recompute metrics on these AOAs using our well-documented, standardized and repeatable methods.

Land Cover and Land Use: Area and Pattern
In the US, habitat loss and fragmentation have profoundly affected biodiversity and other resources important to parks. Measures of habitat availability and pattern ad-

dress these key threats and they can indicate the suitability of landscapes to support species or sustain populations. Many parks are too small, by themselves, to permanently sustain all species that once lived there, particularly in the face of broad-scale environmental change. In these cases, species living in protected areas need adequate expanses of habitat outside parks to persist long into the future.

Related to area, patterns in land cover composition, configuration, and connectivity reflect the dynamics of natural ecological processes, biophysical constraints, and extensive modification resulting from a long history of human occupation and habitat alteration. In turn, these land cover patterns help shape overall patterns in biological

Natural vs. converted land cover around Cowpens National Battlefield and Ninety Six National Historic Site (left map), with corresponding estimates of forest area density (right map).

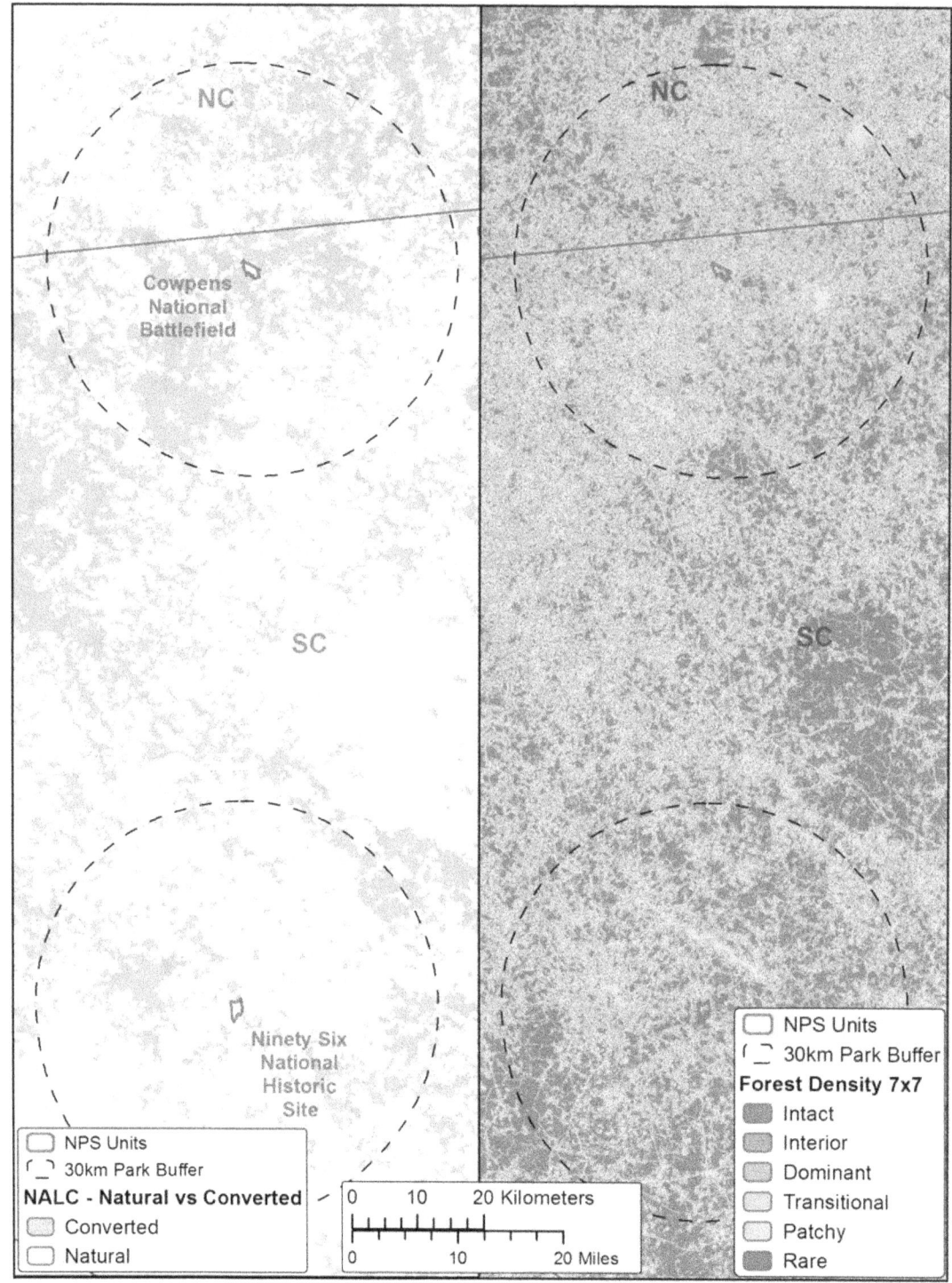

NC

Cowpens National Battlefield

SC

Ninety Six National Historic Site

NPS Units
30km Park Buffer
NALC - Natural vs Converted
Converted
Natural

0   10   20 Kilometers
0   10   20 Miles

NPS Units
30km Park Buffer
Forest Density 7x7
Intact
Interior
Dominant
Transitional
Patchy
Rare

diversity, including the complex array of species occurring in an area, movements of individual organisms, and flows of energy and material. All landscapes are more or less heterogeneous due to variation in topography, geology, and soils; natural disturbances like fire, windthrow, and floods; and anthropogenic disturbances like forest clearing, construction, or agriculture. The major difference between natural and anthropogenic disturbances is that habitats lost to natural disturbances usually 'recover', while anthropogenic disturbances usually result in permanent or semi-permanent conversion of habitat to non-habitat types.

The importance of habitat area and pattern are thus readily apparent for parks, but it is nonetheless difficult to identify a small suite of metrics that adequately describe area and pattern characteristics in ways that generally inform decisions on how to manage park resources. Most or all of the NPScape land cover and pattern data and analyses can be used to assess important attributes of plant and animal habitat. These attributes include indices of availability, connectivity, patch sizes and structure, and multi-scale context. NPScape land cover and pattern metrics are calculated using readily available land cover data from the National Land Cover Database, the North American Land Change Monitoring System, and the NOAA Coastal Change Analysis Program.

Effects of Roads on Natural Resources

Roads provide remarkable access to lands within the continental US, including access to most national parks. While easy access is often deemed a good thing, roads and associated activities can negatively impact a broad range of physical, ecological, and social attributes important to parks. By physically altering the landscape, roads result in the direct loss of habitat, fragmentation of the remaining habitat, altered landscape structure, increased influence of edge effects, and disruption of hydrological processes. Indeed, some have asserted that roads may be the single most destructive element in the process of habitat fragmentation.

Two major distinctions are useful for understanding landscape-level effects of roads on natural resources. The first distinction is between the effects of roads per se that are independent of traffic level, and the effects of road traffic, with strengths dependent on traffic density. Some road effects such as habitat fragmentation, disturbed or open margins for predatory or invasive species, and increased intensity and unpredictability of runoff, vary with road size and construction, but are relatively independent of the traffic volume. Conversely, the magnitudes of effects such as vehicle collision mortality, dust, hydrocarbon and metal runoff, sound, and propagule pressure of invasive species increase relative to traffic volume. This distinction can be blurred by road effects that

are sensitive to very low volumes of traffic, and many resources are impacted by both roads and traffic.

The second major distinction is between direct and indirect effects of roads and traffic. Mortality from vehicle collision is perhaps the most obvious direct effect, but non-lethal direct effects include road avoidance, which may be traffic dependent or independent, and traffic noise masking communication, which is generally traffic dependent. Roads have positive direct effects on some species, notably by creating disturbed habitat for some plants and increasing resource concentration for scavengers. Few direct effects of roads extend beyond 1 km, so roads primarily in or adjacent to parks have direct effects on park resources, but roads near a park can also exert important indirect effects. Indirect effects of roads include road avoidance or mortality modifying home ranges and migrations, limiting access to resources, and leading to subdivided or isolated subpopulations with limited gene flow.

NPScape road metrics are derived from readily available spatial road maps and include road density, distance from roads and – by extension – roadless area. Road density (km/km^2), traffic-weighted road density, and distance from nearest road are perhaps the most common and intuitive road metrics. Distance from road, measured by NPScape as the Euclidean distance (m) between any pixel on the landscape and the nearest road, is useful for considerations of 'road zones' and patch size distributions of roadless area. Together, these metrics provided by NPScape can be used to explore a number of important questions related to the direct vs. indirect effects of roads, as well as the effects of roads vs. traffic.

Human Population and Housing around on Parks

Anthropogenic impacts on park resources may originate directly from the behaviors of humans, or indirectly from the roads, houses, landscaping, and other infrastructure used to support humans. Although the extent of impact is often difficult to measure, data on human population size, density, and

NPScape estimates of distance from road (top map) and corresponding patch size distributions of roadless area, > 500 m from all roads (bottom map), for Crater Lake National Park. In the bottom map, white areas are less than 500 m from a road.

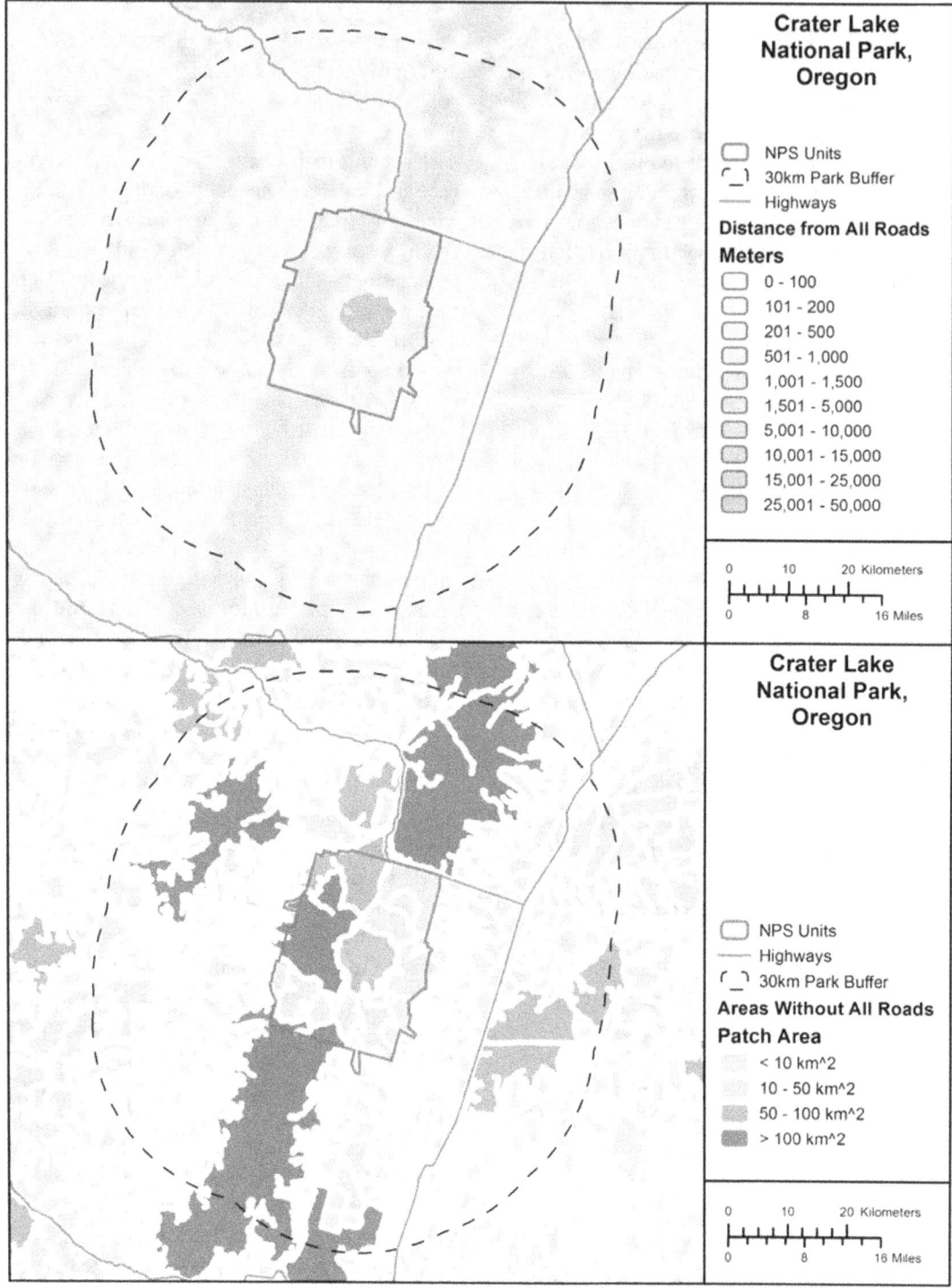

Crater Lake National Park, Oregon

NPS Units
30km Park Buffer
Highways

Distance from All Roads
Meters
0 - 100
101 - 200
201 - 500
501 - 1,000
1,001 - 1,500
1,501 - 5,000
5,001 - 10,000
10,001 - 15,000
15,001 - 25,000
25,001 - 50,000

0   10   20 Kilometers
0   8   16 Miles

Crater Lake National Park, Oregon

NPS Units
Highways
30km Park Buffer

Areas Without All Roads
Patch Area
< 10 km^2
10 - 50 km^2
50 - 100 km^2
> 100 km^2

0   10   20 Kilometers
0   8   16 Miles

infrastructure usually provide relevant and timely information about the magnitude of human impacts in lands adjacent to parks. Because human land uses tend to expand over time, and growth models are available to make projections into the future, these data also provide insights into potential near-term threats to park resources.

High human population density can adversely affect the persistence of habitats and species. In addition, human settlements as measured by housing density can alter ecosystems and affect biodiversity by replacing habitat with structures and non-habitat cover types, fragmenting habitat, increasing disturbance by people and their animals (e.g., dogs, cats, horses), altering vegetation types, and increasing light and noise.

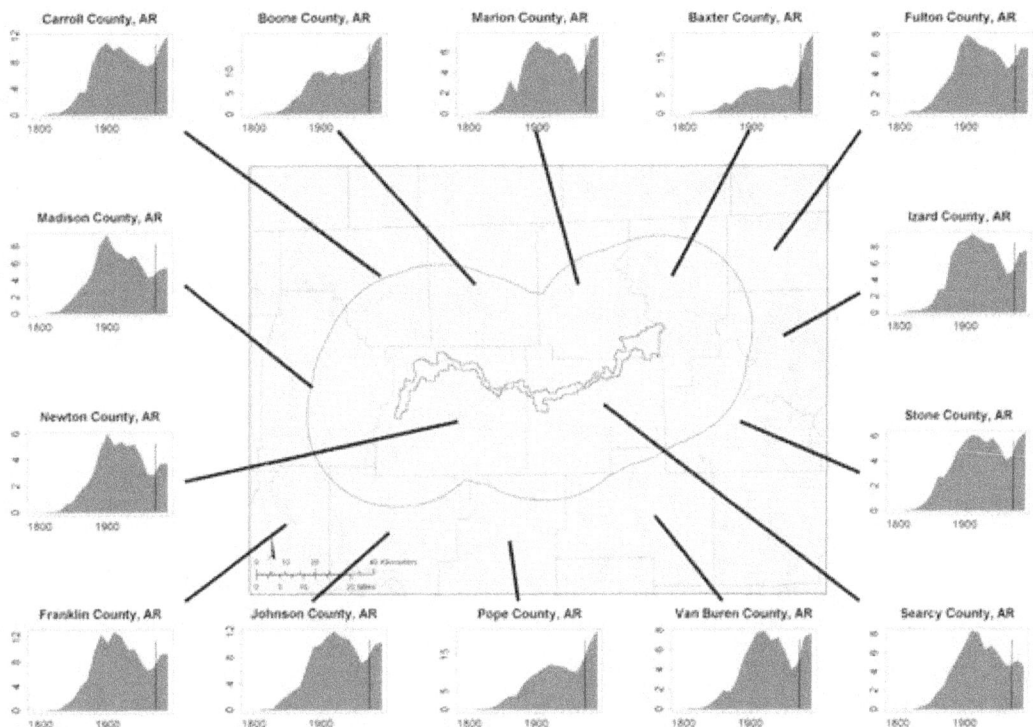

Historic and contemporary changes in human population density by county for counties intersecting the 30 km AOA of Buffalo National River. In time series plots around the map, population density on the y-axis is reported as the number of people per km². Vertical line is 1972, the year Buffalo was established as a park unit.

Population exerts important indirect effects on water quality via housing density, roads, and traffic. By doubling as major sources of anthropogenic impervious surface, such development also affects water quantity (flow and retention) when it is located in park upstream watersheds.

NPScape population metrics are based on historical data from the US Census Bureau and projections from state offices. Derived also in part from Census data, the Spatially Explicit Regional Growth Model provides corresponding estimates of how housing densities have changed over a similar timespan. Combined, the human population and housing metrics furnished by NPScape provide parks with decadal estimates of two major anthropogenic drivers of landscape change occurring around their boundaries.

Evaluating Resource Protection and Risk

The traditional response to preserving biodiversity has been the creation or expansion of protected areas. Yet the conservation status or stewardship of land surrounding these protected areas often dictates and directs potential changes in land use that can have profound impacts on park resources. Impacts – positive or negative – can be categorized by changes in the effective size of reserves, in ecological flows, in the size of critical habitat, and in the amount of exposure to humans. Within each category, the mechanisms that drive these changes include such factors as species area effects, trophic structure, migration habitats outside parks, and hunting and poaching. A common feature of these drivers is that they are known, or at least strongly postulated, to be directly related to land use intensification.

Knowing the condition and changes of land stewardship and resulting land use near and adjacent to parks is important for assessing current threats and impacts and for evaluating how the situation around parks might change in the future. For example, broad-scale patterns of habitat conversion (e.g., to urban or agriculture) and protection (stewardship) are used to estimate conservation risk and help identify areas at greatest risk. Combined with patterns of potential threats (e.g., roads, development), assessments of the level of resource protection have also helped identify areas at risk and refine conservation strategies on a statewide basis.

Although protected areas occur in nearly every country across the globe, they are by no means equal. Even within the United States,

Conservation status of lands surrounding Sequoia and Kings Canyon National Parks (top) and Pipestone National Monument (bottom) as identified by the Protected Areas Database of the United States, version 1.2. NPScape metrics of conservation status identify all GAP status 1 and 2 lands as 'protected'.

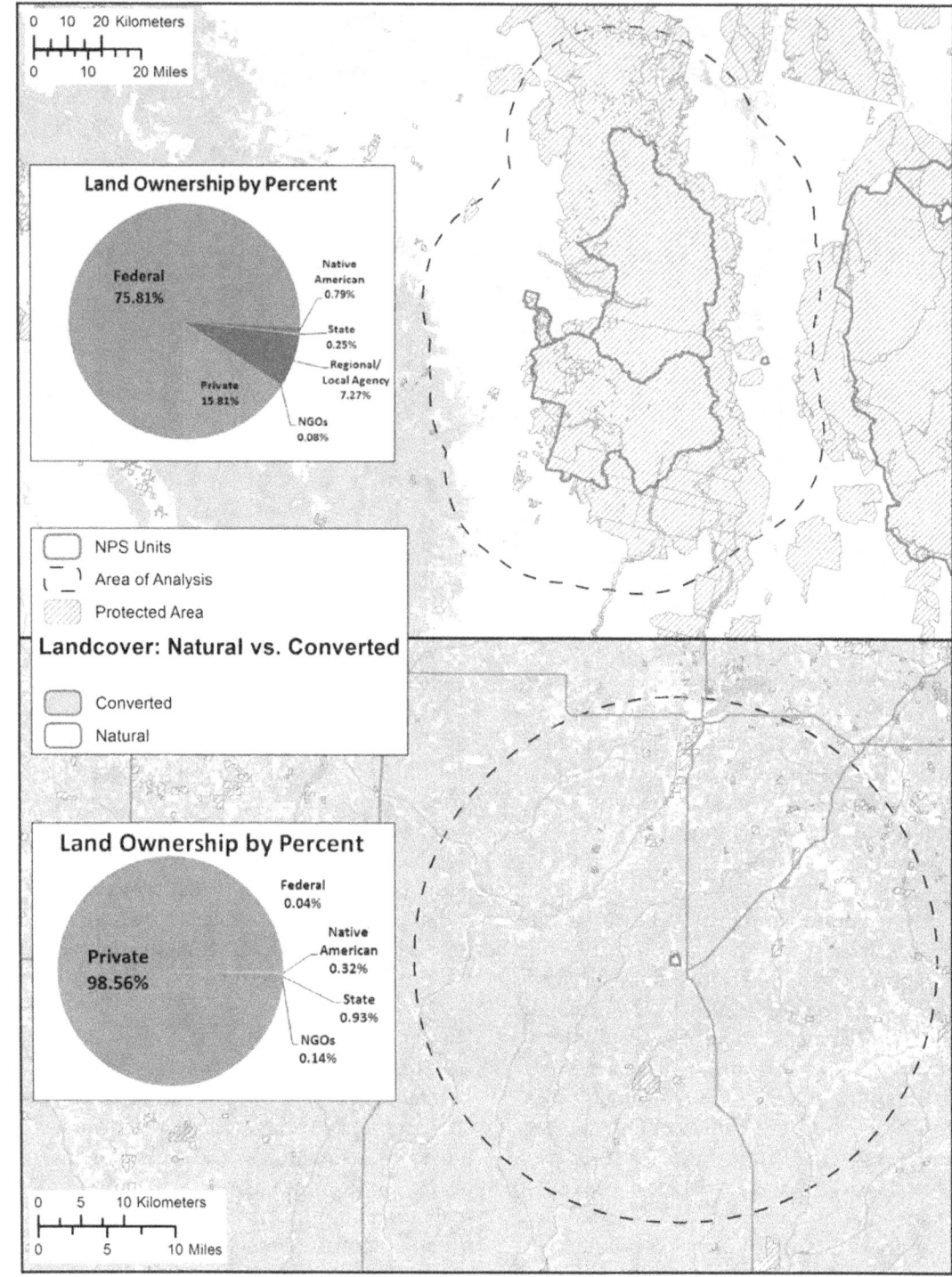

protected areas are managed by many different entities for a wide variety of purposes. Defining what is, or is not, a protected area is no trivial task. For nearly 80 years, the International Union for Conservation of Nature (IUCN) and the World Commission of Protected Areas have discussed, defined, and revised such definitions. In the latest revision by the IUCN, a protected area is defined as, "A clearly defined geographical space, recognized, dedicated and managed, through legal or other effective means, to achieve the long-term conservation of nature with associated ecosystem services and cultural values." The IUCN further categorizes protected areas based on management intent and many countries, including the United States, have similar programs (e.g., US Gap Analysis Program) to further refine and define what is protected.

NPScape metrics used for measuring and monitoring conservation status are derived from the currently available land ownership and management maps, including the Protected Areas Database of the US, the World Database on Protected Areas, and the National Marine Protected Areas database. The first of these metrics, the percentage of land area protected, provides an indication of conservation status by offering insight into potential threats (e.g., how much land is available for conversion and where it is located in relation to the park boundary) as well as opportunities (e.g., connectivity and networking of protected areas) for conserving park resources. Land ownership or stewardship is the second metric, which – by informing parks of who manages other protected areas around them – also provides useful insight into whether and how resources may be effectively co-managed across boundaries of different management units.

Bibliography of Scientific Papers Foundational to Landscape Ecology

In each chapter, we describe the ecological relevance of NPScape metrics based on the scientific literature. This literature is foundational to helping parks understand how the landscape-level data and results originating from NPScape may be used to evaluate the influence of broad-scale dynamics on park resources. The Interpretive Guide concludes with an extensive bibliography of in-text citations, which we encourage readers to consult as they pursue more in-depth analysis and interpretation.

Acknowledgments

This guide for interpreting NPScape products was made possible thanks to the combined effort of the entire NPScape team. While the authors are responsible for the text, the underlying data, analyses, and maps used as illustrations and examples reflect the contributions of many others. Peter Budde, Lisa Nelson, Brent Frakes, Mike Story, Mara Kali, Dave Hollema, Kirk Sherrill, Ursula Glick, Sean Worthington, Bill Hovanec, Nick Viau, Thomas Flowe, and Molly Thomas applied their considerable expertise and skills to the project, and they transformed sometimes unruly source data into the landscape products reflected in this report. In addition to helping compile source data and metadata, they processed enormous quantities of data to derive our landscape metrics, helped design analyses and procedures, produced maps for visualization by broad audiences, and handled data management and product flows. Mike Story, Thom Curdts, Sean Worthington, and Shepard McAninch focused their considerable expertise and skills on land cover data and led efforts to acquire, evaluate, and process NPScape land cover products. Thom Curdts helped us obtain and interpret new source data on marine protected areas from the National Marine Protected Area Center. Shepard McAninch played a major role in the I&M review of park units in the Protected Areas Database of the US (PAD-US), the results of which were incorporated into a recent PAD-US version 1.2 release. Allison Lundeby, Shyla Myrick, and Sara McLaughlin were a great help in the production of this report, and general conduct of the project. The entire team participated in identifying and developing NPScape metrics, as well as the many other NPScape products that include geospatial data, metadata, Standard Operating Procedures, ArcGIS scripts and toolboxes, and analyses that have formed the basis for resource briefs and other reports.

We also acknowledge the extensive advice, data, and support we have received from external collaborators. In particular, Dave Theobald (Colorado State University) generously contributed housing density data, and he has regularly provided feedback and advice on a number of our products. Kurt Riitters (US Forest Service) generously contributed data on land cover pattern, and his willingness to share processing tips and his deep understanding of landscape ecology has greatly facilitated our efforts. Pat Comer (NatureServe) shared pre-release maps and nation-wide data on ecosystem types, and his early advice contributed to the development of our conceptual model for NPScape. Collin Homer (USGS EROS Data Center) provided his insight into the process of developing and using land cover data from the National Land Cover Database and the Commission for Environmental Cooperation North American Land Change Monitoring System. Nate Herold (NOAA Coastal Services Center) provided his insight into the process of developing and using the Coastal Change Analysis Program land cover data. Lisa Duarte (National Gap Analysis Program, University of Idaho) worked with us to incorporate corrections to NPS attribute data identified as part of our I&M review of the protected areas database, PAD-US.

Last but not least, we thank the reviewers who helped us improve earlier versions of this report, listed in alphabetical order: Jeff Albright (NPS Water Resources Division), Jocelyn Aycrigg (National Gap Analysis Program, University of Idaho), Rob Daley (Greater Yellowstone Network), Lisa Duarte (National Gap Analysis Program, University of Idaho), Karen Folger (Sequoia and Kings Canyon National Parks), Lorin Groshong (NPS I&M Klamath Network), Andy Hansen (Montana State University), Mark Huff (NPS I&M North Coast and Cascades Network), Kevin James (NPS I&M Heartland Network), John Kupfer (University of South Carolina), Ben McMillan (NPS I&M Pacific Islands Network), Sean Mohren (NPS I&M Klamath Network), Laura O'gan (NPS I&M Rocky Mountain Network), and Kurt Riitters (US Forest Service).

List of Abbreviations

Abbreviation	Description
AOA	Area of Analysis
BLM	Bureau of Land Management
CCAP	NOAA Coastal Change Analysis Program
CEC	Commission for Environmental Cooperation
CRI	Conservation Risk Index
DOI	US Department of Interior
FRAGSTATS	Fragmentation Statistics, or Spatial Pattern Analysis Program for Categorical Maps
GAO	Government Accountability Office
GAP	Gap Analysis Program
GIS	Geographic Information System
GUIDOS	Graphical User Interface for the Description of image Objects and their Shapes
GYE	Greater Yellowstone Ecosystem
Hab	Habitat
HUC	Hydrologic Unit Code
I&M	Inventory and Monitoring
IBI	Index of Biological Integrity
IRMA	Integrated Resource Management Applications
IUCN	International Union for Conservation of Nature
KML	Keyhole Markup Language
LCC	Landscape Conservation Cooperative
MAUP	Modifiable Areal Unit Problem
MODIS	Moderate-resolution Imaging Spectroradiometer
Mort	Mortality
MPA	Marine Protected Area
MSPA	Morphological Spatial Pattern Analysis
NALC	North American Land Change Monitoring System
NALCMS	North American Land Change Monitoring System
NASA	National Aeronautics and Space Administration
NHS	National Historic Site
NID	National Inventory of Dams
NLCD	National Land Cover Data (or Database, Dataset)
NOAA	National Oceanic and Atmospheric Administration
NPS	National Park Service
NR	National River
PACE	Protected Area Centered Ecosystem
PAD-US	Protected Areas Database of the United States
PALMS	Park Analysis for Landscape Monitoring Support
PDF	Portable Document Format
Pred	Predation
SERGoM	Spatially Explicit Regional Growth Model
SOP	Standard Operating Procedure
UNEP	United Nations Environment Programme
UNSD	United Nations Statistics Division
US	United States

List of Abbreviations (Continued)

Abbreviation	Description
USFS	United States Forest Service
USFWS	United States Fish & Wildlife Service
USGS	United States Geological Survey
WCED	World Commission on Environment and Development
WCPA	World Commission of Protected Areas
WDPA	World Database on Protected Areas

1. Conceptual Foundation and Overview of NPScape

Many park managers have acknowledged that key, defining resources inside parks are being damaged by activities outside park boundaries (US General Accounting Office 1994). Despite the best possible resource management practices being implemented within parks, external anthropogenic landscape stressors originating from such sources as population, housing, and roads have increased around most parks over time (Davis & Hansen 2011), and projections suggest that these stressors will in many instances continue to increase for the foreseeable future (Radeloff et al. 2010). Such trends emphasize the need for the type of landscape information provided by NPScape: a National Park Service (NPS) Inventory and Monitoring (I&M) project that produces and delivers to parks a suite of landscape-scale data, methods, maps, analyses, and guidance to inform natural resource management, planning, and interpretation at local, regional, and national scales. To plan and implement actions that preserve park resources "unimpaired for the enjoyment of future generations" (NPS Organic Act of 1916), we must identify important landscape-scale resources, assess levels of protection and risk, and determine appropriate management actions (National Academy of Public Administration 2010; National Park Service 2011).

The overall goal of NPScape is to support park natural resource management, planning, and interpretation by providing relevant landscape-scale information to park units with significant natural resources (National Park Service 1999).

Key NPScape objectives are to provide:

- A coherent conceptual and analytical framework for conducting landscape-scale analyses and evaluations that can inform park-level decisions.

- Credible and well documented methods, founded on strong science, and readily repeatable and extensible with local data.

- Informative and useful data and derived products at broad spatial extents not typically available at the park level.

- Assistance in interpreting results, including an introduction to relevant literature and illustrative examples (this guide).

This report serves as an interpretive guide for understanding and evaluating landscape data and results from NPScape. In particular, the guide focuses on how landscape-scale dynamics evaluated by NPScape relate to past, current, and potential future conditions of park natural resources. Example questions that may be addressed using NPScape and are illustrated in this guide include:

- What types of human mediated landscape change are occurring around my park? How do these vary in intensity? How do they vary spatially in relation to park boundaries? What are the mechanisms by which human mediated drivers of landscape change might impact park resources?

- What are the major forms of land cover change occurring around my park, and how do these affect the amount, intactness, and connectivity of natural habitats? How much habitat loss is too much? What are some habitat thresholds that – when exceeded – lead to large ecological change?

- Who owns and manages lands around my park? To what extent do they manage their resources to meet the same goals and objectives? How much protected area around my park is sufficient for maintaining park natural resources?

- What are ecologically relevant areas of analysis? How does the selection of an appropriate analysis area vary according to landscape metric? By extension, how should the spatiotemporal resolution of the source data affect my choice of analysis area?

These and related questions are addressed below in the introductory chapter, and in subsequent chapters that focus on specific landscape metrics (Chapter 2: land cover and landscape pattern; Chapter 3: roads; Chapter 4: human population and housing; Chapter 5: conservation status). We include a series of park examples in an effort link the questions to topics and issues important to park scientists, managers, planners, and interpreters. However, because parks are part of a larger protected areas network, comprised of management units facing similar landscape-scale challenges and opportunities for achieving conservation, the examples are also applicable to areas managed by other agencies. In this context, NPScape has shared its data, methods, maps, and analyses with partner agencies that are also engaged in landscape-scale conservation, including USFWS (I&M Program), BLM (Rapid Ecological Assessments), and DOI Landscape Conservation Cooperatives. What makes NPScape unique compared to these other landscape-scale efforts is the fact that it (1) is heavily geared towards standardized and repeatable landscape-scale monitoring for all geographies with NPS units, which allows us to analyze and evaluate park landscapes at many spatiotemportal scales; and, (2) produces a diverse set of landscape-scale products, broadly encompassing data, methods, maps, analyses, and interpretations (e.g., this report), that are foundational to any landscape-level assessment or planning effort.

NPScape products are developed under a conceptual framework that links measurable attributes of landscapes to resources within parks. NPScape focuses on broadscale factors and measures that are founded on consistent data available at a regional to national scale. Most NPScape data sources and products are best (or only) suited for analysis of areas that are hundreds to thousands of square kilometers. Information at these broad scales is increasingly needed to identify wildlife corridors, isolated habitats, and areas with important resources that may be at risk from projected land use changes around parks. As source data are updated, or new sources become available, NPScape

will update its products to meet the latest standards, and also provide new estimates of landscape status and trend.

The use of consistent data and methodologies by NPScape maximizes the benefits of centralized processing of landscape measures that are fundamentally important to the vast majority of parks. However, there is little benefit to centralized analyses of fine-scale measures when the availability, content, and format of data differ between sites. Local data usually require separate and often unique processes for acquisition, aggregation, and analysis. In this sense it is important to distinguish between NPScape data and analyses, which are reflected in this interpretive guide, and NPScape methods, which are documented in great detail elsewhere (see below) and intended to help parks and networks replicate NPScape analyses using other, more localized landscape datasets.

This interpretive guide describes the scientific underpinnings of NPScape vital sign indicators (Fancy et al. 2009) or 'measures' and their associated 'metrics' (explained further in Section 1.2). The guide provides literature summaries, sources of more detailed information, and park examples to help readers put specific results and principles in context. We emphasize information to help readers understand existing NPScape products and how to use them to evaluate conditions and threats to resources and values. We have attempted to provide thorough and balanced assessments based on current knowledge, but we also welcome comments and suggestions that can help us improve future versions of this report.

1.1 Conceptual Foundation
The conceptual models and frameworks presented in this section illustrate connections among key environmental attributes and relate NPScape products to the evaluation of landscape condition and the context of parks. No single model or framework can meet all needs; we present these select models because they are easily understood, can be applied to most systems, and are readily modified to better represent specific situa-

A.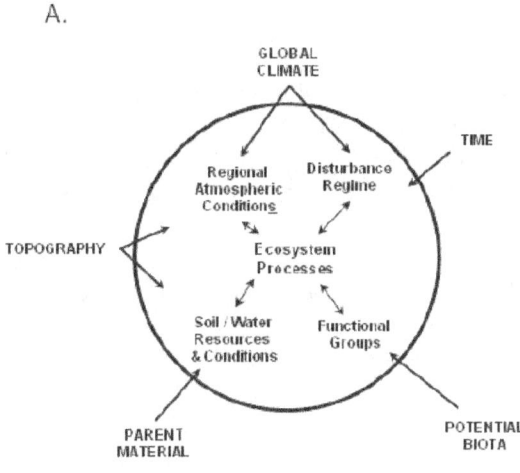

B.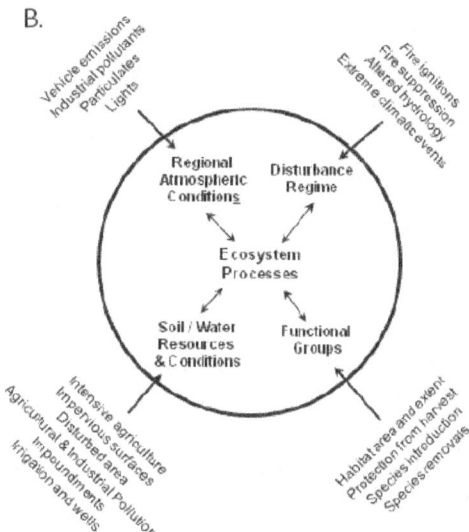

Figure 1.1. (A) General ecosystem model showing primary constraints (upper case) and ecosystem attributes or 'interactive controls' (lower case). (B) Factors that commonly alter ecosystems at local to landscape scales. Modified from Chapin et al. (1996) and Miller (2005).

tions or needs. The models are presented in order from more general and broad in scale to the more specific and detailed in scale.

At the most general level, Figure 1.1 (A) illustrates factors that are the primary determinants of ecosystem state and sustainability over broad scales of time and space. Five 'state factors' (Figure 1.1 A, in upper case) impose fundamental constraints on ecosystem processes and these factors largely determine such features as dominant vegetation type (e.g., deciduous forest, tundra, grassland). These state factors are external to the ecosystem (as represented by the circles in Figure 1.1). The specific characteristics of a particular ecosystem are determined by the 'interactive controls', which regulate and respond to ecosystem processes. Implicit in this model is the assertion that a significant change to any interactive control will lead to a different ecosystem. Figure 1.1 (B) includes anthropogenic factors and activities that can significantly alter one or more of the interactive controls, and thus threaten the sustainability of the system. NPScape provides direct measures of some of these general stressors (e.g., land cover types), and strong indices to oth-

ers (e.g., road and population density are strongly related to vehicle emissions and to night lights).

At a somewhat finer level of resolution, the model in Figure 1.2 more directly focuses on the types of measures and interactions evaluated by NPScape. Consider by way of example a focal resource occurring inside a particular management unit such as a national park. That resource is capable of persisting in part because of the ecological attributes of the larger natural system within which it exists. However, the value of the natural system with respect to the focal resource can be challenged by human-mediated drivers of landscape change. Precisely how these drivers interact with the natural system to impact

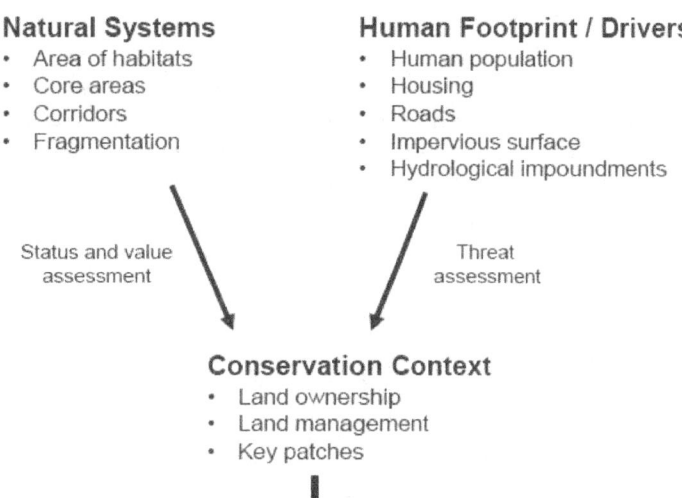

Figure 1.2. Broad categories of measures considered in this guide, and how they contribute to understanding the landscape context of parks and park resources.

the resource and, by extension, resource conservation vulnerability and opportunity, depends further on the stewardship of all management units within the natural system.

Together, these measures in Figure 1.2 describe landscape condition at a range of scales of space and time. Historical information provides a context for change: how, and how fast, did we reach our present state or condition? Historical rates and magnitudes of change help determine the urgency of decisions, and they provide a social context important for understanding and relating to people who experienced these changes. Current information reflects status, and projections help identify trajectories in resource conditions or ecological drivers that are important for planning.

The historic, current, and future context provided by NPScape can help identify and evaluate opportunities to prevent resource damage or loss, assess actions for restoration, and identify key areas or threats to park resources. The relationships between park natural resources, nearby protected areas, and connecting corridors can determine opportunities for preserving resources. Users will generally want to integrate multiple measures to evaluate the status or trend of a resource, as the sum of this information can provide a much richer picture of the history, status, risks, and opportunities for conservation decisions than the independent use of one or a couple of measures (Exhibit 1.1).

The conceptual models illustrated in Figures 1.1 and 1.2 provide general frameworks for considering landscape-scale factors that affect park resources, but more detailed models are necessary to directly link landscape dynamics mechanistically to ecological processes and specific resources. The more detailed model in Figure 1.3 links landscape changes associated with land use intensification to key ecological processes and effects on natural resources, and it identifies attributes suitable for monitoring. The ecological relationships and processes articulated in Figure 1.3 are common to many parks, and they provide a sound basis for evaluating the potential effects of landscape-scale attributes on park natural resources. Key attributes include natural disturbances, (e.g., fire, floods), critical habitats, ecological flows (e.g., pollutants, nutrients), and both direct and indirect effects of humans (e.g., poaching, noise, behavioral disturbance).

Exhibit 1.1. Land use outside Yellowstone National Park influences the status, condition, and population trends of bird populations inside the park.

Hansen et al. (2002) quantified population dynamics for two common bird species in the Greater Yellowstone Ecosystem (GYE), the yellow warbler (*Dendroica petechia*) and the American robin (*Turdus migratorius*), as well as their land use determinants at low and high elevations. Importantly, the GYE is generally characterized by protected areas at high elevations – which due to climatic constraints tend to have short breeding seasons for birds – and non-protected areas at low elevations, where the breeding season is comparably long. Hansen et al. discovered remarkably different responses for the two bird species.

The American robin reproduced at rates well above replacement level at low elevations and at rates close to replacement at high elevations. Meanwhile, yellow warbler reproduction was well below replacement levels at both low and high elevations. Combined, these results suggest that the entire study area is currently a population sink for the warbler, while high-elevation sink populations of the robin are subsidized by low elevation source populations.

Exhibit 1.1. (continued) Land use outside Yellowstone National Park influences the status, condition, and population trends of bird populations inside the park.

Land use dynamics are hypothesized to be at the root of this discrepancy. As background, the brown-headed cowbird (*Molothrus ater*) is a major brood parasite of certain bird species. Robin nests remained unparasitized by cowbirds. However, warbler nests were heavily parasitized, and cowbird density was positively correlated with home density. Hence, land use at low elevations adjacent to protected areas exerted prominent indirect negative population effects on the warbler and – in the case of the robin – are still noteworthy in the context of low elevations serving as population sources for sinks existing in protected areas at high elevations.

To further investigate whether the warbler may have once exhibited source-sink dynamics similar to the robin, Hansen et al. used a computer simulation to examine replacement rates under pre-human settlement conditions. The simulation reflecting current conditions closely approximated observed population dynamics. After removing the housing density effect (and, by extension, the cowbird effect), low elevation sites became population sources that fed population sinks throughout high elevations of Yellowstone National Park.

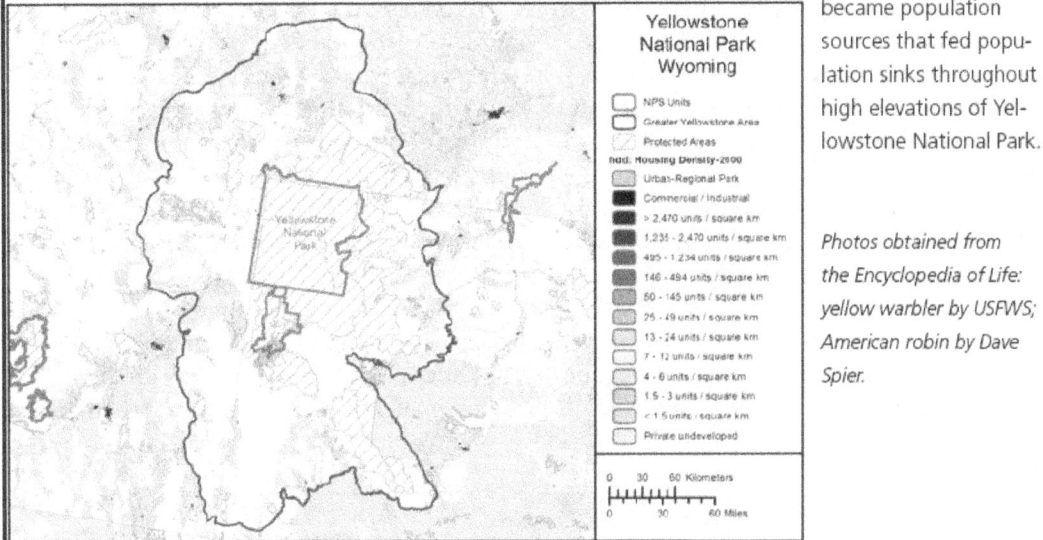

Photos obtained from the Encyclopedia of Life: yellow warbler by USFWS; American robin by Dave Spier.

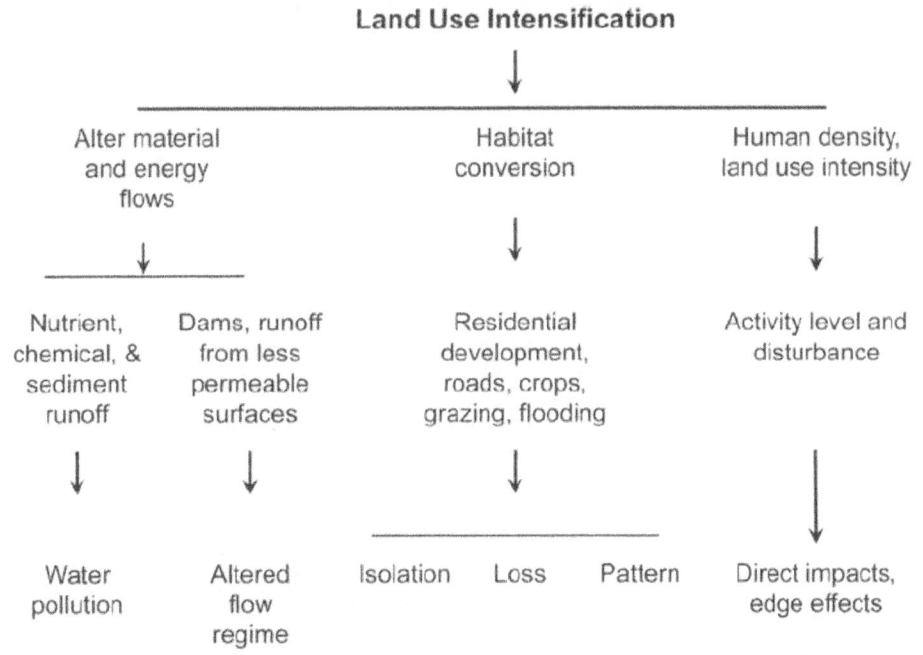

Figure 1.3. Mechanistic links between attributes of land use intensification and natural resources, depicting the relationships described by Hansen & DeFries (2007).

1.2 Measures, Metrics, and Related Products

NPScape delivers a suite of products that focus on a set of information-rich, landscape-scale measures and metrics (Figure 1.4). Analyses summarize and deliver measures in six major categories (population, housing, roads, land cover, pattern, and conservation status) that broadly address the environmental drivers, natural attributes, and conservation context of NPS units (Table 1.1, Figure 1.2).

In addition to the measures and metrics, NPScape products include a series of methodological reports or Standard Operating Procedures (SOPs), and ArcGIS Python scripts and toolboxes that enable users to recompute NPScape metrics for other data sources and spatial extents. These analytical resources for computing population, housing, road, land cover, landscape pattern, and conservation status metrics are available for download through the NPScape website: http://science.nature.nps.gov/im/monitor/npscape/methods.cfm. For example, metrics could be recomputed from higher-resolution land cover data that are only locally avail-able for a park, or on existing NPScape data layers for a particular park planning region. We emphasize the importance of our SOPs and GIS processing scripts and toolboxes as resources to help parks repeat the computation of NPScape measures and metrics on local data using expert knowledge. All of these products are available for download through IRMA and the NPScape website (Figure 1.5).

1.3 Spatial Scales of Analysis

Landscape attributes important to park resources often vary with scale or spatial extent. Relevant scales or areas of analysis (AOAs) include the landscape within the park itself, the 'boundary' area immediately adjacent to the park (e.g., within 1-3 km), the local area surrounding a park (e.g., within approximately 15-40 km), watersheds upstream from the park, and the ecoregion. All of these AOAs are relevant for at least certain measures and metrics included in NPScape. The park examples that follow provide basic guidance on when and how to select a particular AOA from this list. We also provide standardized GIS data for all AOAs referenced above in an effort to streamline

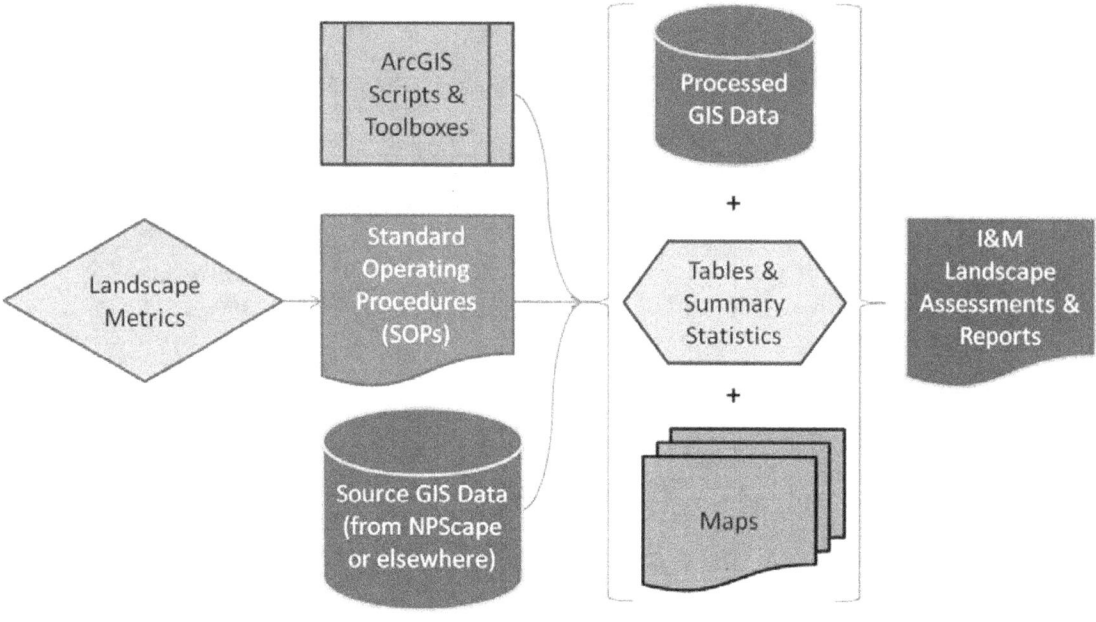

Figure 1.4. Overview of processing steps and products produced and delivered by NPScape to I&M networks, parks, and other agencies. We begin by defining a core set of landscape metrics that are of fundamental value to all or at least most parks (see Table 1.1). We then document in great detail the GIS methods needed to quantify the landscape metrics, including the source GIS data inputs and ArcGIS scripts and toolboxes to assist with computations. Importantly, these methods enable others to recompute the landscape metrics using local source data, where available. Primary outputs from our processing methods include processed GIS data, tables with summary statistics, and maps to assist visualization by non-GIS audiences (Adobe Reader geo-enabled PDF maps and KML maps for Google Earth). These outputs are then used to generate I&M assessments and reports, designed to assist parks with management, planning, and interpretation.

Table 1.1. NPScape measures, metrics, and key data attributes (years of coverage, spatial resolution and park coverage by geographic area). Where possible, metrics and related GIS data are provided for Canada and Mexico for the benefit of parks located near these international boundaries.

Measure	Metric	Years	Resolution	Geographic coverage					
				Alaska	Lower 48	Pacific	Caribbean	Mexico	Canada
Population	Current: total and density	1990, 2000, 2010	Census block group	X	X	X	X		
	Historic: total and density	1790-1990, by decade	County		X				
	Projected: total and desnity	2010-2050, by decade	County	X	X				
Housing	Housing density	1970-2100, by decade	100 m cells		X				
Roads	Road density	varies, up to 2005	km/km²	X	X	X	X		X
	Distance from roads	varies, up to 2005	30 m cells	X	X	X	X		X
	Roadless area	varies, up to 2005	varies, down to 30 m	X	X	X	X		
Land cover	Natural vs. converted	varies, 1992-2006	30 or 250 m cells	X	X	X		X	X
	Anderson Level I & II	varies, 1992-2006	30 or 250 m cells	X	X	X		X	X
	Impervious surface	2001, 2006	30 m cells		X	X			
Pattern	Patch size	2001, 2005, 2006	30 or 250 m cells	X	X			X	X
	Morphology	2001, 2005, 2006	30 or 250 m cells	X	X			X	X
	Area density	2001, 2005, 2006	30 or 250 m cells	X	X			X	X
Conservation status	Area protected	varies	varies	X	X	X	X	X	X
	Ownership	varies	varies	X	X	X	X	X	X

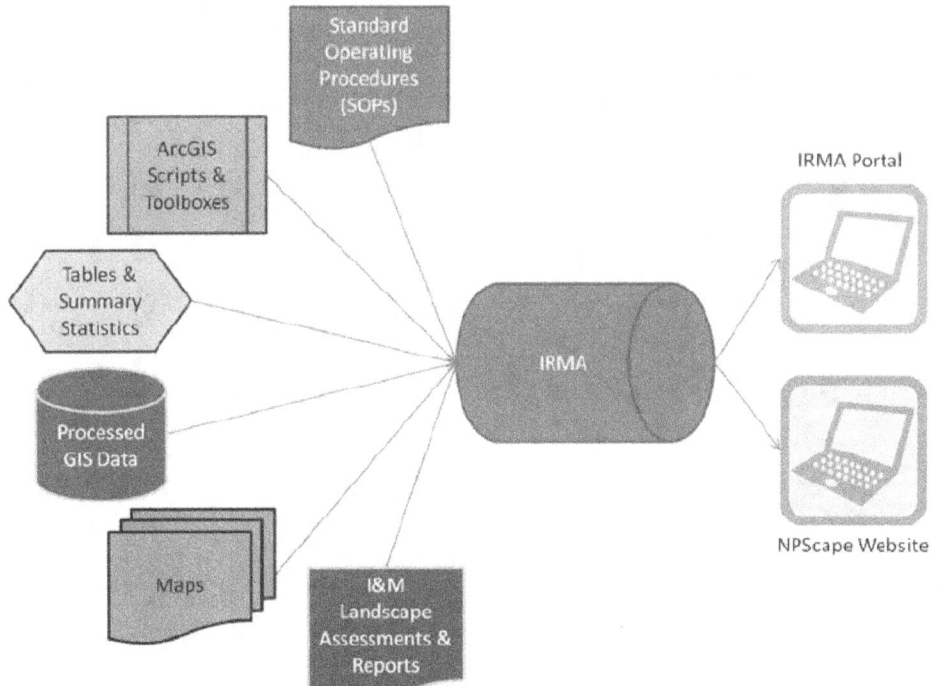

Figure 1.5. Overview of how NPScape products are managed and distributed for use by parks and other agencies. NPScape products listed on the left are managed through the Integrated Resource Management Applications (IRMA) system. All NPScape records are publically accessible and may be viewed/downloaded through either the IRMA Data Store (http://irma.nps.gov) or the NPScape website (http://science.nature.nps.gov/im/monitor/npscape/). The NPScape website streamlines access to the products and provides additional useful information on the project.

Exhibit 1.2. Land cover estimates (year 2006) for different AOAs around Pinnacles National Monument.

Summaries show how the percentage land cover area by category can vary depending on one's choice of AOA. This comparison involves three AOAs: (i) the park plus 30 km buffer, (ii) the upstream watershed with respect to the park, and (iii) critical habitat for the California tiger salamander (US Fish and Wildlife Service 2005), a species of conservation concern that inhabits grasslands and occasionally breeds in seasonal ponds along the eastern side of the monument. Notice how cultivated crops vary in area from 0-12%, grassland/herbaceous from 30-52%, and scrub/shrub from 31-60%. These types of differences illustrate the importance of selecting an appropriate AOA.

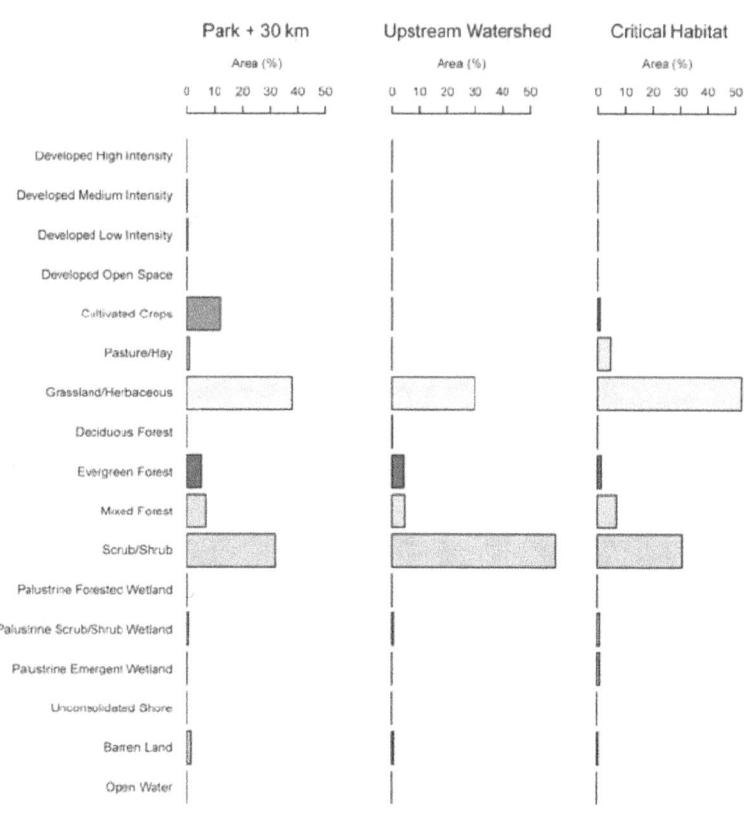

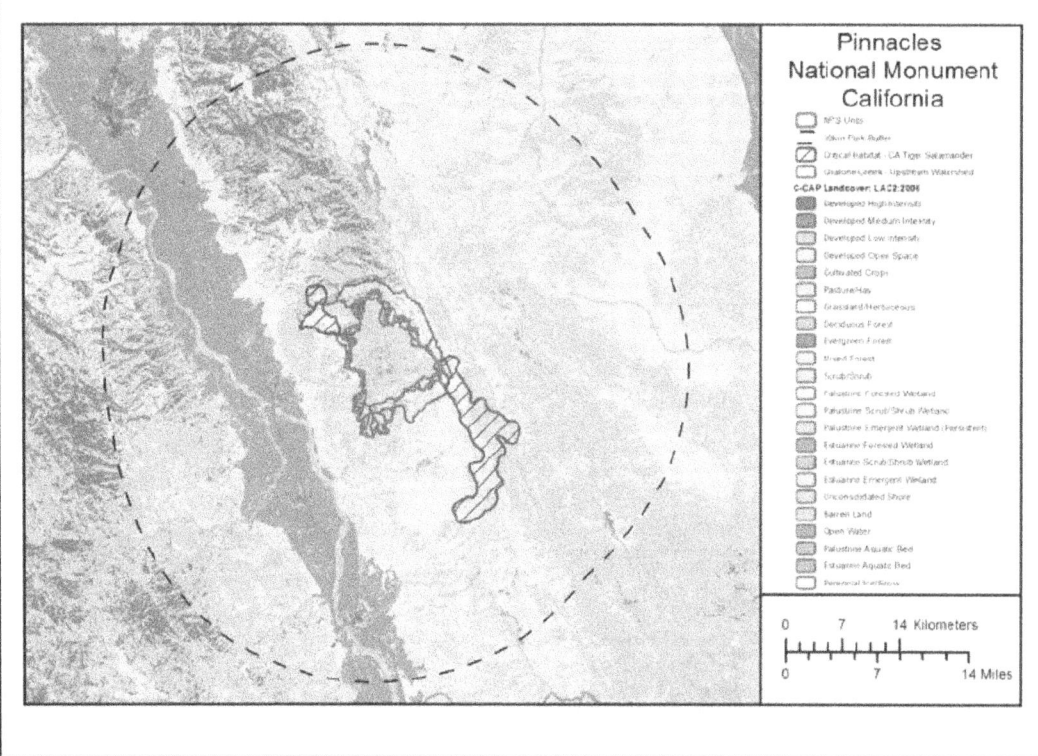

analysis and statistical reporting of NPScape metrics (http://science.nature.nps.gov/im/monitor/npscape/methods_aoas.cfm). With that said, we encourage users to consider other AOAs that may be more relevant to a particular park or question, such as AOAs established by 'protected area centered ecosystems', or PACEs (Piekielek et al. 2010a,b; Hansen et al. 2011), developed originally as part of the NASA-funded project, Park Analysis for Landscape Monitoring Support (PALMS: http://science.nature.nps.gov/im/monitor/lulc/palms/index.cfm). Parks may also wish to consider NPScape statistics within the distributions of particular resources, or more generally how the choice of an AOA can affect statistics used in reporting (Exhibit 1.2). In all such cases, NPScape users can recompute metrics on these AOAs using our methods. A summary of ecologically relevant AOAs used by NPScape is provided in Table 1.2.

For many park decisions, the most relevant spatial scale of NPScape data will consist of the area within park boundaries (Figure 1.6). Wildlife may move among areas within the park, plants disperse and colonize, and development and visitor use have impacts that extend spatially from their locations within the park. This is also the scale where NPS management has the greatest control over landscape change. The size, spatial location, and geographical context of the park determine the relative importance of landscape factors within the park compared to those in the surrounding area. A few of the very largest NPS units may approximate self-con-tained or self-sufficient ecosystems, but the vast majority of park units are embedded in larger ecosystems, and relatively few wildlife populations or food webs are sustained solely by resources within the park boundary (Coggins 1987).

The landscape immediately adjacent to the park has a large effect on permeability or connections between the park and the surrounding landscape, and thus on the importance of landscape attributes in the broader local area (Hansen & DeFries 2007, Figure 1.3). Roads and highly developed areas can act as barriers to movement of wildlife between the park and surrounding areas, isolating park resources from important habitats outside the park. Land cover characteristics at this local scale can have a strong effect on fire management strategies and the probability that wildfires ignited on the surrounding lands will burn into the park. Activities and processes occurring within the area immediately adjacent to a park are sufficiently close that even small effects can propagate into the park and affect park resources. Housing adjacent to the park boundary can increase pet-wildlife interactions, exotic plant introductions from yards and gardens, and the ignition frequency of small fires. Roads near park boundaries provide additional visitor access, and may increase the potential for poaching within the park.

Although analyses within and immediately adjacent (< 3 km) to the park are important, many NPScape datasets are unsuited

Table 1.2. Summary of AOAs considered by NPScape and why they are relevant to parks.

AOA	Relevance
Park	The scale at which park units have maximum management control.
Park + 3 km buffer	Captures the effects of human drivers that are most proximate and direct to the park.
Park upstream watersheds	Important for evaluating the degree to which a park provides watershed services downstream versus - in the case of a non-headwater park - is dependent on water flowing in from areas beyond its boundaries, with perhaps varied uses and levels of protection.
Park + 30 km buffer	A local park landscape that tends to integrate the combined effects of human drivers, natural systems, and conservation context outlined in Figure 1.2.
Viewsheds	Areas that are visible from key observation points inside the park; informative AOAs for such 'visual' park resources as visitor experience and wilderness character
Ecoregions	Geographies at scales suitable for management units that share major common ecosystems.

for analysis at such fine scales. Local aerial photography and fine-scale vegetation maps, county property records, and county/state road and traffic data are usually better suited to analyses that focus on relatively small areas within a few kilometers of a park. Instead, most NPScape data excel at analyses that focus on larger areas and on park resources that are dependent on landscapes that extend well beyond park boundaries. For example, many ecological processes operate at a local scale on the order of 15-40 km (Clark 1985; Wiens 1989). Specific examples include the propagation of wildland fires, dispersal of local pollutants, daily to weekly movements of birds and larger mammals, and yearly to multi-decadal dispersal of amphibians, reptiles, and smaller mammals. There is no unique and uniform distance that defines the local scale, and for reporting purposes we chose 30 km from the park boundary as a rough and hopefully robust distance for quantifying landscape effects of this type. Hereafter, we refer to this park plus 30 km buffer as a 'local scale'. The 'protected area centered ecosystems' (PACEs, Hansen et al. 2011) referenced above provide an alternative means for determining park-centered local scales that are important for supporting ecological systems and processes.

Watershed boundaries also delineate a relevant and useful area for landscape analysis, largely because of the downhill and downstream transport of materials and energy. For example, landscape processes in the upstream watershed affect hydrology, water chemistry, and aquatic biota; aboveground and belowground flows can rapidly transmit the effects of actions outside parks to aquatic resources within park boundaries. When there is intensive development in the upstream contributing area to a park, the effects of upstream activities may constitute the most important stressors or drivers of aquatic conditions within the unit. The upstream watersheds delineated by NPScape are shown in Figure 1.7, and our methods for determining these boundaries are described in an SOP (http://science.nature.nps.gov/im/monitor/npscape/methods_aoas.cfm).

Landscape attributes at broader, regional scales often affect park resources on time scales of decades to centuries. This regional perspective is necessary to plan for or respond to issues such as the ability of altered landscapes to support regional biodiversity, and to evaluate impacts from broad-scale drivers like climate change. At this scale, species are most likely to interact through gene flow and long-term extinction and recolonization processes. As the NPS confronts challenges of global changes, including climate change, a regional perspective will be essential for long-term conservation of biodiversity (National Park Service 2010).

NPScape summarizes landscape attributes and provides regional-scale data within the general boundaries of the 21 Landscape Conservation Cooperatives (LCCs, DOI Secretarial Order 3289; US Fish and Wildlife Service 2010a; Figure 1.8). The boundaries of these regions are biologically based, incorporating the Bird Conservation Regions, Freshwater Ecoregions of the World, and Omernick Level II ecoregions (US Fish and Wildlife Service 2010b). While LCCs provide an especially convenient spatial framework for serving up GIS data in a way that is useful for a number of different agencies, they are not generally considered ecologically informative regional units for many park-based questions. For our regional analyses and results, we report NPScape statistics using the internationally recognized ecoregional classification put forth by the Commission for Environmental Cooperation (CEC, Figure 1.9). When parks are on or near the boundary of two or more CEC ecoregions, evaluation of the regional context will likely require consideration of multiple nearby regions.

1.4 Appropriate Uses

Several assumptions described below are inherent to the types of GIS analyses provided by NPScape, and they need to be considered when applying NPScape data, maps, or statistical results towards particular problems or questions. NPScape assumptions can be broadly categorized as those related to the actual GIS mapping (e.g., the land cover map) and those related to the statistical properties or calculation of the metric

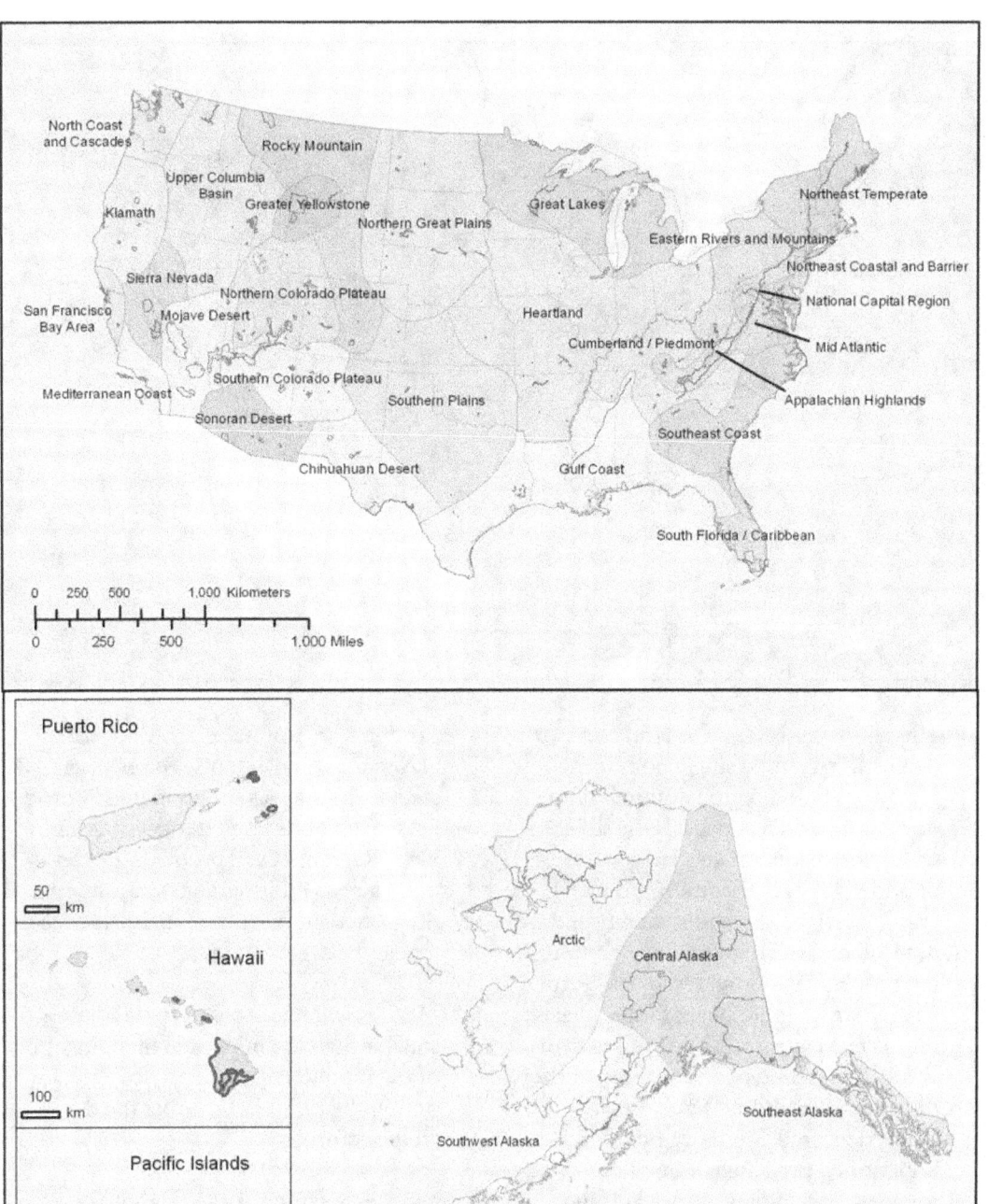

Figure 1.6. Map of all 291 natural resource park units (red outlines) and 32 I&M Networks (solid polygons, labeled) serviced by NPScape.

(e.g., proportions). Each of the NPScape measures (population, housing, roads, land cover, landscape pattern, and conservation status), and many of the associated metrics (e.g., percent natural cover, road density), are dependent on these assumptions. We provide here a brief overview; additional details may be found in the SOPs.

1.4.1 Mapping

The assumptions related to mapping are typically a result of thematic scale, spatial scale, spectral scale, and overall study objectives. The standards and methodologies employed in each mapping effort will differ, thus so will the overall applicability of those data to any given question or situation. In general, the following apply to all map-derived products:

Figure 1.7. Map of upstream contributing watersheds (aqua polygons) for 152 focal parks (red outlines), as calculated by NPScape. The NPScape SOP and ArcGIS toolbox for computing park upstream watersheds is available for download at http://science.nature. nps.gov/im/monitor/ npscape/methods_ aoas.cfm.

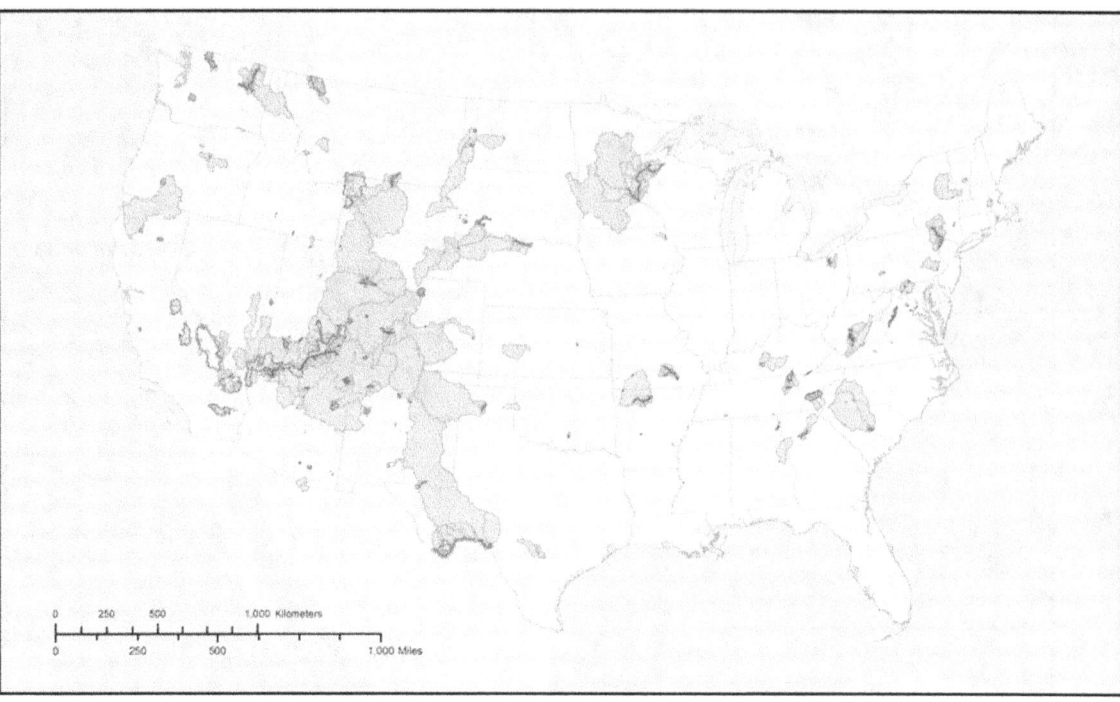

- Thematic classes, such as land cover or ownership, assume single homogeneous categories based on the dominant type or value and do not necessarily differentiate finer characteristics (e.g., stand age or understory composition). In many cases, the classes assume stability and do not isolate disturbances. For example, in land cover maps provided by NPScape, an area with a great deal of forest clearing may be classified as forest, grass, or shrub, depending on the severity of the disturbance and time since the disturbance occurred. Similarly, private land is identified as a single homogeneous category, and individual private land units, owners, and management status are not differentiated unless the information was provided voluntarily (typically to recognize a long-term commitment to biodiversity through binding conservation easements, covenants, or institutional dedication).

- Boundaries between thematic classes (e.g., land cover types) along real environmental gradients are seldom as sharp as implied by maps. Transition areas between classes represent gradients of condition that likely change with time.

- Products are not necessarily consistent across mapping extents. For example, state Gap Analysis Program (GAP) products may not be consistent across state lines. Regional GAP products are developed across multiple states to minimize this issue, but there may still be inconsistencies between regions.

- Metrics will not account for land units smaller than the minimum mapping unit of the input data and are strictly valid only at the point in time that the data were acquired.

By way of an example using our land cover measure, mapping is generally done by adopting a land cover classification system, delineating areas of relative homogeneity, and then labeling these areas using classes defined by the classification system. This mapping often takes many forms; no single mapping strategy will work best in all locations. The usefulness, efficiency, and cost-effectiveness of any land cover map is dependent on the scope and scale of questions being addressed, the spatial and temporal scale of imagery, the comprehensiveness of field and classification methods employed, and the level of desired accuracy.

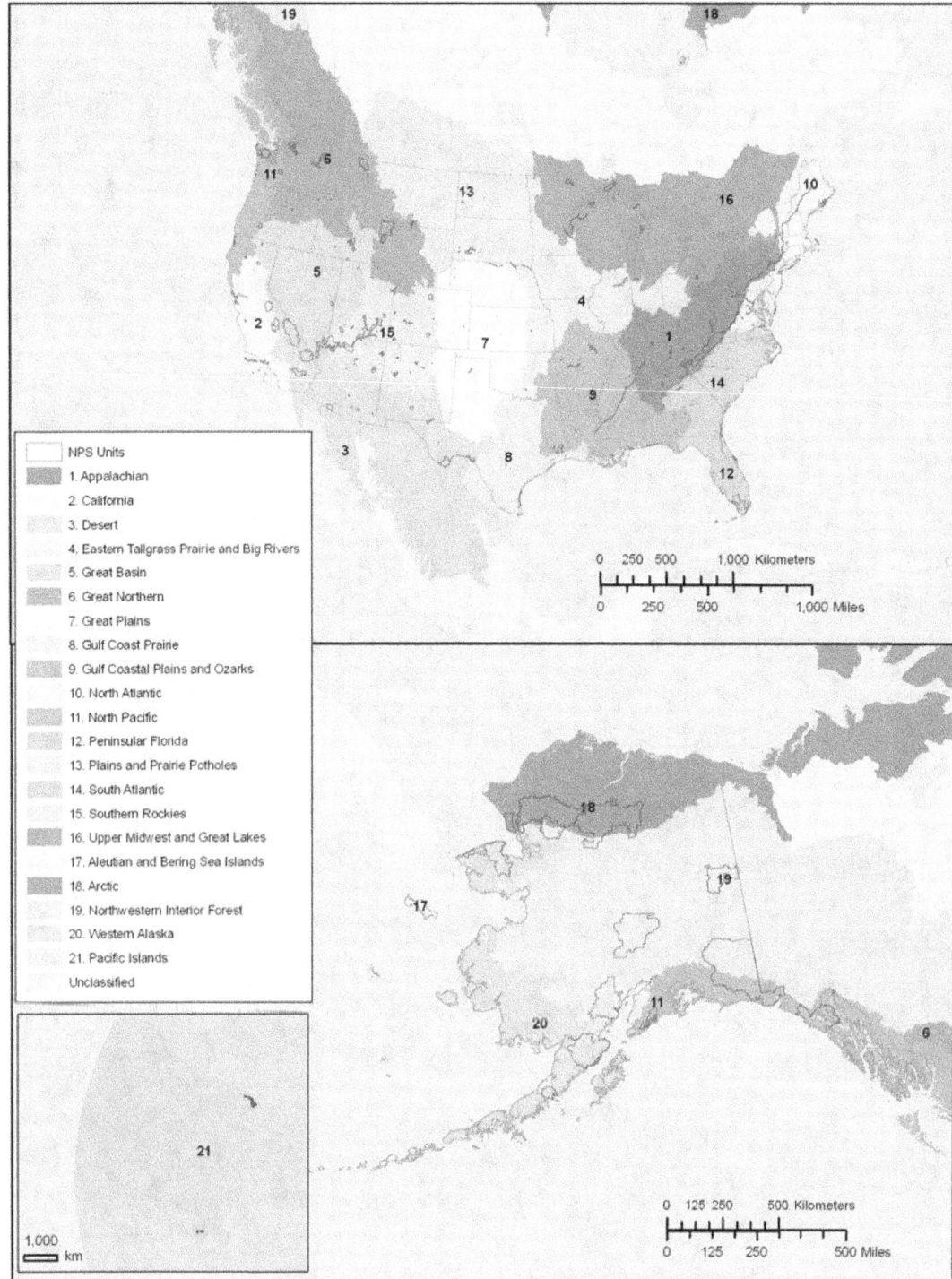

Figure 1.8. The 21 Geographic Areas (solid polygons) proposed by the DOI as Landscape Conservation Cooperatives (LCCs). Park unit boundaries shown as red outlines.

NPS Units
1. Appalachian
2. California
3. Desert
4. Eastern Tallgrass Prairie and Big Rivers
5. Great Basin
6. Great Northern
7. Great Plains
8. Gulf Coast Prairie
9. Gulf Coastal Plains and Ozarks
10. North Atlantic
11. North Pacific
12. Peninsular Florida
13. Plains and Prairie Potholes
14. South Atlantic
15. Southern Rockies
16. Upper Midwest and Great Lakes
17. Aleutian and Bering Sea Islands
18. Arctic
19. Northwestern Interior Forest
20. Western Alaska
21. Pacific Islands
Unclassified

Clearly identifying what is being managed (e.g., species, habitat, processes; Beatley 2000) and the scales at which those species or processes respond is key to selecting an adequate scale for evaluating the status and trends of land cover composition, configuration, and connectivity. Appropriate application of remotely-sensed imagery (e.g., aerial photos, multispectral, hyperspectral, laser) and methods (e.g., photo interpretation, maximum likelihood classification, object oriented image analysis) at relevant spatial and temporal scales is necessary (Turner et al. 2003; Gross et al. 2006). All of which depend on the timeframe, cost allowance, and accuracy level desired. Kennedy et al. (2009) provide detailed guidance for determining the suitability of remotely sensed data for

Figure 1.9. Map of all marine and terrestrial Commission for Environmental Cooperation (CEC) Level I (colored, labeled) and Level III (gray outlines) ecoregions used by NPScape. Park unit boundaries shown as red outlines.

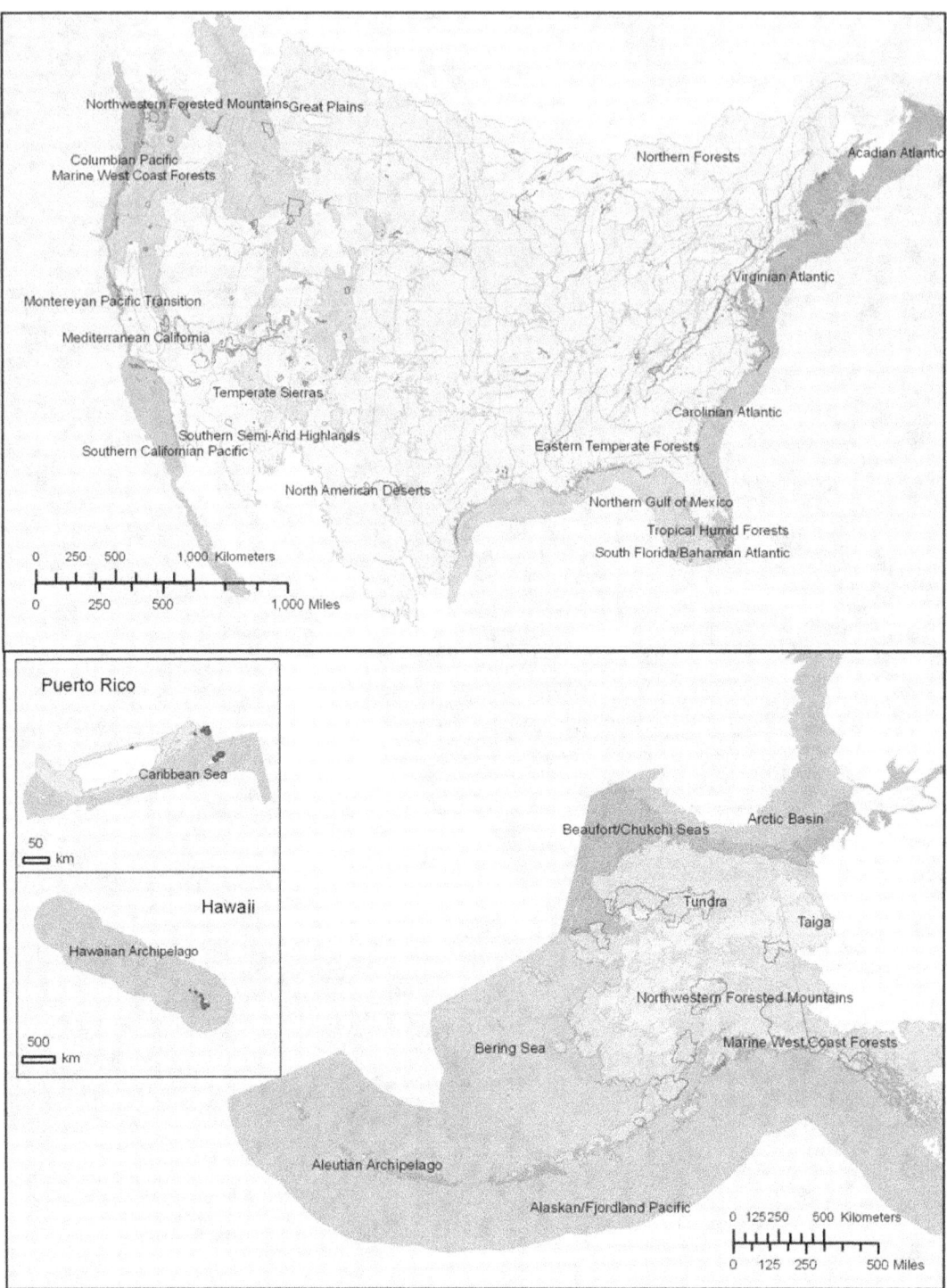

natural resource monitoring, and describe a four-phase process for conducting a natural resource remote sensing project. For NPScape and similar analyses, Story et al. (2009) evaluated the suitability of land cover data from a number of common sources and determined that the National Land Cover Database (NLCD, Vogelmann et al. 2001; Homer et al. 2004; Fry et al. 2009) was most

appropriate for NPScape because it is: (1) best suited to assessing distribution and pattern of broad land cover types, and (2) the only dataset that measures change in land cover types over time for most of the US.

1.4.2 Calculations

Many of the metrics calculated by NPScape reflect a proportion or percentage of area (e.g., 10% of the park's local AOA). Calculating the proportion of area in any manner is always a function of the sampling unit being measured (e.g., county, buffer, grid cell size) and must be interpreted in that context. The proportion of land in a particular thematic class is dependent on the underlying map and – for land cover maps – Stranko et al. (2008) have shown that using various imagery methods (e.g., 2001 NLCD vs. high-resolution aerial photography) interchangeably to assess potential thresholds can produce inconsistent results. Related, the modifiable areal unit problem (MAUP) must also be considered when interpreting NPScape products. MAUP describes how differences in the spatial units of aggregation (e.g., census block, moving window of grid cells) can result in different statistical results. The extent to which these issues introduce bias varies depending on the starting question, and it is thus important for NPScape users to think critically about sampling units and MAUP in relation to a particular application of NPScape products.

Important assumptions also exist regarding the distribution of the data in relation to the species or processes under consideration. For example, the response of species to ecological thresholds is thought to be non-linear and to occur at diverse spatiotemporal scales (Groffman et al. 2006; Utz et al. 2009), though some species exhibit linear responses at some scales (Morley & Karr 2002). Given this, it is often difficult to generalize potential species or community responses to the various data and metrics provided by NPScape (Karr & Chu 2000; Bledsoe & Watson 2001; Morley & Karr 2002).

1.5 Summary of Where to Go for More Information on NPScape Products

The NPScape webiste prodives easy, direct access to a number of the products that are used throughout this guide, including:

- Metric processing methods (SOPs and ArcGIS toolboxes): http://science.nature.nps.gov/im/monitor/npscape/methods_sops.cfm

- Standardized areas of analysis: http://science.nature.nps.gov/im/monitor/npscape/methods_aoas.cfm

- GIS data: http://science.nature.nps.gov/im/monitor/npscape/gis_data.cfm

- Data sources: http://science.nature.nps.gov/im/monitor/npscape/methods_sourcedata.cfm

- Maps (dynamic online map viewer, map services, and map movies): http://science.nature.nps.gov/im/monitor/npscape/maps.cfm

- Other case studies: http://science.nature.nps.gov/im/monitor/npscape/casestudies.cfm

1.6 Preview of Chapters

Following the conceptual model shown in Figure 1.2, we proceed by describing each of the three main landscape elements that relate to resource vulnerability and opportunity:

- Natural systems (Chapter 2, Land Cover and Land Use: Area and Pattern)

- Human drivers (Chapter 3, Effects of Roads on Natural Resources; Chapter 4, Human Population and Housing around Parks)

- Conservation context (Chapter 5, Evaluating Resource Protection and Risk)

In each chapter, we describe the ecological relevance of NPScape metrics based on the scientific literature and include illustrative examples of the metrics for select parks. Combined, the information presented in these chapters is designed to help parks understand how the landscape-level data and results originating from NPScape may be used to evaluate the influence of broad-scale dynamics on park resources. We conclude with an extensive bibliography of in-text citations included in the other chapters (Chapter 6, References).

2. Land Cover and Land Use: Area and Pattern

The importance of habitat area and pattern are readily apparent for parks, but it is nonetheless difficult to identify a small suite of metrics that adequately describe area and pattern characteristics in ways that generally inform decisions on how to manage park resources. This fundamental difficulty accounts for the number and complexity of NPScape metrics that address land cover and landscape pattern.

In this chapter, we begin by discussing metrics that focus primarily on habitat. We proceed to metrics that address landscape pattern, in terms of individual patch characteristics and the composition of landscapes. The final section focuses more specifically on watershed condition, a topic of great interest to many parks. In this final section, we illustrate how to use a variety of NPScape metrics to assess condition of watersheds and aquatic resources. Throughout this chapter, we review studies that link the metrics and landscape attributes to resources, but one should appreciate that the metrics, by themselves, are important to communicate the status of an area. Many people want to know, for example, whether large intact patches of habitat still exist, without reference to any particular species or other resource.

Most or all of the NPScape land cover and pattern products can be used to assess important attributes of plant and animal habitat. These attributes include indices of availability, connectivity, patch sizes and structure, and multi-scale context (Table 2.1). The most important habitat features vary according to question, species, or issue. NPScape products are designed to be diverse enough to provide useful information for a very wide range of analyses, and each has its strengths and limitations, including those summarized in Table 2.1.

Most NPScape area and pattern metrics are based on the National Land Cover Database (NLCD), although NPScape also provides metrics calculated based on NOAA Coastal Change Analysis Program (CCAP) and Commission for Environmental Cooperation (CEC) North American Land Change Monitoring System (NALCMS, hereafter shortened to NALC) data. CCAP data provide more accurate and higher-resolution data for coastal and near-coastal areas, while NALC covers all of North America at a coarser (250 m) resolution than NLCD and CCAP (30 m). Exhibit 2.1 summarizes important information about NLCD products and their appropriate uses.

Table 2.1. A very condensed summary of NPScape land cover and land use metrics, and some of their key strengths and limitations. While maps can be used to display the spatial context of all metrics, some metrics are not explicitly spatial.

Metric	Strengths and/or appropriate uses	Limitations
Habitat area	Easily interpreted. May be the single most important indicator of landscape condition. May be most relevant to wide-ranging, generalist species. Data on area of cover or habitat types is a basis for many analyses.	No explicit spatial information. Not informative about individual patch attributes or spatial pattern. Must define what constitutes "habitat".
Natural and converted cover	Simple metric of overall biotic condition. When expressed as a proportion it may be informative about the overall condition of e.g. an area around a park. Easily computed.	Uninformative about specific habitat types. May be misleading if high-value habitats are disproportionately converted. No spatial information.
Forest and grassland density	Easily interpreted. Can detect changes in spatial patterns of patches not identified by other metrics. Moving window relatively insensitive to pixel-level classification errors. Multiple window sizes can identify scale-specific or scale-dependent habitat changes. Scales of analysis more easily linked to species-specific requirements than other metrics.	Can mask changes in patches of particular sizes. May be insensitive to some relatively homogenous changes in habitat area. Can be computationally demanding.

Table 2.1. (continued) A very condensed summary of NPScape land cover and land use metrics, and some of their key strengths and limitations. While maps can be used to display the spatial context of all metrics, some metrics are not explicitly spatial.

Metric	Strengths and/or appropriate uses	Limitations
Patch size distribution	Clear relevance to some species, especially where there is a strong contrast between patch and non-patch habitats. Can identify largest patches, which may be most important. Statistical properties often well known.	Care is needed to handle patches that cross boundary of AOA. Does not identify shape effects.
Morphological spatial pattern analysis	Sensitive to changes at the pixel level. Rule-based methodology unambiguously identifies spatial context of individual pixel. Identifies key landscape elements including corridors, edge, and core area. Multiple edge widths provide powerful means to evaluate aspects of patch shape and other fine-scale landscape attributes.	Sensitive to changes at the pixel level. Computationally demanding. Some categories hard to interpret. May not be informative for large areas. Trend analyses can be very sensitive to classification errors. New process; few studies linking results to ecological attributes.
Impervious developed surface	For some areas there are well-studied and reasonably clear relationships with condition of many hydrologic and aquatic values. Broad literature base can contribute to making locally-relevant interpretations.	Relevant values often small (< 10%) and can be very sensitive to classification errors. Relevant changes may be difficult to detect. Not inherently spatially explicit, but topographical locations can be very important.

NPScape users will need to define 'habitat' in an appropriate way and this definition will vary between applications. NPScape data on land cover type, natural/converted habitats, and forest/grassland may be suitable definitions of 'habitat', or habitat maps can be constructed from other maps. Regardless of the source of an input habitat map, NPScape methods (SOPs and ArcGIS toolboxes) can be used to estimate the metrics described in this chapter, and the literature reviews will describe and provide an entry into the relevant scientific studies.

2.1 Habitat Area and Biodiversity

Habitat loss and fragmentation have profoundly affected biodiversity and other park resources (Turner 1989; US General Accounting Office 1994; Trzcinski et al. 1999; Fahrig 2003). Measures of habitat availability and pattern address these key threats and they can indicate the suitability of landscapes to support species or sustain populations. Many parks are too small, by themselves, to permanently sustain all species that once lived there (Newmark 1986, 1987), particularly in the face of global climate change (Burns et al. 2003; Svancara 2010). In these cases, species living in protected areas need adequate expanses of habitat outside parks to persist long into the future (Hansen et al. 2011).

One of the most pervasive effects of land use intensification is habitat loss, and the ecological implications of habitat loss and fragmentation have been extensively reviewed (Andrén 1994; Harrison & Bruna 1999; Debinski & Holt 2000; Fahrig 2003; Ewers & Didham 2007; Mantyka-pringle et al. 2012). In brief, habitat loss is non-random in both location and in the cover types converted (Seabloom et al. 2002), and in most areas habitat loss is one of the most important threats to biodiversity. The effects of habitat loss and associated fragmentation vary with species' habitat preferences and requirements, interactions with predators and competitors, parasites, and the time and magnitude of habitat changes. Effects of habitat area or pattern on species can vary with spatial and temporal scale, and the effects may be strongly expressed at some scales, while absent at others (Wiens et al. 1987; Thompson et al. 2002). In the extreme case, long-lived plant species or communities may show no response to landscape changes for decades or centuries (Kuussaari et al. 2009; Cole 2010). While habitat loss, almost by definition, usually leads to reduced abundance or fitness of species, fragmentation can benefit edge-dwelling species. Creation of artificial 'hard' edges, like those between a forest and parking lot, are usually highly detrimental to native biota, whereas 'soft' edges between native communities can create valuable habitats. For example, Hansen & Urban

Exhibit 2.1. NLCD versions and their pervasive impact on NPScape cover and pattern products.

NLCD – the National Land Cover Database – is the most important source of land cover data for NPScape. NLCD provides seamless, 30 m resolution land cover products for the contiguous US for circa 1992, 2001, 2006, and a 2011 cover targeted for completion in 2013. This is the only land cover data for such an extended period for such a broad area.

Most NPScape land cover and pattern metrics are based on NLCD. The only real national or continental alternative is the North American Land Change Monitoring System product, which is based on 250 m images from MODIS sensors for a single year (2005). Finer-resolution (30 m) NPScape land cover metrics, and most pattern metrics (forest density, grassland density, morphological spatial pattern analysis [MSPA]), are based on NLCD land cover maps.

Why are there relatively few examples of land cover change products in this guide?

The classification methods used to develop NLCD land cover maps have been continuously improved. In addition, the legend (classification scheme) was improved in the 2001 product. Direct comparisons of NLCD products are inappropriate because an end user cannot distinguish real change from change due to use of different methods.

To partially address this problem, the 2006 version of the National Land Cover Data was released in mid February 2011. Additional data that were released at the same time include an updated (2006) Developed Impervious Surface, a 2001–2006 Impervious Surface Change product, a 2001–2006 Land Cover Change map, and an updated version (version 2) of the Land Cover for 2001. As they did in 2001, the USGS improved the methods for creating NLCD 2006. Use of different methods makes comparisons with the previous versions of NLCD problematic. To estimate land cover changes between 2001 and 2006, the USGS re-created or updated the 2001 Land Cover data using methods developed for the 2006 version. Additional changes in the updated 2001 version include; coastlines synced with NOAA coastlines, wetlands issues were fixed (i.e., more accurate wetland delineation), various roads issues were addressed and classification of oil pads in the SW US was improved.

The circa 2011 version of NLCD has a planned release in 2013. This rapid release is possible due to improvements in classification methods.

How does this impact NPScape?

The 2006 data is now the preferred version, rather than the 2001 Land Cover data that NPScape used and previously distributed. The NPScape team will evaluate the NLCD versions and determine whether changes to NPS areas of interest justify the considerable time and expense to rerun NPScape analyses with a newer version of NLCD. In the meantime, users can download the latest NLCD source data from our NPScape references posted online; these data work with our Land Cover ArcGIS toolbox, which in the absence of us recomputing metrics for the entire US at least gives users the ability to update the metrics for local AOAs.

The 2001–2006 Land Cover change data does not relate well to the 1992–2001 Land Cover change that NPScape has used for analyses conducted through April 2011 because these data were created using very different methods. Direct comparison of these products is inappropriate, and careful consideration is necessary when comparing NPScape products or using NPScape methods with earlier NLCD maps.

The NPScape and NLCD teams are engaged in discussions on options that may permit using NLCD to evaluate land cover changes over the full period of NLCD data. However, satellite sensors, data acquisition, and data processing methods will continue to improve, and it seems likely that future NLCD (and other) products will use the best available methods to produce maps more quickly and with greater accuracy than previous versions. These methodological changes will likely complicate direct comparisons between data.

(1992) noted that openings in largely intact forests may represent a rare habitat type and be disproportionately important to supporting native open canopy birds.

Habitat loss, typically by conversion to a non-natural cover type, results in reduced natural area, creation of edges, and increased isolation of resulting remnants (Kupfer 2006; Ewers & Didham 2007). These changes in the arrangement of habitats can inhibit or prevent species' movements between patches, influence species' dispersal behavior, mode and scale of movement, and change overall habitat requirements (O'Neill et al. 1988; With & Crist 1995; Pearson et al. 1996; McIntyre & Hobbs 1999; Kupfer et al. 2006; Fischer & Lindenmayer 2007; Vranckx et al. 2012). The response of species to an overall reduction in habitat or loss of special habitats, like summer or winter range, can include reductions in distribution and abundance, and changes in behavior, physiological state, or vital rates. Simple measures of habitat area may seem crude, but Wiersma et al. (2004) found that the area of effective habitat within a park had the greatest support from a broad range of variables for accounting for the loss of species within a set of 24 Canadian parks. It is important to remember that overall habitat area is perhaps the most fundamental characteristic of landscape pattern. In a hierarchical sense it imposes constraints on many other attributes. When habitat area is nearly complete (e.g., > 90%), it is nearly impossible to have a highly fragmented system. Similarly, when there is little area of habitat, the system will not be composed of large, intact, and connected patches. The simple measure of habitat area may be the 'best' first measure of ecosystem condition for many organisms.

Land cover types are often used to identify broad habitat areas, and the NPScape area by cover category metric is designed to address this use. Area by cover is calculated for both Anderson Level I and II cover types using NLCD (Table 2.2) and CCAP, and is limited to just Level I for NALC. These cover types provide an opportunity to identify and map major habitat types, and the classification lends itself to broad-scale analyses.

2.2 NPScape Natural and Converted Metric

Proportional change in natural land cover is possibly the simplest indication of biotic condition (O'Neill et al. 1997). Calculating the proportion of natural land cover remaining in an area provides a general indication of overall landscape condition surrounding protected areas and offers insight into potential threats (i.e., how much land has been converted and how much natural habitat remains) and opportunities for conservation. Calculating the proportion of converted (agriculture and urban) land, also known as the U-index (O'Neill et al. 1988), can be used to measure general land use pressure by humans. The definition of 'natural' will vary depending on the ecological question and land cover classification but typically requires aggregating the original land cover/land use data into broad 'converted' versus 'natural' categories. NPScape used the aggregation scheme in Table 2.2 to combine NLCD land cover categories into the two broad classes of 'converted' and 'natural'. A comparable aggregation scheme was applied to NALC.

On average, parks are predominantly surrounded by 'natural' cover. At the national scale, an average of 76% of land within 30 km of parks was classified as natural. But the relationship between natural cover and park resources must be evaluated in the context of other information. For example, Cowpens National Battlefield and Ninety Six National Historic Site are two Cumberland-Piedmont I&M parks in relatively close geographic proximity, yet surrounded by strikingly different amounts of natural vs. converted land (Figure 2.1, left map). In the case of Cowpens near the border between North and South Carolina, the park seems to provide an important corridor linking mostly natural habitats located immediately to the southeast and northwest of the park. Furthermore, when these largely forested natural habitats are considered in relation to the intactness or density of forest as a land cover type (described in detail in the next section), it is apparent that these corridors are even more narrow and less contiguous for forest-dependent species (Figure 2.1,

Table 2.2. NLCD land cover classes used in analyses of Natural/Converted and pattern analyses. Numbers are the class numbers used in NLCD legends and databases.

Anderson Level I	Anderson Level II	Natural/Converted	Forest or grassland pattern
Open Water	11 Open Water	Natural	
	12 Perennial Ice/Snow		
2 Developed	21 Developed Open Space	Converted	
	22 Developed Low Intensity		
	23 Developed Medium Intensity		
	24 Developed High Intensity		
3 Barren/Quarries/Transitional	31 Barren Land	Natural	
	32 Unconsolidated Shore		
4 Forest	41 Deciduous Forest	Natural	Forest
	42 Evergreen Forest		
	43 Mixed Forest		
5 Shrub/Scrub	51 Dwarf Scrub	Natural	
	52 Shrub/Scrub		
7 Grassland/Herbaceous	71 Grassland/Herbaceous	Natural	Grassland
	72 Sedge/Herbaceous		
	73 Lichens		
	74 Moss		
8 Agriculture	81 Pasture/Hay	Converted	
	82 Cultivated Agriculture		
9 Wetlands	90 Woody Wetlands	Natural	Forest
	95 Emergent Herbaceous Wetlands		

right map). In contrast, Ninety Six is embedded in a much larger and more contiguous matrix of natural land cover (Figure 2.1, left map), which affords multiple paths or corridors that species may use to move between the park and neighboring lands (e.g., within the 30 km AOA shown). Ninety Six is also surrounded by much larger patches of forest that are classified as intact (Figure 2.1, right map).

2.3 NPScape Forest and Grassland Density Metric

The NPScape forest and grassland density metrics estimate the proportion of these land cover types within a moving window surrounding each focal pixel on a landscape (Figure 2.2). NPScape estimates density for these two Anderson level I land cover classes because they are reliably mapped in most land cover classifications, and they provide coverage for most natural resource parks considered by NPScape. Where other cover types are important, NPScape methods can be used to replicate density metric calculations for other land cover classes. As illustrated in Figure 2.2, the value of a pixel represents the context of surrounding pixels within a moving window, rather than the content of a specific pixel.

To facilitate interpretation of density metrics, observed cover density is categorized into seven classes with correspondingly less forest (or grassland) cover: intact, interior, dominant, transitional, patchy, rare, and none (Table 2.3; following Riitters 2011). Trends in habitat density across broad areas are clearly illustrated by this metric (Figure 2.3). If a window contains at least one pixel with the density cover type (forest, grassland), then the focal pixel is categorized as something other than 'none'. Hence, as window sizes increase, the apparent area of forest increases (Figures 2.3 and 2.4). Similarly, as window size increases, there is an increasing likelihood that the window will contain a cover type other than the density cover type (Figure 2.5). For most parks, the NPScape density metric summary table can be used

Figure 2.1. Natural vs. converted land cover around Cowpens National Battlefield and Ninety Six National Historic Site (left map), with corresponding estimates of forest density (right map, forest density described in detail in section 2.3).

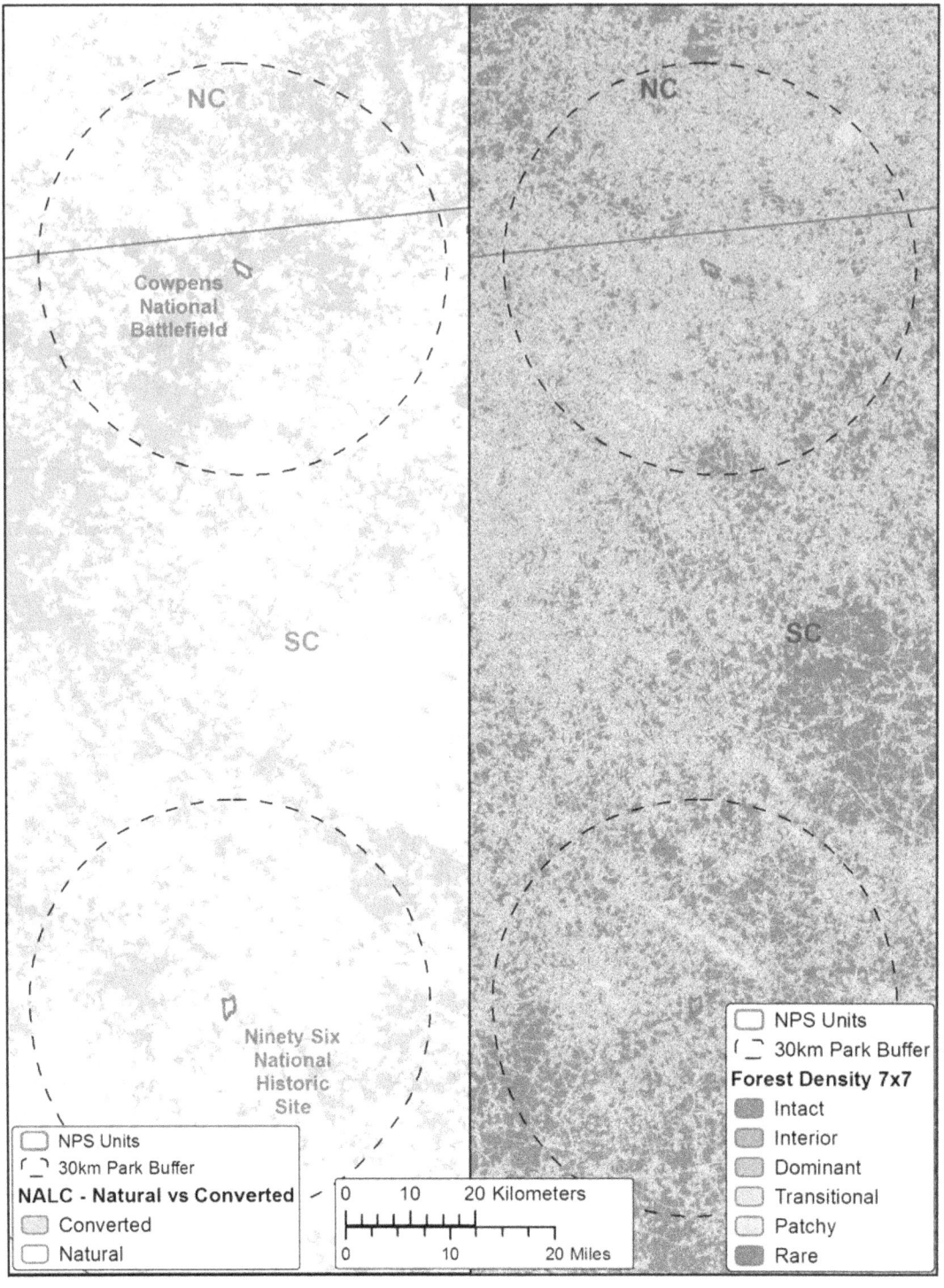

to quickly produce plots like that shown in Figure 2.5, and for AOAs that vary in size.

The NPScape density metric emphasizes the landscape context of a particular pixel, rather the attributes of that pixel. The density metric can also be calculated only for pixels that contain the cover of interest (e.g., forest or grassland). When calculated this way, the apparent expansion of forest with window size, as exhibited in Figure 2.3, does not occur.

Forest and grassland density metrics can be used 'as is' to assess habitat for species that exhibit a strong affinity to forests or grassland, or a mix of cover types. Riitters et al. (1997) used habitat density of forest and

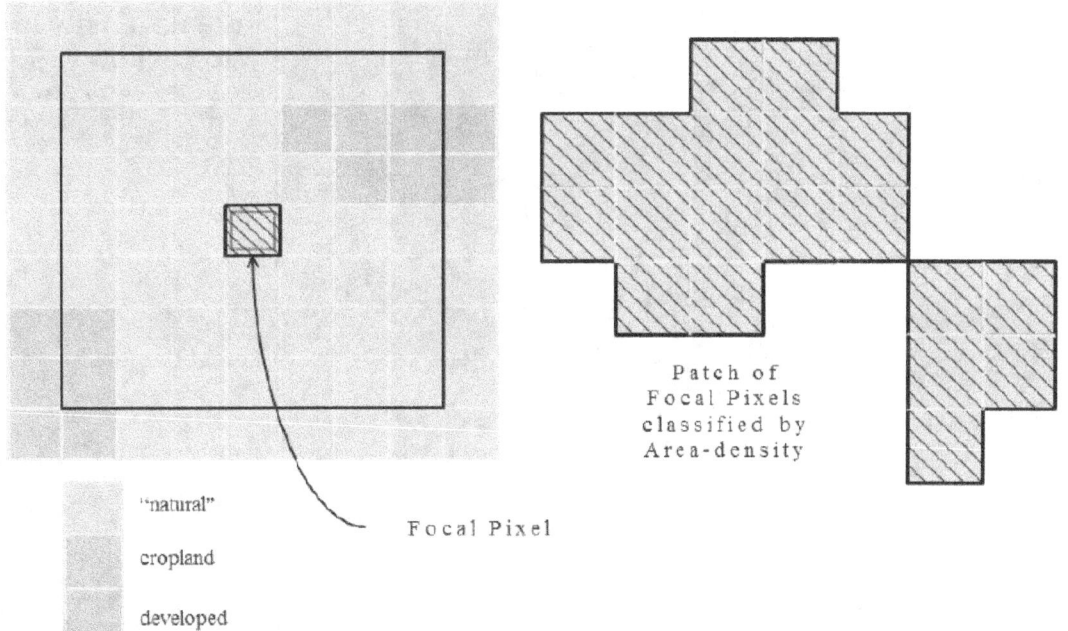

Figure 2.2. Conceptual diagram of how a moving window area-density analysis is performed, in this case for "natural" land cover and a 7x7 pixel moving window (left diagram). As the window moves across the landscape, the percentage of "natural" pixels in the window is calculated for each focal pixel (at the center of the window). If the percentage of "natural" pixels exceed some predefined threshold (e.g., >90%), then center pixel is assigned to an ecologically meaningful category (e.g., "core"). Then, in a separate step (right diagram), the classified pixels are aggregated into spatially contiguous sets of cells to define patches. NPScape uses the classification in Table 2.3.

"natural"

cropland

developed

Focal Pixel

Patch of
Focal Pixels
classified by
Area-density

Table 2.3. Area density class definitions for forest or grassland cover within the moving window. These classes follow Riitters (2011).

Area density class	Area density (p)
Intact	$p = 1.0$
Interior	$0.9 \leq p < 1.0$
Dominant	$0.6 \leq p < 0.9$
Transitional	$0.4 \leq p < 0.6$
Patchy	$0.1 \leq p < 0.4$
Rare	$0.0 \leq p < 0.1$
None	$p = 0.0$

grasslands in the 178,000 km² Chesapeake Bay Watershed, measured with window sizes of 5, 46, and 410 ha (see Table 2.4 for window sizes evaluated in NPScape), to assess habitat availability for archetypic species that prefer 'woody', 'herbaceous', or 'woody-edge' habitats. Their results illustrated the application of habitat density measurements to identify suitable habitat for a matrix of species defined by patch size requirements (i.e., from 5-410 ha), and species that prefer woody to herbaceous habitat types. Similarly, the Heinz Center explored national trends in land cover patterns based on variable-scale moving win-

dows and recommended their inclusion in the State of the Nation's Ecosystems report (Heinz Center 2008a,b). Appropriate scales for analysis of density maps depends on the accuracy of the underlying land cover map. Riitters et al. (1997) analyzed sub-watersheds that varied in size from 622 to 6,200 km².

The multi-scale nature of the density metric lends itself to detecting trends at scales of change that may go undetected by other pattern metrics. Wickham et al. (2007) examined changes in forest area in the Chesapeake Bay / New Jersey region. They compared changes in area-density scaling to changes in the distribution of patch size. Area-density proved to be sensitive to loss in the area of dominant forest, while patch size distribution was unchanged. They found a

Table 2.4. Area within analysis windows for forest and grassland density estimates.

Window Size (pixels per edge)	NLCD (30 m pixel) Area (ha)	NLCD (30 m pixel) Area (ac)	NALC (250 m pixel) Area (ha)	NALC (250 m pixel) Area (ac)
7	4.4	10.9	306	756
13	15.2	37.6	1,056	2,610
27	65.6	162	4,556	11,258
81	590	1,459	41,006	101,328
243	5,314	13,132	369,056	911,957
729	47,829	118,189	3,321,506	8,207,620

Figure 2.3. Forest density in the central US evaluated with a 4.4 ha window (top) and 5,314 ha window (bottom). Forest density (and grassland density in other examples), following Table 2.3, varies from intact (darkest green), to dominant, transitional, patchy, and rare (red). See text for further explanation of these results.

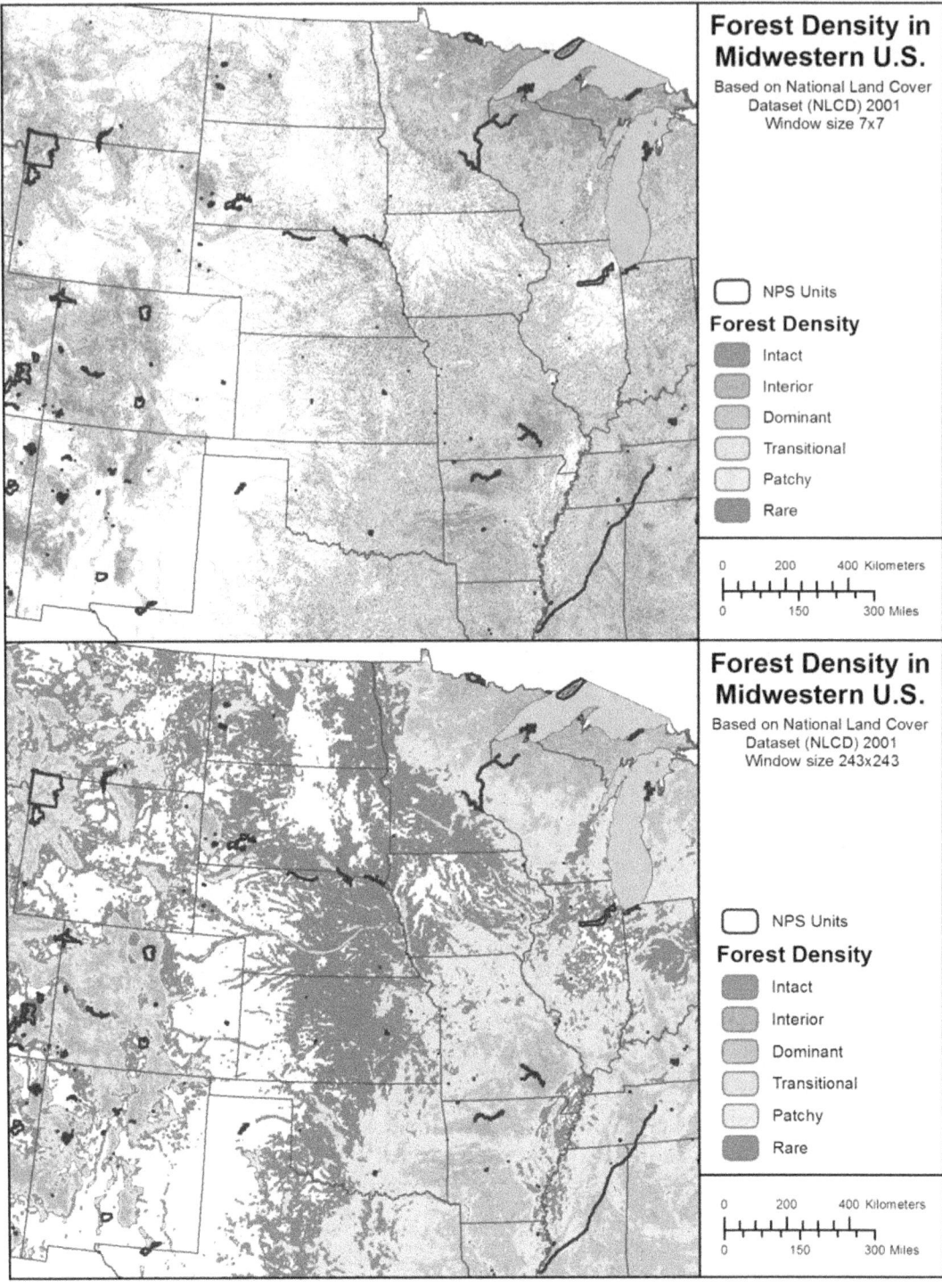

non-linear relationship between the rate of overall forest loss and loss of dominant forest across scales – the loss of dominant forest at the largest scale was approximately 6 times that of the smallest scale.

There are conflicting views about the relative importance of habitat density versus the structure of patches within an area of

analysis. Most studies of landscape pattern and composition have failed to simultaneously account for effects of patch pattern and the amount (density) of habitat. From the studies that independently assessed these traits, a growing number are finding that habitat density has as much or more effect on wildlife populations. These include studies of mammals (Kurki et al. 1998; Umetsu et

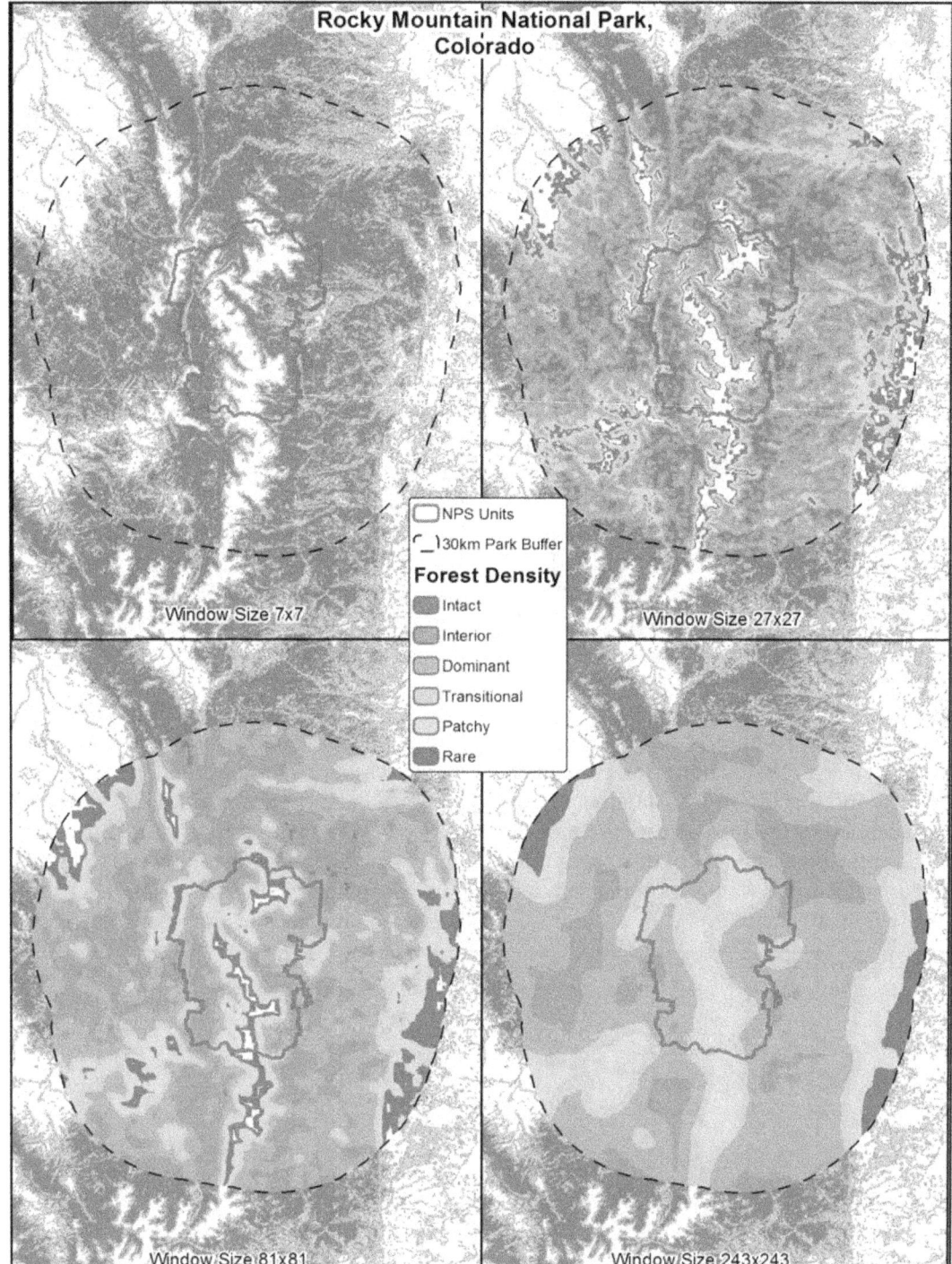

Figure 2.4. Forest density maps of the Rocky Mountain National Park (ROMO) area using window sizes of (top left) 7x7 (4.41 ha), (top right) 27x27 (65.6 ha), (bottom left) 81x81 (590 ha), (bottom right) 243x243 (5,314 ha). ROMO and 30 km AOA boundaries shown in black. The area outside the AOA for all maps is forest density in 7x7 window to emphasize the grouping that occurs with analyses based on larger window sizes.

al. 2008; Ritchie et al. 2009), birds (Trzcinski et al. 1999; Drapeau et al. 2000; Radford & Bennett 2007), and amphibians (Guerry & Hunter 2002; Van Buskirk 2005). Ritchie et al. (2009) noted that these results are sometimes scale dependent and the mechanism of effect varies. Overall, it is clear that pattern matters when 'habitat' is rare, but almost by definition habitat density has some effect,

whether measurable or not, across the entire spectrum of densities. The NPScape Arc-GIS Pattern Density toolbox requires raster inputs for a given land cover type, which may be pure forest or grasslands, or they may be used to represent other user-defined habitat types.

**Figure 2.5.
Relationship
between moving
window size and
percent of area for
Rocky Mountain
National Park within
a 30 km AOA (see
previous figure).
As window size
increases, less area
is categorized as
either without forest
(none) or intact, and
a greater proportion
falls within the
middle classes. Table
2.3 defines density
classes.**

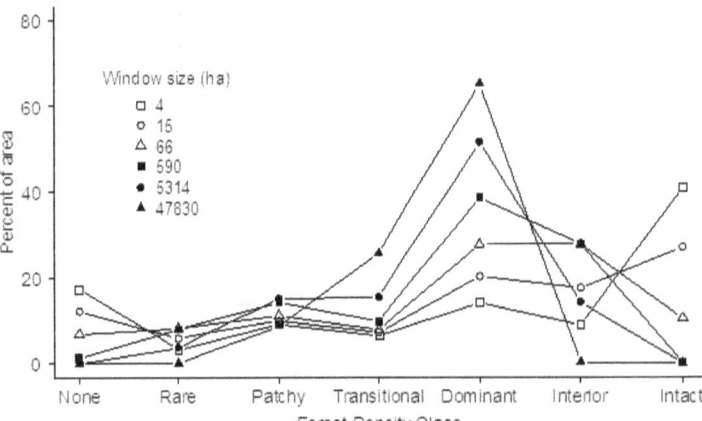

Even where other landscape traits are well known to affect species' abundances, habitat density can be important. As an example, rates of parasitism by cowbirds have often been used in examples of edge effects. Despite the strong affinity of cowbirds for edge habitats, Thompson et al. (2000, their Fig. 4) found a strong relationship between the percentage of forest cover within 10 km of a nest and the percentage of nest parasitism (r = –0.86). In fact, Thompson and collaborators (Donovan et al. 1997; Thompson et al. 2000, 2002) found that broad-scale landscape context, defined by the area-density of forest, was a critical determinant of the magnitude of edge effects and was more important than local patch attributes.

Extra care should be taken when interpreting the forest and grassland density metrics for landscapes that naturally support multiple cover types, such as western landscapes where patches of sagebrush, grasslands, and conifer (or aspen) woodlands are naturally intermixed. In intermixed systems, areas typically classified as background, or 'matrix' (sensu Kupfer et al. 2006), are important natural components of the landscape. In recognition of the complexities of evaluating landscapes that naturally have very mixed cover types, the Heinz Center (2008a) reported a similar metric that included natural cover types to report on forest composition at regional and national scales.

A series of additional examples of NPScape forest and grassland density metrics are given in Figures 2.6, 2.7, and 2.8. Tallgrass Prairie National Preserve and surrounding areas are dominated by intact grasslands that provide important habitat for many species (Figure 2.6). Meanwhile, Wind Cave National Park is located on a steep transition between

**Figure 2.6. Grassland
density for Tallgrass
Prairie National
Preserve and
surrounding 30 km.
This map was made
using the NPScape
grassland density
metric calculated
using NLCD and a 7x7
pixel (4.41 ha) moving
window.**

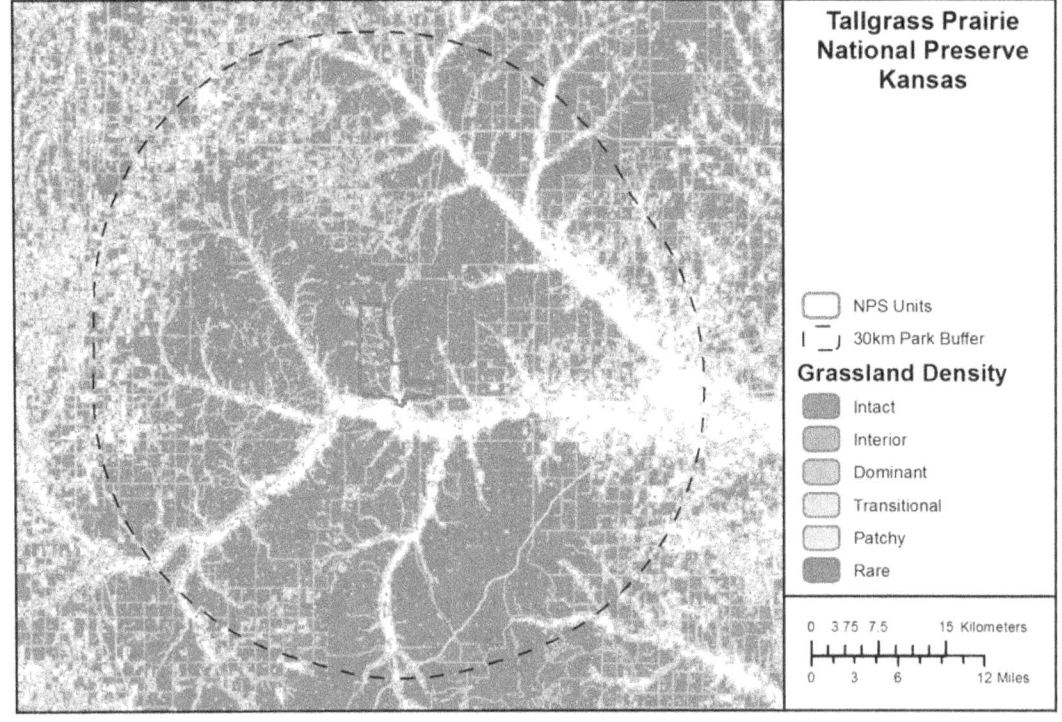

grassland and forested habitats, many of which are classified as intact inside the park and connect with even larger intact patches to the southeast (grassland) and northwest (forest) (Figure 2.7). Finally, Big Thicket National Preserve contains large tracts of forest that are considered intact or interior across multiple spatial scales (Figure 2.8, top maps). Also evident in these maps are corridors of intact/interior forest that connect several of the sub-units of the park. Importantly, these corridors traverse areas with low housing density and are further classified as core habitat based on a morphological spatial pattern analysis (Figure 2.8, bottom maps). The NPScape housing density metric is described in detail in Chapter 4. Forest morphology is detailed later in this chapter.

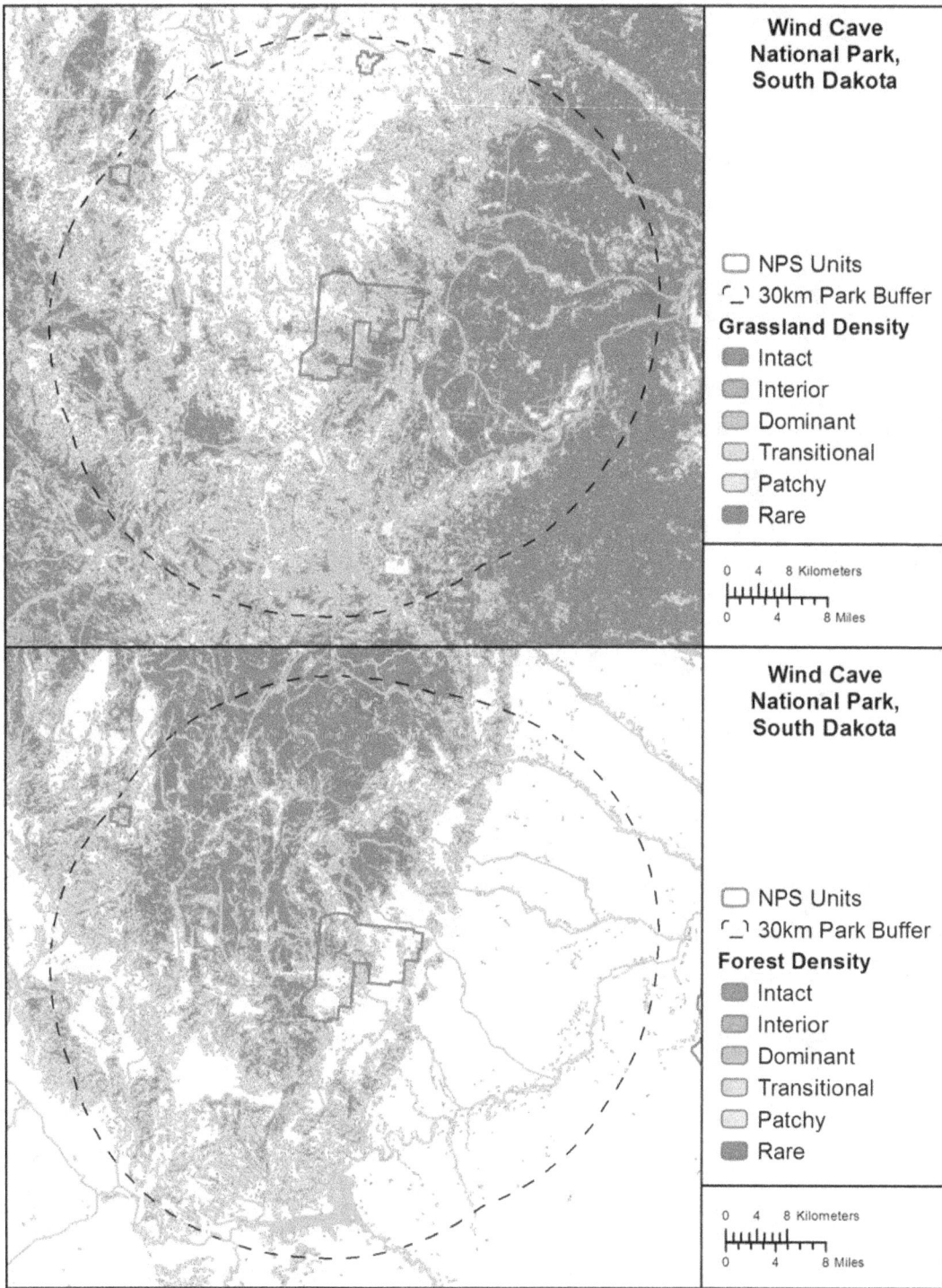

Figure 2.7. Grassland density (top) and forest density (bottom) for Wind Cave National Park, both shown for NLCD with a 7x7 pixel (4.41 ha) window size. This park is located on a transition between the two land cover types, and the density analyses expose areas both within and adjacent to the park with intact habitat.

Figure 2.8. Forest density (top maps), housing density (bottom left), and forest morphology based on MSPA (bottom right) in the area of Big Thicket National Preserve, TX. Note the forested areas that might be used as corridors. See text for description.

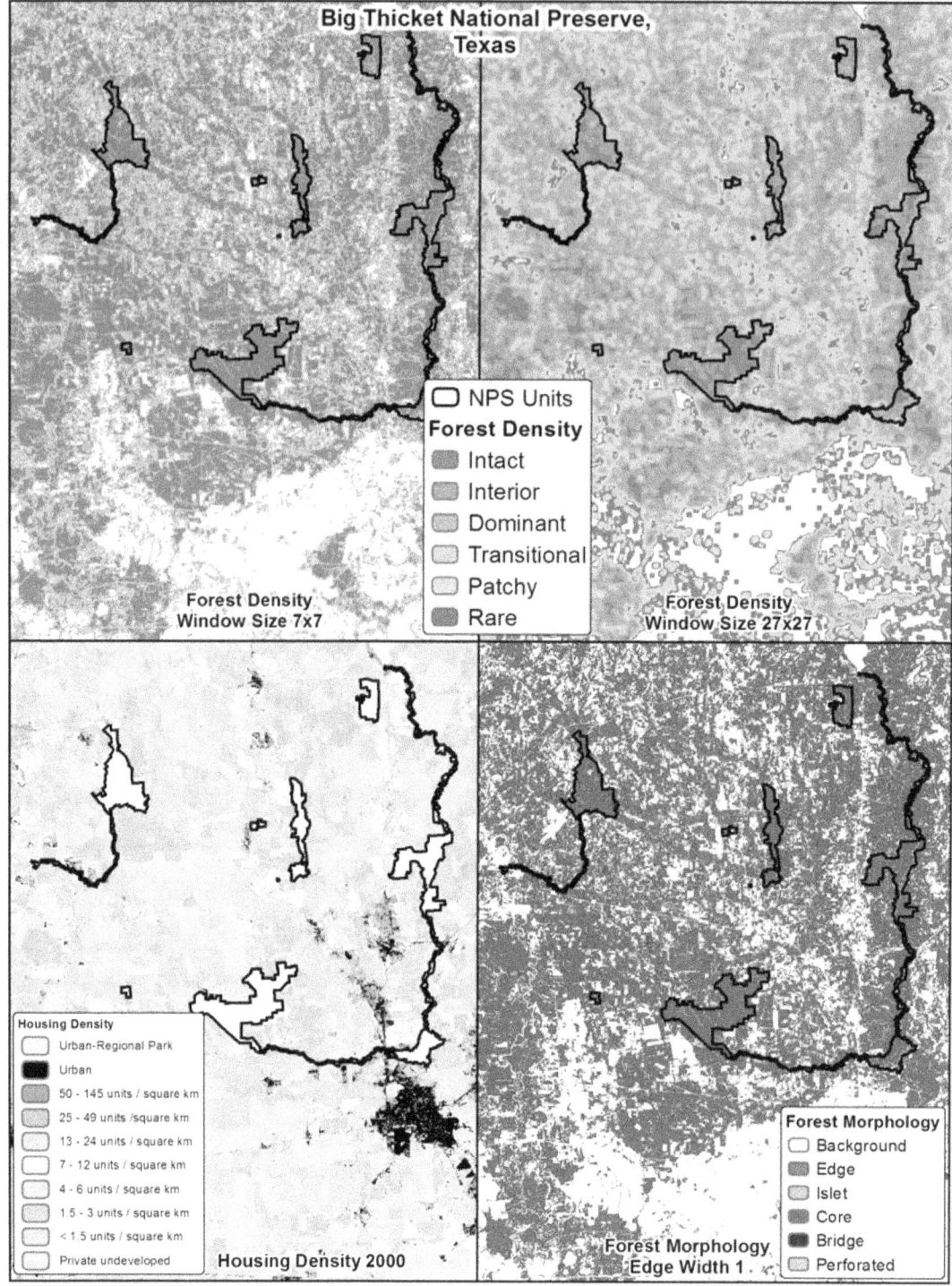

2.4 Habitat Thresholds

NPScape metrics can indicate the loss of habitat, but interpretation tends to focus on questions such as:

- How much habitat loss is too much?

- How does the conversion of land cover from natural to urban or natural to agri-

culture impact species, communities, or ecological processes?

- At what values of land cover might we observe thresholds, or discontinuities, where a small change in land cover catalyzes a larger ecological change?

Along the gradient from completely natural

to completely developed, we want to be especially sensitive to ecological discontinuities or thresholds, where a relatively small change in habitat area or quality results in a large change in biodiversity or ecosystem function (Turner & Gardner 1991; Muradian 2001; Huggett 2005; Groffman et al. 2006; Suding & Hobbs 2009). Management interventions are particularly effective near thresholds, and management targets are generally related to known or postulated thresholds. The challenge is that ecologists are usually unable to accurately identify thresholds until they have been exceeded, and many ecological functions probably change slowly, without any dramatic threshold or abrupt change in behavior (Bennetts et al. 2007). In general, field-based studies suggest that species will almost certainly be affected when the landscape is composed of less than 60 or 70% natural habitat, although results vary (Table 2.5). Less sensitive species may only exhibit a detectable response in landscapes with far more converted habitat. Depending on the context, species, and conservation objective, model-based studies have estimated habitat area requirements that range from almost no habitat to fully intact (100%) natural habitat (Table 2.6). The proportion of land near parks that is still considered 'natural' spans almost the entire range from 0 to 100 percent (Figure 2.9).

Table 2.5. Empirical study estimates of the percentage of natural land cover or suitable habitat necessary for maintenance of various wildlife species in North America. Additional studies from Australia, Europe, and Africa are not included (modified from Svancara et al. 2005).

Taxa	Area	% Habitat	Conclusions	Reference
Birds				
Kirtland's warbler	Michigan	30	Population of male Kirtland's Warblers increased fourfold when the proportion of suitable habitat on the landscape increased above 30%. Patch size, age and distance to occupied patches were important variables.	Donner et al. 2009
Forest species	Panama	40	Bird species richness declined significantly when remaining forest cover dropped below 40% of the historical forest cover.	Rompré et al. 2009
Wetland species	South Dakota	50	Wetland species were more likely to occupy wetlands if <50% of the upland matrix was tilled.	Naugle et al. 2001
Breeding birds	Seattle, Washington	48	Bird species richness was high and many native forest species were retained when urban land cover comprised <52% of landscape.	Donnelly & Marzluff 2006
Forest birds	Oregon	1-25	All 12 species examined showed a positive response to broad-leaf forests, and threshold models received greater support for 8 of 12 species.	Betts et al. 2010
Fish				
Trout	Maryland	96	Brook trout were almost never found in watersheds with >4% impervious surface.	Stranko et al. 2008
Insects				
Beetles	Colorado	20	Tenebrionid beetles in experimental micro-landscapes exhibited a strong threshold in movement parameters when the proportion of grass was <20%.	Wiens et al. 1997
Butterfly	Ohio	40	Though results were species-specific, over half of the butterfly and skipper species surveyed were never observed in plots with <60% suitable habitat remaining. Rare species were disproportionately more affected by habitat fragmentation.	Summerville & Crist 2001

Table 2.5. (continued) Empirical study estimates of the percentage of natural land cover or suitable habitat necessary for maintenance of various wildlife species in North America. Additional studies from Australia, Europe, and Africa are not included (modified from Svancara et al. 2005).

Taxa	Area	% Habitat	Conclusions	Reference
Mammals				
Grizzly bear	US Northern Rocky Mtns	60	Predicted 60% of region in suitable habitat was necessary to maintain an effective population of 500 grizzly bears.	Metzgar & Bader 1992
American marten	Utah, Maine, Wyoming, Newfoundland	70-75	Compared results from different spatial scales and study sites and demonstrated that American marten populations are reduced to near zero density when only 25-30% of forest is lost.	Bissonette et al. 1997
Eastern chipmunk	SE Ontario	30	Predicted that 70% habitat loss was a critical threshold for population size and persistence of eastern chipmunks, though species-specific habitat dependencies produced different vulnerabilities to habitat loss.	Henein et al. 1998
Florida panther	SE US	60-70	Predicted 60-70% of historical range was necessary to maintain an effective population of 500 Florida panthers, actual population of 1000-2000.	Noss 1991
Reviews				
Multiple taxa	Literature Review	20-60	Recommended 20-60% suitable habitat necessary to sustain long-term populations of area-sensitive species and rare species.	Enviornmental Law Institute 2003
Birds, Mammals	Literature Review	10-30	10-30% suitable habitat in the landscape might be a critical threshold for birds and mammals.	Andrén 1994

Table 2.6. Model-based estimates of the percentage of natural land cover or suitable habitat necessary for maintenance of various wildlife species in North America (modified from Svancara et al. 2005). Studies from Australia, Europe, and Africa not included.

Taxa	Area	% Habitat	Conclusions	Reference
Models				
Multiple	Model	75-98	For species with poor dispersal abilities and low reproductive potential, thresholds varied from 75-98% suitable habitat as fragmentation increased.	With & King 1999
Birds	Model	60-100	Model results indicate the numbers of individuals a location can support depends not only on the amount of habitat loss but, whether the loss is restricted to the best or worst patches. If best patches were removed first, decline in number of individuals began immediately. Birds could withstand 40% loss of worst patches.	Sutherland & Anderson 1993
Multiple	Model	30-40	Landscape structure and dispersal behavior affected dispersal success in landscapes with <30-40% suitable habitat; spatial pattern was generally not a factor in dispersal success when habitat >40%.	King & With 2002
Multiple	Model	20-30	Occupancy probability of single hypothetical species decreases with the percentage of habitat loss due to biological parameters.	Bascompte & Solé 1996
Northern spotted owl	Model	19-23	Predicted that extinction of Northern spotted owls would result if suitable habitat (old growth forest) is reduced to <19-23% of the total area in a large region.	Lande 1988

Table 2.6. (continued) Model-based estimates of the percentage of natural land cover or suitable habitat necessary for maintenance of various wildlife species in North America (modified from Svancara et al. 2005). Studies from Australia, Europe, and Africa not included.

Taxa	Area	% Habitat	Conclusions	Reference
Models (continued)				
Multiple	Model	10-30	Model results suggest that real landscapes may have a lower threshold than the theoretical value of 60%, population performance likely declines past threshold of 70-90% habitat loss.	Gardner et al. 1987
Multiple	Model	1-99	Determined minimum amount of habitat needed for persistence varies among regions with species reproductive potential and dispersal strategy, quality of the matrix also has strong influence. These extinction thresholds should not be confused with the 20% fragmentation threshold (see Fahrig 1997, 1998; Andrén 1994).	Fahrig 2001
Multiple	Model	10-80	Results indicated that thresholds depend on demographics of species of interest with 80% suitable habitat required for species with low demographic potential.	Lande 1987
Multiple	Model	59.28	In an infinite, random landscape, percolation theory predicts an organism can move freely if it's critical resource or habitat occupies 59% of the landscape.	Stauffer 1985; Orbach 1986
Birds, Ants	Model	55	Predicted that 45% habitat loss led to extinction of army ants, consequently bird species (n=50) dependent on the ants also showed threshold responses.	Boswell et al. 1998
Multiple	Model	50	Expected occupancy dropped below 0.6 with all simulations when the proportion of suitable habitat was <50%.	Keymer et al. 2000
Grass-hoppers	Model	40	Models of 2 grasshopper species indicated that >40% of suitable habitat was needed for habitat specialists to maintain dispersed populations and >35% for habitat generalists.	With & Crist 1995
Trees	Model	25	Simulated migration rates for the tree species *Tilia cordata* slowed markedly when habitat availability fell below 25%, though patch size and connectivity were also important	Collingham & Huntley 2000
Northern spotted owls	Model	25	Model predicted that >25% of suitable habitat was necessary for an 80% probability of survival of Northern spotted owl for 250 years with environmental variance.	Lamberson et al. 1992
Multiple	Model	20	Model results suggest that when breeding habitat covers more than 20% of landscape, species survival is virtually ensured no matter how fragmented and the effects of habitat loss far outweigh effects of fragmentation.	Fahrig 1997, 1998
Beetles	Model	20	Predicted that the ability of ladybird beetles to track prey populations was affected when suitable habitat dropped below 20%.	With et al. 2002

Thresholds in the extent of natural land cover have been used to define four broad types of landscapes, each associated with particular levels of habitat loss and connectivity (McIntyre & Hobbs 1999, 2000; Hobbs 2005). These landscapes cover a gradient from intact (more than 90% habitat remaining) to variegated (60-90% remaining), fragmented (10-60% remaining), and relictual (less than 10% remaining). A threshold of about 60% habitat is supported by percolation theory where, assuming a random distribution of habitat patches, landscapes rapidly flip from consisting largely of

Figure 2.9. Proportion of the 30 km AOA that is a natural land cover type, as a function of park size. Note: The *x* axis is limited to AOAs < 25,000 km2 in size, and park units are restricted to the Lower 48 (i.e., those covered by NLCD).

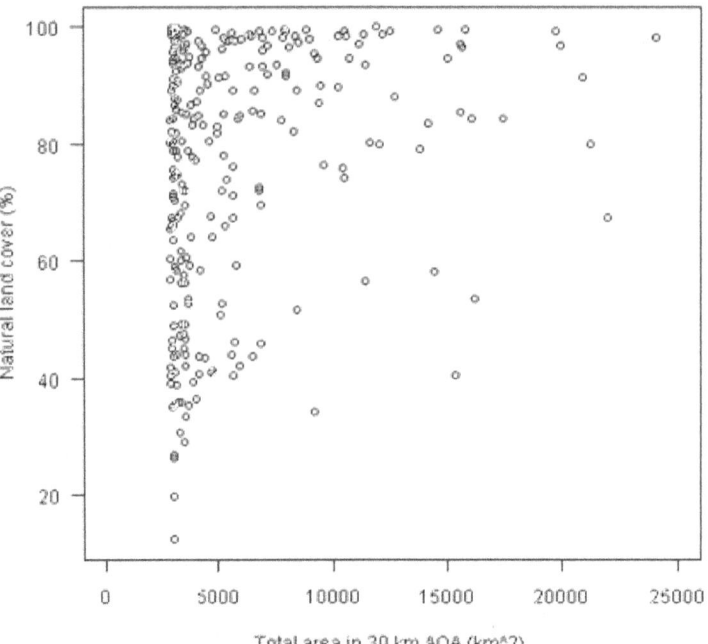

Total area in 30 km AOA (km^2)

interconnected areas of habitat to consisting of a number of small, isolated patches (Stauffer 1985; Gardner et al. 1987; With & Crist 1995). With (2005) postulated that this loss of connectivity can initiate a "threshold cascade". While there is strong theoretical support for a connectivity threshold at about 60% habitat, field studies have suggested that in real landscapes, the habitat area threshold may be much lower. At least in some habitats, 30% natural land cover may represent a more realistic threshold and below 30% natural land cover, loss of connectivity is particularly severe and there is a distinct loss of species dependent on natural land cover (Andrén 1994; With & Crist 1995; Fahrig 2003; Radford et al. 2005). The lower empirical threshold for natural cover likely results, in part, from a methodological requirement to classify areas as 'habitat' or 'not habitat'. The limitations of such a binary classification are widely appreciated, and the importance of the background matrix is receiving more attention as recent analyses question the usefulness of conservation goals dependent on overly simplistic habitat classifications (Kupfer et al. 2006; Prugh et al. 2008; Franklin & Lindenmayer 2009).

Critical habitat area thresholds, such as those supported by percolation theory, have been suggested as landscape targets at the state level (O'Neill et al. 1997) and provide general

guidance on broad management decisions related to total habitat area. For example, when the percentage of natural land cover is ≥ 60%, protective measures may be considered sufficient, while values between 40 and 60% might indicate a need for restoration (Wade et al. 2003). At the national level, such assessments may supply information useful from both a management and policy perspective (Kupfer 2006). Regional and national assessments can provide context for more local evaluations, but they cannot replace local level monitoring (Svancara et al. 2009). Thresholds are "not just a property of landscapes, but one that emerges from species' interactions with landscape structure" (With & Crist 1995).

While a single threshold value cannot adequately describe responses of all species to changes in landscape pattern or extent, certain levels of land cover conversion may act like 'red-flags' for some species (Hansen & Urban 1992; Andrén 1994; With & Crist 1995; Bascompte & Solé 1996; Parker & Mac Nally 2002; Lindenmayer et al. 2005; Svancara et al. 2005). Among terrestrial species, Lande (1987) suggests that species with a large dispersal range, high fecundity, and high survivorship, may be able to persist when suitable habitat covers only 25-50% of the landscape, while species with low demographic potential may be lost when as much as 80% of the landscape remains suitable habitat.

2.5 Habitat Pattern
Patterns in land cover composition, configuration, and connectivity reflect the dynamics of natural ecological processes (Watt 1947), biophysical constraints (Whittaker 1967; Stephenson 1990), and extensive modification resulting from a long history of human occupation and habitat modification (Heilman et al. 2002; Riitters et al. 2002; Mann

2005; Schulte et al. 2007). In turn, these land cover patterns help shape overall patterns in biological diversity, including the complex array of species occurring in an area, movements of individual organisms, and flows of energy and material (Levin 1981; Noss 1990; Dunning et al. 1992; Franklin 1993; Taylor et al. 1993; Turner 2005; Hansen & DeFries 2007; Table 2.7).

All landscapes are more or less heterogeneous due to variation in topography, geology, and soils; natural disturbances like fire, windthrow, and floods; and anthropogenic disturbances like forest clearing, construction, or agriculture. The major difference between natural and anthropogenic disturbances is that habitats lost to natural disturbances usually 'recover', while anthropogenic disturbances usually result in permanent or semi-permanent conversion of habitat to non-habitat types (e.g., forest to road, agricultural field, parking lot, etc.). Changes in habitat availability and pattern are typically measured using independent methods, but they are usually correlated and it is often difficult to separate effects of area and shape on species' responses (Trzcinski et al. 1999). Landscape composition as described simply by the proportion of cover types is a very important attribute of a system, and there are strong theoretical relationships between cover and attributes like landscape percolation (Gardner & O'Neill 1991, and discussed above). The effects of habitat area, patch isolation, and pattern likely interact. Betts et al. (2006), for example, found that landscape pattern was important to ovenbirds, but only when patches were isolated. Theoretical studies (reviews in Betts et al. 2006) have identified threshold effects due to the interaction of habitat loss and pattern, but these sorts of complex ecological relationships, which may be pervasive, are very difficult to study in the field.

Pattern metrics can describe individual patches (size, shape), properties of cover classes (connectivity, isolation), or landscape-level metrics that are functions of the composition and arrangement of patches throughout the entire area of analysis (richness, evenness, diversity). While metrics of landscape composition (abundance, variety of patches) are relatively straight-forward to calculate, they do not account for or describe effects of location, size, shape, or spatial configuration of patches. Conversely, spatial configuration is difficult to quantify in simple metrics, and metrics of spatial configuration are most valuable when combined with other information. Some metrics, like patch size distribution, reflect the aggregate of individual patch characteristics across an area of analysis, while other metrics, like isolation or connectivity, describe the spatial relationship between patches.

The description of pattern metrics can further be divided between those that describe structural versus functional characteristics of the landscape. Structural metrics measure

Table 2.7. Example effects of landscape pattern on ecological functions and biodiversity.

Effect	Description	Reference
Movement between patches	Most strongly correlated with amount of habitat in a buffer around patch (simulation study).	Bender et al. 2003; Tischendorf et al. 2003
Percolation across a landscape	For random pattern, occurs when 60-70% of landscape is composed of habitat.	Gardner et al. 1989
Number of forest interior bird species	Increases with patch size.	Forman et al. 1976; reviewed by Fahrig 2003
Sediment and nutrient absorption / buffering	Vegetation fragmentation and natural vegetation along waterways strongly affect stream biological condition.	Shandas & Alberti 2009
Forest cover in riparian buffers is associated with fish Index of Biological Integrity (IBI)	Riparian forest cover and length slope were most important watershed-scale variables and mostly positively correlated with IBI scores in the eastern corn belt.	Frimpong et al. 2005

physical attributes without regard to any specific species or ecological function. Structural metrics include patch size distribution and nearest-neighbor distances between patches. The determination of structural pattern metrics is – in theory – invariant across applications. By contrast, functional pattern metrics measure spatial landscape attributes that are relevant to properties of particular species or processes. Functional metrics thus require parameters that apply to focal resources, and different applications may yield very different results. Connectivity metrics are typically functional, and they include parameters that account for the dispersal ability of a species or group of species. For example, graph analyses (Townsend et al. 2009) can evaluate landscape connectivity at a scale relevant at the relatively short movements characteristic of amphibians or squirrels (Lookingbill et al. 2008, 2010), or at broader scales that reflect the movement abilities of species such as spotted owls (Keitt et al. 1997).

2.5.1 Morphological Spatial Pattern Analysis

NPScape provides land cover pattern metrics based on Morphological Spatial Pattern Analysis (MSPA), a pixel-level analysis of cover maps using image segmentation to classify individual pixels into a set of pattern types, including core, patch, connector, perforation, edge, and background (Vogt et al. 2007a,b, 2009; pattern types are defined in Table 2.8). The behavior of these metrics across scales and in landscapes with defined statistical properties has been examined (Riitters et al. 2007; Ostapowicz et al. 2008; Riitters et al. 2009a), as has their ability to characterize landscape connectivity and identify corridors (Vogt et al. 2007b, 2009). Vogt et al. (2007a) describe the process of MSPA, provide an example application, and highlight the advantages of this method over approaches that require identification and delineation of specific patches. Software used to calculate the landscape metric is part of the GUIDOS package, available from the European Commission Joint Research Centre (http://forest.jrc.ec.europa.eu/download/software/guidos/) and is described by Soille & Vogt (2009).

NPScape has included MSPA for forest and grasslands. Advantages of MSPA for these cover types are that, at Anderson Level

Table 2.8. Landscape pattern metrics and their description. These metrics can be sensitive to both areas of analysis, and to the scale at which the metric is defined.

Effect	Description	Reference
Composition	Proportion of area. Usually an aggregate class (forest/non-forest, natural/converted). Can be elegantly expressed at multiple scales.	Heinz Center 2008a; Riitters et al. 2009a
Patch size distribution	Simple and understandable metric. Does not describe spatial relationships between patches.	Turner 1989; Gardner et al. 2008 (and many others)
Landscape morphology	A pixel-based, structural approach to identify specific types of landscape elements. The key types are described below. Analyses used by NPScape are based on maps that aggregate classes in to forest/non-forest, or natural grassland/non-natural-grassland. See text for a more detailed and complete description.	Riitters et al. 2007; 2009b; Ostapowicz et al. 2008; Vogt et al. 2007a,b, 2009
- Core	Foreground pixels that are more than a defined 'edge' distance from the background.	
- Edge	Pixels within a defined distance ('edge') to the background. NPScape reports analyses with edges of 30 m (1 pixel) and 150 m (5 pixels) for NLCD-based analyses data.	
- Patch	Distinct area with foreground pixels that does not contain any core pixels. i.e., all edge or other classes.	
- Connector	A cluster of non-core pixels connected at two or more locations to edge.	
- Perforation	Inner boundary of a core area that is adjacent to a hole in the core area.	

I, they are reliably mapped in most land cover classifications, and they are further important to many park natural and cultural resources and values. Like other NPScape pattern metrics (Table 2.7), MSPA may be objectively repeated over time to detect changes at multiple scales. MSPA metrics are sensitive to fire, land type conversions, and other common types of landscape change that occur over broad extents. Three key attributes of MSPA are (1) analyses can be conducted over very large spatial extents, (2) its sensitivity to pixel-based maps, and (3) its ability to detect changes in patterns over time. The number of pixels in each morphological pattern class are easily summed and the composition of an area of interest described in terms of the proportion or area of core and edge habitats. Areas of other morphological types can also be calculated, but interpretation of the significance or ecological function of some types is difficult. NPScape MSPA results are based on methods detailed in Riitters (2011), and the current data distribution includes results with edges defined as the area within 30 and 150 m of a core area of forest or grassland (i.e., there are four data layers: forest with 30 m edge, forest with 150 m edge; same edge definitions for grassland; Figures 2.10 and 2.11). Responses to edges vary across species, and they may even vary within a species but across habitats (e.g., Mazerolle & Hobson 2003).

NPScape MSPA metrics, roads, and patch size summaries and maps provide information on core and edge habitat abundance and distribution. Figure 2.10 illustrates results from MSPA for the Chesapeake and Ohio Canal (CHOH) and the broader context of the park. Overall, 52% of the AOA is natural land cover (e.g., unconverted forest), but the proportion of 'habitat' varies with location and spatial scale. By varying the edge width used in the analysis, MSPA provides an effective and scalable means to evaluate landscapes for species or processes that are sensitive to edges. NPScape reports MSPA with edge widths of 30 m and 150 m habitat because these widths allow comparison to other studies, and these widths are clearly relevant to many park-based resources.

NPScape methods may be used with the GUIDOS software to replicate MSPA metrics for other edge widths and land cover types. A comparison of results from MSPA of CHOH with a small edge width (30 m) and larger edge width (150 m) clearly shows the spatial distribution of core forested areas. Together, these results suggest that species that require core forested areas and large home ranges are at risk in this AOA.

2.5.2 Ecological Effects of Edges

An important consequence of increased habitat patchiness is the greater proportion of edges in the landscape. At fine scales, edges influence virtually every ecological property and there have thus been thousands of studies on the ecological roles of habitat edges. Forman (1995) and Ries et al. (2004) provide very good general syntheses and reviews. Chalfoun et al. (2002) focus on edges and nesting success of birds. Ewers & Didham (2006) and Fletcher et al. (2007) investigate additional factors that influence species at the boundaries of ecological types and the interaction of edge and area effects.

The MSPA data provided by NPScape show where edges are and how much edge habitat exists. The appropriate distance to use as an edge width varies with the species, question, and other characteristics, such as the contrast between habitat types.

Ries & Sisk (2004) developed a general framework for evaluating the likely consequences of changes in patchiness and edge habitat at a specific site. Direct effects of edges are usually measured at fine scales and across distinct boundaries (e.g., forest-grassland edges) because changes in the proportion of habitat edge accompanies changes in, for example, core habitat, proportional land cover, and habitat pattern (at a variety of scales).

Ries & Sisk (2004) identified four primary mechanisms that account for most ecological effects of edges:

- Ecological flows: changing the rate of transport of energy and materials across the boundary

Figure 2.10. Landscape pattern around the Chesapeake & Ohio Canal NHP. Distribution of natural and converted land cover (top) and forest pattern with an edge width of 30 m (middle) or 150 m (bottom). Pattern types are defined in Table 2.8.

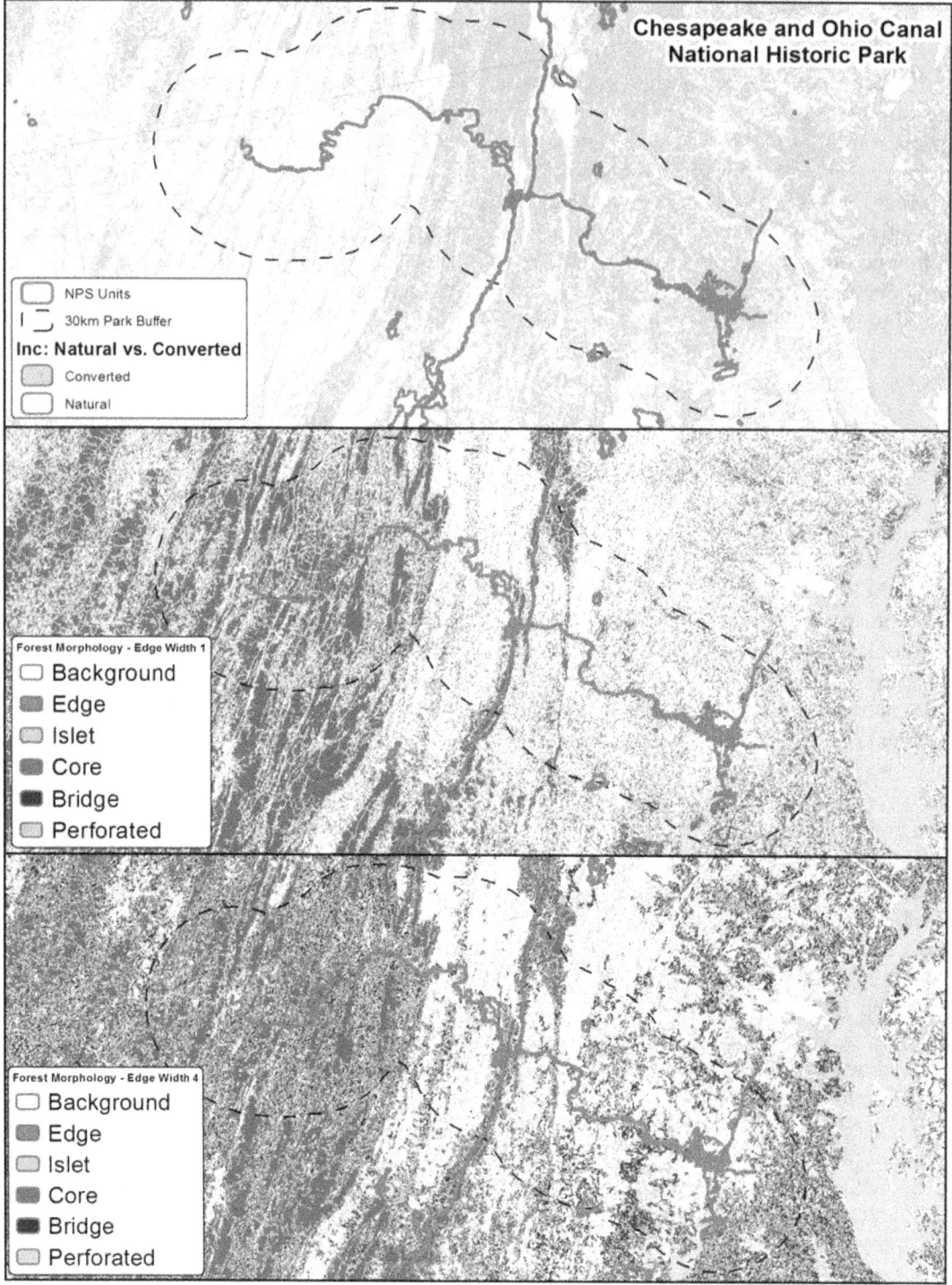

- Access to spatially separated resources: a result of the juxtaposition of different cover types

- Resource mapping: where a species' distribution maps directly to its resources

- Species interactions: changes in predator-prey, parasitism, etc. that result

directly or indirectly from the contrast in adjacent cover types

Ecological Flows across Edges: There are often sharp gradients in moisture, temperature, wind, and light across forest ecotones, and these can dramatically influence the composition and structure of vegetation (Didham & Lawton 1999). Forest

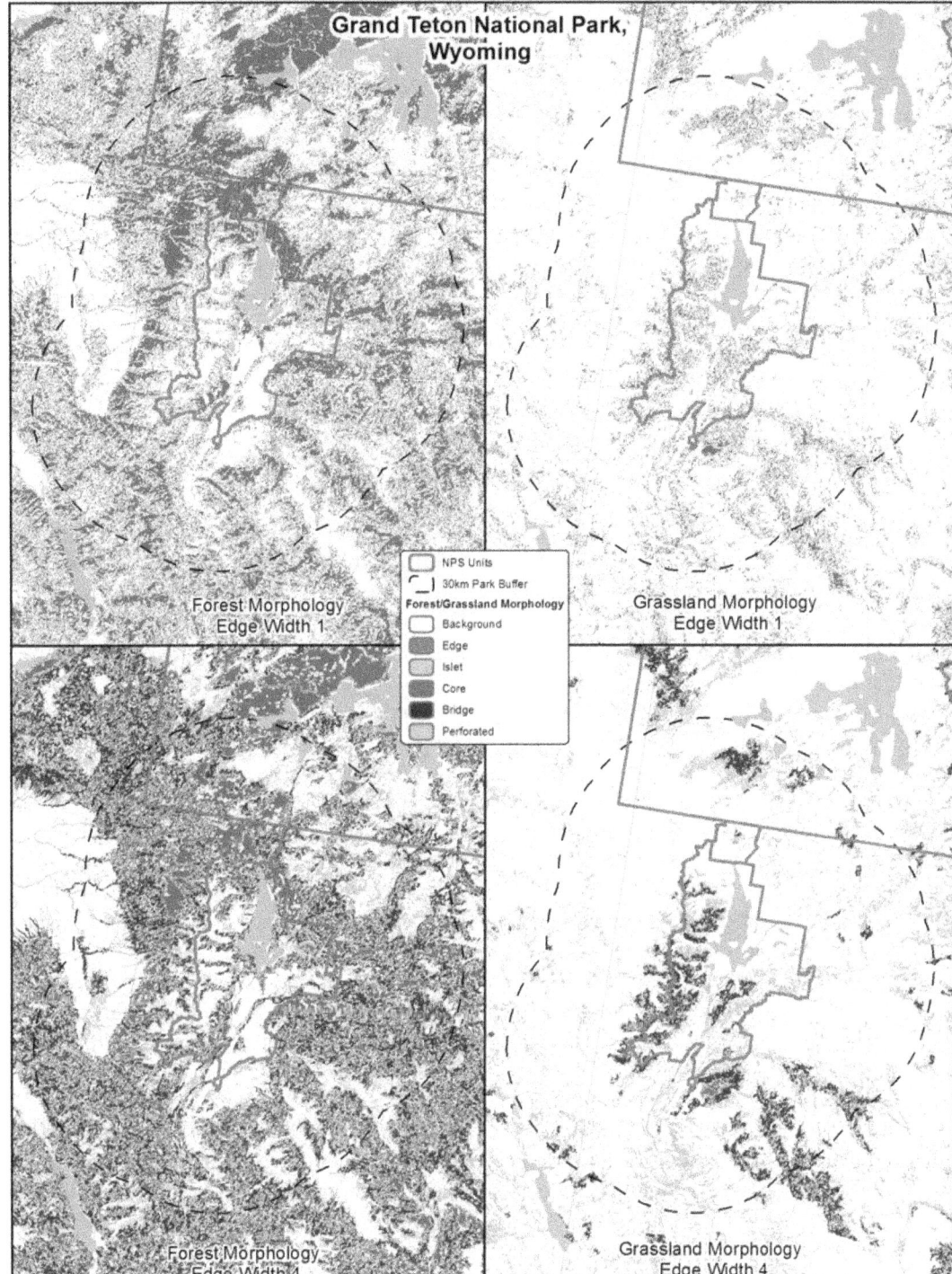

Figure 2.11. Examples of morphological landscape pattern metrics provided by NPScape, here illustrated for Grand Teton National Park with forest (left maps) and grassland (right maps) land cover types. A scale factor (edge width) establishes the degree of buffer or permeability between land cover types: 30 m edge (top maps) vs. 150 m edge (bottom maps). Note how smaller edge widths equate to larger areas defined as 'core'. In general, setting appropriate edge width(s) will be question dependent. For example, a single edge width might be selected based on the dispersal capability of focal taxa. Alternatively, the inclusion of a range of edge widths could allow one to bracket the range of plausible pattern metrics that characterize a landscape.

edges adjacent to open habitats are drier, lighter, and hotter than forest interior, and thus often suitable for a different suite of species (Chen et al. 1999). Open habitats near forests are likely to be cooler and more shaded than those farther from forest edges. Edges can facilitate or inhibit movement of species or their propagules (pollen, air-transported eggs or organisms).

Access to Resources: Until the 1970s, habitat edges were widely considered to be beneficial because of the higher density of animals and richness of species in these ecotones (Leopold 1933; Johnston 1947). Deer and other game species – the focus of many early studies – prefer mixed habitats, and thus management recommendations often included the creation or enhancement of edges. These species benefit from the close proximity of habitats that provide different resources – in this case cover and forage. Some species may require both core and edge features. Brown-headed cowbirds, for example, parasitize the nests of forest song-birds (often in edge habitats), but they forage in open pasture/grassland. Access to different habitat types and/or habitat structural features may be particularly important for species where habitat requirements vary with life stage (Ponsero & Joly 1998). In cases where resource access is believed to result in edge effects, it is important to be able to demonstrate that multiple habitats provide different/complementary resources.

Resource Mapping: Species' distributions at edges are influenced by resource mapping via multiple pathways. Many plants and animals track abiotic gradients in moisture, light, or nutrients. For example, Monahan & Hijmans (2008) showed how a northward winter range expansion in the field sparrow (*Spizella pusilla*) tracked climatically induced changes in ecosystem net primary productivity until the 1960s, at which point the species reached its lower lethal temperature limit imposed by physiology.

Ries et al. (2004) noted that the most common studies of resource mapping focused on vegetation structure and habitat selection by birds. Another common form of resource mapping is the overlap in the distribution of plants and animals. For example, in the spotted owl (*Strix occidentalis*), individuals that prey primarily on wood rats (*Neotoma* sp., an edge related species) are more abundant near forest edges, whereas individuals that feed mainly on flying squirrels (*Glaucomys sabrinus*, a non-edge related species) exhibit no edge effect (Zabel et al. 1995; Ward et al. 1998).

Most studies of resource mapping are correlational and thus do not necessarily identify the resource variables or gradients that cause edge effects. In these instances, it is possible that edge effects are most proximately mediated by an entirely different set of variables that are correlated with the variables measured in the study. As a unique example of

a study that quantified the importance of different resource gradients, Kristan et al. (2003) tested the hypothesis that changes in vegetation features near habitat edges account for observed edge effects. In the case of two birds and one mammal, they found that species abundances tracked changes in vegetation with respect to the edge, while another three species failed to show a vegetation-mediated edge response. Studies like this illustrate the importance of thinking mechanistically and testing hypotheses about observed species-resource associations.

Species Interactions: Species interactions at edges include predation, parasitism, herbivory, and competition. Parasitism by birds is a well-know example. Hartley & Hunter (1998) found that rates of parasitism of nests in US forested habitats were higher near edges. Cowbirds are particularly well studied. The preferred foraging habitat for cowbirds is open pasture, but they exhibit a very strong preference for forested breeding sites within about 200 m of the forest edge (Howell et al. 2006). Nests of other bird species in edge habitats can experience very high rates of parasitism (Thompson et al. 2000; Howell et al. 2006).

Ries et al. (2004) discuss a variety of other situations where species interactions result in edge effects. These include bird predation on insects (Ries & Fagan 2003), mammals avoiding edges due to higher predation rates (Bowers & Dooley 1993), higher predation of seeds and herbs (by mice) near edges (Tallmon et al. 2003). But the direction and magnitude of effects are inconsistent, and other studies reveal lower rates of predation (e.g., seeds: Nickel et al. 2003).

A Predictive Model for Edge Effects: The mechanisms proposed by Ries et al. (2004, discussed above) are important to understanding how organisms can respond to edges, such as the various edges mapped by NPScape. Ries & Sisk (2004) incorporated this understanding into a predictive conceptual model of edge effects, based on resource distributions and the projected response of organisms to changes in resources across ecotones. In theory, the model can be applied to all species and all edge types. Model predictions of change in organismal abundance are founded on the relative distribution of resources in habitats on either side of the edge and include: (1) a decrease in abundance in the preferred habitat and an increase in the non-preferred habitat when resources are concentrated in just one of the two habitats, (2) an increase in abundance near both edges when resources are divided between the two habitats, (3) no directional change in abundance when resources are spread equally among habitats, and (4) an increase in abundance near the edge in both habitats when resources are concentrated along the edge. An initial test of the model using data for 52 bird species demonstrated strong support for these predictions (Ries & Sisk 2004). One advantage of the conceptual model is that it readily accommodates differing edge types and responses; in so doing it accounts for apparently conflicting results of studies that have shown how responses of a single species to edges can be positive, negative, and neutral.

2.5.3 Structural and Functional Connectivity

The only NPScape analysis that provides direct information on corridors (structural connectivity) is MSPA. However, MSPA is best suited to identify specific, fine-scale corridors or connectors, and MSPA will probably be of limited use for identifying important corridors at broader scales. Although NPScape does not presently offer much in the way of direct quantitative measures of connectivity, many of the analyses and underlying base layers can be used as important inputs to analyses of connectivity. For example, a biologist may wish to identify least-cost paths between intact forest patches larger than 10,000 ha. NPScape data can be used to locate large intact forest patches, and to estimate travel costs that are a function of other factors like housing density, roads, and topography. Additionally, NPScape metrics can be overlaid on a map to visualize opportunities for connectivity, which may then be evaluated more formally using quantitative approaches.

Increased habitat patchiness erodes landscape connectivity and it imposes the need for patches to connected if they are to support viable populations, ecological integrity, and ecosystem function. The importance of maintaining connectivity varies depending on the conservation target and – in the case of species – dispersal potential and other life history attributes. The habitat connectivity literature has grown tremendously over the past couple decades and we are now confronted with a confusing set of related concepts and different ways to address conservation issues.

Corridors versus Connectivity: The concept of landscape connectivity was introduced by Merriam (1984) and later defined by Taylor et al. (1993) as "the degree to which the landscape facilitates or impedes movement among resource patches". This definition emphasizes how landscape connectivity is largely a functional rather than structural concept and something that is shaped by both habitat pattern and the attributes of what is moving (e.g., species, nutrients, materials). Conversely, structural connectivity exists irrespective of what is moving and is thus largely a product of habitat pattern. Habitat corridors represent one possible form of structural connectivity. NPScape pattern metrics similarly reflect a structural view of connectivity but may be expressed functionally when considered in relation to a particular organism.

To illustrate the difference between structural and functional forms of connectivity, consider a landscape consisting of two habitat patches connected by a long, narrow corridor. Despite being structurally connected, the length, shape, and matrix condition (e.g., Vergara 2011) of the corridor would prevent some species from moving between the two habitat patches. But after removal of the corridor, these (now) structurally isolated patches could still be functionally connected for highly vagile organisms like birds, or for plants with windblown propagules. Clear definitions of connectivity are necessary to ensure the method used is suitable for a particular application.

Patch Connectivity versus Isolation: The degree of isolation among habitat patches may also be thought of in terms of structural or functional forms. In a functional sense, it is a product of the rates of immigration and emigration among patches, which again are determined by a combination of habitat pattern and the attributes of what is moving on the landscape. According to this view, connectivity is synonymous with the inverse of the average degree of patch isolation (Tischendorf & Fahrig 2000). Hence, patch isolation and connectivity are related concepts, and one may be preferentially used in place of the other depending on context.

How to Measure Connectivity?: Tischendorf & Fahrig (2000) describe several examples of how to measure functional landscape connectivity, which they broadly categorize into model-based and empirical approaches. Model-based approaches include measuring dispersal success, search time (i.e., the number of movements made by individuals before finding a new habitat patch), and the spatial distribution of populations, which are not direct measures of connectivity but in many instances are assumed to be related to connectivity. Meanwhile, empirical approaches include measuring functional distances (i.e., the sum of weighted distances between all pairs of points on a landscape, where weights are determined based on movement intensity and mortality rate) and obtaining direct estimates of movement using techniques like mark-recapture.

Galpern et al. (2011) articulated and discussed nine conservation-relevant questions that connectivity (or fragmentation) metrics can address. A full discussion of these questions is beyond the scope of this report, but the questions are clearly relevant to selecting, evaluating, and applying NPScape metrics.

The questions are:

1. Which areas of the landscape are connected?

2. Which areas of the landscape are highly connected?

3. What are the critical thresholds at which the landscape is aggregated?

4. What are the implications of the network topology for connectivity?

5. How does connectivity differ between graphs?

6. Which patches are important for connectivity?

7. Which patches are important as sources and which as sinks?

8. What types of patches are important for connectivity?

9. Which connections among patches are important for connectivity?

For more information, readers can refer to the following: Galpern et al. (2011) for information on conservation applications of graph theory; Theobald (2006) and Theobald et al. (2011, 2012) for a variety of connectivity methods and applications; and Hilty et al. (2006) for an unusually broad context for corridor studies and conservation applications.

As an illustration of the potential application of NPScape data, Goetz et al. (2009) identified the location of forest 'core' areas in the Northeastern and mid-Atlantic US and evaluated the connectivity of these areas. Forest cores were defined as areas > 5,000 m from the nearest improved road and with an area > 2,000 ha. Their analyses found that 19% of core areas were within NPS park units and that more than a third of core areas had no long-term protection (i.e., were not identified in the Protected Area Database of the US as GAP status codes 1 or 2, see Chapter 5). Goetz et al. (2009) used a graph-based approach to identify a number of parks in the area that have a key role as connecting 'links' between core areas.

2.5.4 Other Pattern Metrics
Many other landscape pattern metrics are easily calculated using widely available software such as r.le (Baker & Cai 1992),

FRAGSTATS (McGarigal & Marks 1995), and Patch Analyst (Rempel 2009) with either vector or raster-based land cover maps. The basic attributes of most of these pattern metrics have been extensively studied and reviewed, and it is apparent that many metrics are highly correlated and that only a small number contain most of the available information (Riitters et al. 1995; Cain et al. 1997; Calabrese & Fagan 2004; Cushman et al. 2008). The real challenge, then, is to figure out which metrics are informative. The FRAGSTATS web site provides a particularly useful overview of many commonly used pattern metrics.

2.6 Land Cover Effects on Water and Watershed Condition

Aquatic resources within parks can be strongly influenced by conditions in upstream watersheds. The NPScape upstream watershed AOA (Figure 1.7) and other NPScape metric processing SOPs and ArcGIS toolboxes can greatly facilitate analyses of these upstream catchment areas (Monahan & Gross 2012). The relative influence of landscape attributes on watershed condition varies with the size of the analysis area. In general, spatial characteristic of landscape features (e.g., proportion of forest within 100 m of a stream) affect analyses of smaller watersheds to a much greater extent than analyses of large watersheds. Over time, some landscape factors may have only transient effects on aquatic resources, such as sedimentation or temporarily altered flow during road or housing construction that ceases once roads or buildings are completed (Wheeler et al. 2005). Most landscape attributes have more persistent effects on aquatic resources: paved roads and developed areas have long-term effects on hydrology and they contribute nutrients and contaminants such as salts and metals to streams. Finally, historic land use can have impacts that last well beyond the duration of that use. Examples are colonial-era clearing and mining that resulted in runoff and sedimentation that has persisted long after the land cover reverted to forest (Harding et al. 1998; Noe & Hupp 2009).

Table 2.9. Environmental factors altered by land use changes, and the mechanisms by which they alter stream ecosystems (reproduced from Allan 2004).

Factor	Effects	References
Sedimentation	Increases turbidity, scouring and abrasion; impairs substrate suitability for periphyton and biofilm production; decreases primary production and food quality causing bottom-up effects through food webs; in-filling of interstitial habitat harms crevice-occupying invertebrates and gravel-spawning fishes; coats gills and respiratory surfaces; reduces stream depth heterogeneity, leading to decrease in pool species.	Wood & Armitage 1997; Walser & Bart 1999; Henley et al. 2000; Quinn 2000; Burkhead & Jelks 2001; Hancock 2002; Sutherland et al. 2002
Nutrient enrichment	Nutrient increases autotrophic biomass and production, resulting in changes to assemblage composition, including proliferation of filamentous algae, particularly if light also increases; accelerates litter breakdown rates and may cause decrease in dissolved oxygen and shift from sensitive species to more tolerant, often non-native species.	Lenat & Crawford 1994; Carpenter et al. 1998; Delong & Brusven 1998; Mainstone & Parr 2002; Niyogi et al. 2003
Contaminant pollution	Increases heavy metals, synthetics, and toxic organics in suspension associated with sediments and in tissues; increases deformities; increases mortality rates and impacts to abundance, drift, and emergence in invertebrates; depresses growth, reproduction, condition, and survival among fishes; disrupts endocrine system; physical avoidance.	Cooper 1993; Woodward et al. 1997; Liess & Schulz 1999; Schulz & Liess 1999; Clements et al. 2000; Rolland 2000; Kolpin et al. 2002
Hydrologic alteration	Alters runoff-evapotranspiration balance, causing increases in flood magnitude and frequency, and often lowers base flow; contributes to altered channel dynamics, including increased erosion from channel and surroundings and less-frequent overbank flooding; runoff more efficiently transports nutrients, sediments, and contaminants, thus further degrading in-stream habitat. Strong effects from impervious surfaces and stormwater conveyance in urban catchments and from drainage systems and soil compaction in agricultural catchments.	Poff & Allan 1995; Allan et al. 1997; Paul & Meyer 2001; Walsh et al. 2001; Wang et al. 2001

Table 2.9. (continued) Environmental factors altered by land use changes, and the mechanisms by which they alter stream ecosystems (reproduced from Allan 2004).

Factor	Effects	References
Riparian clearing/ canopy opening	Reduces shading, causing increases in stream temperatures, light penetration, and plant growth; decreases bank stability, inputs of litter and wood, and retention of nutrients and contaminants; reduces sediment trapping and increases bank and channel erosion; alters quantity and character of dissolved organic carbon reaching streams; lowers retention of benthic organic matter owing to loss of direct input and retention structures; alters trophic structure.	Lowrance et al. 1984; Gregory et al. 1991; Osborne & Kovacic 1993; Gurnell et al. 1995; Martin et al. 1999; Stauffer et al. 2000; Bourque & Pomeroy 2001; Findlay et al. 2001
Loss of large woody debris	Reduces substrate for feeding, attachment, and cover; causes loss of sediment and organic material storage; reduces energy dissipation; alters flow hydraulics and therefore distribution of habitats; reduces bank stability; influences invertebrate and fish diversity and community function.	Ehrman & Lamberti 1992; Gurnell et al. 1995; Maridet et al. 1995; Stauffer et al. 2000; Johnson et al. 2003

Figure 2.12. Mapping of NPScape landscape measures affecting each of Allan's (2004) environmental factors, which effect aquatic ecosystems.

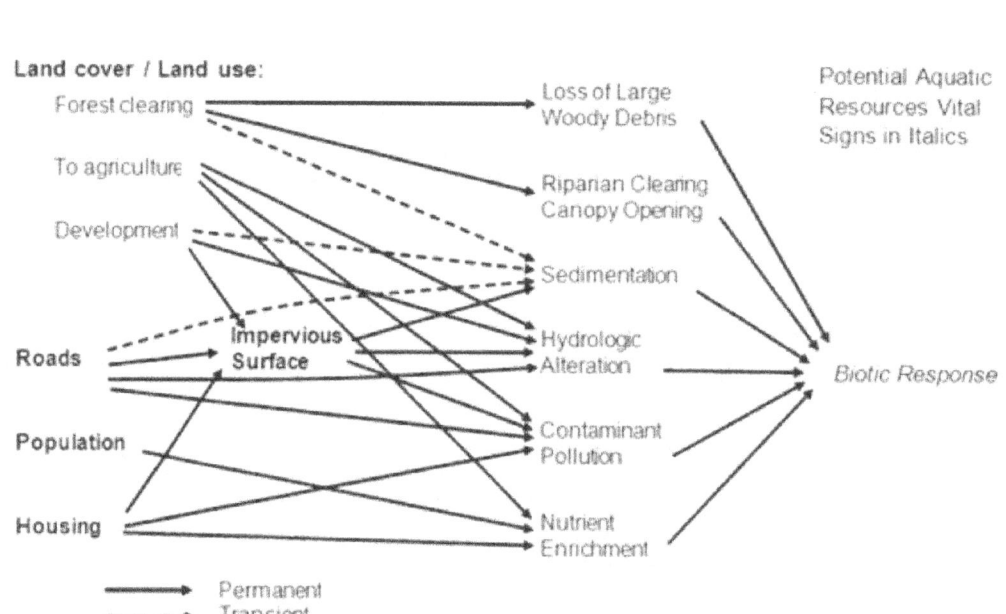

Allan (2004) provides an excellent synthesis and review of the effects of land cover and land use changes on watersheds. Allan articulated six primary mechanisms by which land use affects stream ecosystems (Table 2.9). All of these factors can significantly impact park resources. Figure 2.12 illustrates the relationships between NPScape measures and Allan's six factors.

Natural land cover types can provide more water storage capacity by dissipating the pulse flow following a storm, reducing the peak flow, and extending the flow duration. In addition, they have substantial capacity to hold nutrients and support processes such as denitrification. Conversely, impervious surfaces (e.g., roads, urban development) reduce the upland storage of precipitation and increase the rate of runoff into streams and rivers, thereby increasing the magnitude of peak flow and reducing the base flow between storms (Allan et al. 1997).

It can be difficult to independently evaluate and distinguish whether an observed response in watershed condition is due to the increase in one land cover type or the decrease in another type (King et al. 2005). For example, Poff et al. (2006) compared hydrologic responses to land cover (urban, agriculture, or least disturbed) across catchments within different ecoregions and found different responses. They found that agricultural land cover was negatively correlated with flow flashiness in the Central US and suggested that this counterintuitive result was explained by greater variation in conversion from agriculture to developed urban than from natural forests and grasslands to agriculture.

2.6.1 Aquatic Connectivity

Like terrestrial habitats, some aquatic systems have also been heavily affected by alterations that disrupt the natural flow of water, organisms, and aquatic processes. There are more than 80,000 large dams in the United States (US Army Corps of Engineers 2011), and these impoundments have profound impacts on natural waterways. Impoundments alter the timing and magnitude of water flows, sediment flows, the upstream and downstream movement of organisms, and the temperature and chemical characteristics of water. Virtually every ecological processes in freshwater systems can be altered by impoundments (e.g., Ward & Stanford 1979). In many cases, the magnitude of impact is related to the size and degree of change that a dam imposes on a system. Thus the size, distribution, and density of impoundments (dams and diversions) has been used as an indicator of the connectivity and intactness of freshwater systems. Data on dam locations and attributes (height, width, volume, etc.) are available from the U.S. Army Corps of Engineers National Inventory of Dams (NID; http://nid.usace.army.mil). Access is restricted, so NPScape cannot redistribute its copy of the NID database, but others may similarly request access through the above website. Various metrics based on the location of impoundments and their size have been proposed and evaluated. The Heinz Center task group recommended use of a metric calculated at the HUC-12 (subwatershed) level (Heinz Center 2008a), whereas others have used the NID to evaluate anthropogenic impacts and resource conditions at much broader scales (Sabo et al. 2010; Lawrence et al. 2011; Monahan & Gross 2012).

NPScape does not currently calculate any metrics from information on impoundments. However, the studies cited above provide background information and NPScape provides information on upstream watersheds, land cover, landscape pattern, and other attributes that are directly relevant to evaluating watershed condition. Lawrence et al. (2011) and Monahan & Gross (2012) specifically address NPS resources.

2.6.2 Impervious Surfaces

Impervious surface is a land cover classification that includes bare rock, paved roads, and most developed areas (note difference from NPScape data classification, which maps only 'developed' impervious cover types; Figure 2.13). Impervious surfaces prevent the infiltration of precipitation into the ground. The consequences for hydrology are quicker runoff into streams, more rapid rising and dropping of streamflow following storm events (flashiness of storm response), and reduced evapotranspiration and percolation to aquifers, thus increasing the cumulative flow out of the catchment. Nutrient enrichment and contaminant transport are increased, as chemicals picked up by the water are transported directly into the stream, without the opportunity for uptake or decomposition by soil organisms.

The effects of impervious surface on hydrology can be more important in smaller catchments. Where a storm can cover most or all of the catchment at the same time, and the time delay for stream flow from the top of the catchment is small relative to the duration of the storm event, increasing impervious surface can result in a large increase in peak flow. As watershed size and thus stream length increases, the effects of even a large storm will be spread out temporally by the difference in arrival times of flows from upstream versus downstream in the watershed. Increasing the amount of impervious surface still increases peak flow for storm events that last longer than the flow time in the watershed, but the flashiness is at least partially attenuated. In very large watersheds, larger than the largest storm system, impervious surface presumably should have even less effect, but the variation in percentage impervi-

Figure 2.13.
An example of anthropogenic impervious surface, as calculated by NPScape for Whitman Mission National Historic Site and its contributing upstream watershed.

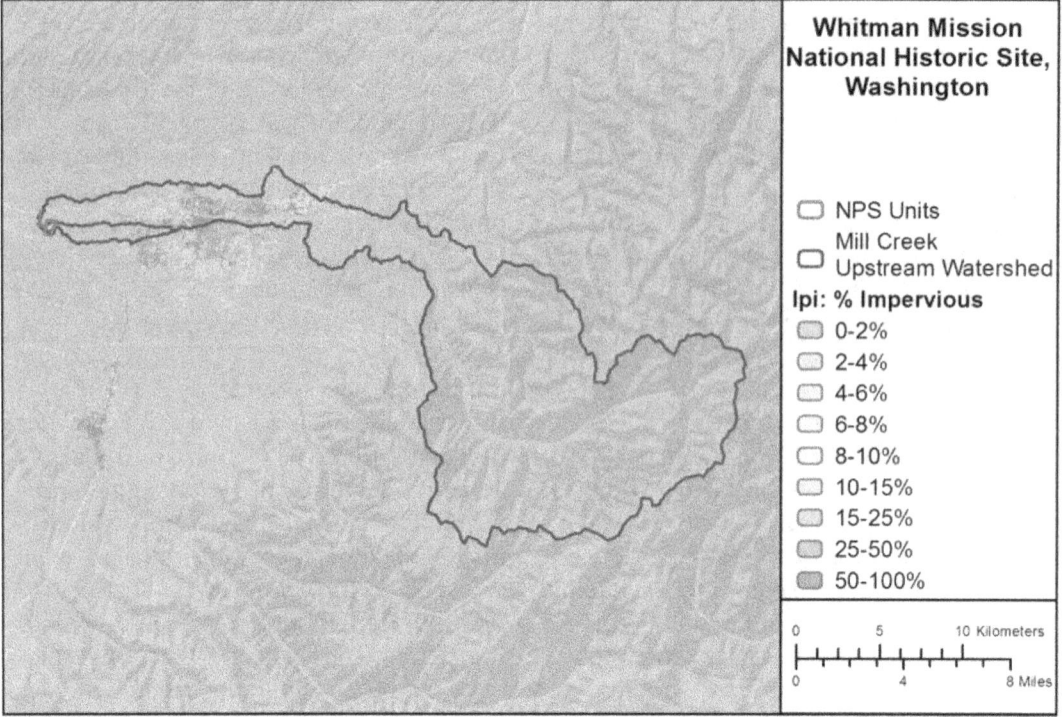

ous surface between such large watersheds is much smaller than the variation in precipitation patterns, so any such pattern cannot be quantified or confirmed.

The effects of impervious surfaces on nutrient enrichment and contaminants are a function of the availability of nutrients and contaminants. Therefore, the effects are greatest in smaller, highly-developed watersheds where impervious surfaces receive higher concentrations of both nutrients and contaminants. In smaller urban and suburban watersheds, storm water retention ponds and other engineered solutions are often required to mitigate both the hydrologic and nutrient/contaminant effects of impervious surfaces.

Multiple ecological studies have quantified thresholds for the effects of the proportion of impervious surface. Paul & Meyer (2001) review studies of the effect of impervious surface from urbanization and report thresholds of 2-10% for effects on stream geomorphology, 10-15% for effects on fish diversity, and 1-33% for invertebrate diversity. For example, when total impervious cover exceeds 10-15%, stream biota is not maintained (Klein 1979; Schueler 1994; Wang et

al. 2001). However, impacts to more sensitive species can occur at 3-5% impervious cover (Booth & Jackson 1997; Angermeier et al. 2004; Stranko et al. 2008). These thresholds vary geographically (Utz et al. 2009) and with a variety of physical and biotic factors (Allan 2004).

Geographical differences in biotic responses to developed impervious surfaces can also be important, and populations at the edge of a species' range may be more sensitive to disturbance (Stranko et al. 2008). For instance, aquatic invertebrates negatively affected by urbanization responded at lower threshold levels (10-45% converted) in the Piedmont compared to the Coastal Plain physiographic province (15-60% converted, Utz et al. 2009). Additionally, Booth et al. (2002) questioned whether the varying thresholds of effect reflect differences in the systems studied, or are functions of the imprecision of measurement, and argue that biological effects are more continuous rather than threshold effects, with small responses at lower levels of development than the inferred thresholds may suggest.

3. Effects of Roads on Natural Resources

Roads provide remarkable access to lands within the continental US, including access to most national parks. Riitters & Wickham (2003) estimated that 50% of the land in the conterminous 48 states is within 382 m of a road, and only 3% of the land is greater than 5 km from a road. While easy access is often deemed a good thing, roads and associated activities can negatively impact a broad range of physical, ecological, and social attributes important to parks. By physically altering the landscape, roads result in the direct loss of habitat, fragmentation of the remaining habitat (Carr et al. 2002), altered landscape structure (Saunders et al. 2002), increased influence of edge effects (Carr et al. 2002), and disruption of hydrological processes (Jones et al. 2000; Trombulak & Frissell 2000). Noss (1993) asserted that roads may be the single most destructive element in the process of habitat fragmentation. Table 3.1 lists some of the more pervasive effects of roads.

There is a substantial body of literature on the effects of roads. Table 3.2 lists references we found to be particularly useful, and Chapters 2 and 4 discuss the larger effects of roads as precursors to land conversion and development. Comprehensive reviews document extensive direct and indirect impacts of roads on both terrestrial and aquatic environments (Spellerberg 1998; Ercelawn 1999; Trombulak & Frissell 2000; Forman et al. 2002; Wheeler et al. 2005), the effects of which may be undetectable in some taxa for decades (Findlay & Bourdages 2000). Even in areas where human population densities are relatively low and landscapes are perceived as natural, the impacts of roads are pervasive (Saunders et al. 2002) and may extend hundreds to thousands of meters from the roadside (Forman 2000; Forman & Deblinger 2000; Forman et al. 2002).

Two major distinctions are useful for understanding landscape-level effects of roads on natural resources. The first distinction is between the effects of roads per se that are independent of traffic level, and the effects of road traffic, with strengths dependent on traffic density. Some road effects such as habitat fragmentation, disturbed or open margins for predatory or invasive species (e.g., kudzu), and increased intensity and unpredictability of runoff, vary with road size and construction, but are relatively independent of the traffic volume. Conversely, the magnitudes of effects such as vehicle collision mortality, dust, hydrocarbon and metal runoff, sound, and propagule pressure of invasive species increase relative to traffic volume. This distinction can be blurred by road effects that are sensitive to very low volumes of traffic, and many resources are impacted by both roads and traffic.

Table 3.1. Pervasive effects of roads relevant to natural resources, park visitors, and park operations.

Physical Effects	Biological Effects
Alter temperature, humidity, and other climate attributes	Collisions between animals and cars
Increase rate and amount of water runoff	Physical barrier to movement
Alter surface and ground water flows	Habitat loss
Alter rates of sediment and nutrient dispersal	Habitat fragmentation
Runoff of chemicals applied to road surface	Behavioral avoidance of disturbances
Alter geological and soil substrates	Corridor for invasive species
Increase production and propagation of noise	Indirect effects like poaching, fire ignition, trash
Alter light	Noise interference with species communication
Physical barrier to many species	Habitat alteration

Table 3.2. Useful sources of information on roads and their effects on resources important to parks.

Topic	Description	Citation
Road Ecology	This book is the 'go-to' source and is a comprehensive guide to ecological and other aspects of roads. More than 1000 citations. A bit dated.	Forman et al. 2003
Anurans	Web site with extensive list of references on effects of roads on reptiles and amphibians. See: http://community.middlebury.edu/~herpatlas/roads_biblio.php	Carter & Andrews 2007
Many species and communities	Broad review of ecological effects of roads on terrestrial and aquatic communities.	Trombulak & Frissell 2000
Wildlife	Short, concise review of multiple effects of roads on wildlife.	Jackson 2000
Wildlife (books)	Detailed treatment and review of effects on wildlife.	Spellerberg 1998; Sherwood et al. 2003
Ecological effects	Very broad scope of topics with examples (a few too many citations) of studies for about 25 types of effects.	Spellerberg 1998
Ecological effects	A review of the impacts of road, powerline, gasline and canal fragmentation on tropical forest ecosystems. Also provides a solid review of the road ecology literature in all ecosystems.	Laurance et al. 2009
Wildlife populations	Special feature in Ecology and Society 2009-2011.	http://www.ecologyandsociety.org/issues/view.php?sf=41
Small mammals	Generally found no effect on abundance, density, or diversity in desert community near I-15. Good concise literature review for small mammals.	Bissonette & Rosa 2009
Breeding birds	A comprehensive review of noise impacts to bird behavior and populations in relation to overall traffic load and noise intensity.	Reijnen & Foppen 2006
Birds	A recent review of the direct and indirect effects of paved roads on bird populations.	Kociolek et al. 2011
Habitat & Conduits for exotic invasives	A broader study than most, plus a good review in the introduction.	Gelbard & Belnap 2003
Effects on aquatic resources	A general review of the effects of roads on aquatic resources	Wheeler et al. 2005
Traffic noise and birds	Noted response of birds with higher frequency song; Recent literature review of traffic noise effects.	Parris & Schneider 2009
Noise and terrestrial organisms	Comprehensive review of effects of chronic noise exposure on a variety of terrestrial species.	Barber et al. 2009
Direct mortality	Reduced abundance of anurans as a function of distance to road varied by species; thresholds from 250 to > 1000 m from road. Heavy truck traffic.	Eigenbrod et al. 2009
Noise	Interferes with auditory communication and ability of orient to calls among birds and amphibians.	Reijnen et al. 1996; Rheindt 2003; Bee & Swanson 2007
Release from predators	Moose cows with calves preferentially forage near roads, apparently to avoid wolves and bears. Some mammalian predators – foxes, wolves, and bears – avoid roads (see below).	Berger 2007
Avoidance	Bears in NC and grizzly bears elsewhere shift home ranges away from roads. Elk prefer feeding away from roads. Elk and mule deer in Colorado prefer winter feeding area more than 200 m from roads.	Rost & Bailey 1979; Grover & Thompson 1986; McLellan & Shackleton 1988; Brody & Pelton 1989; Coleman & Fraser 1989
Prefer roads	Caribou in AK use roads during migration; Caribou are reputed to rest on roads in summer due to lower insect harassment. Turkey and black vultures establish home ranges in areas with higher road density.	Banfield 1974, Coleman & Fraser 1989
Amphibians and Reptiles	A comprehensive literature review.	Andrews et al. 2008
Research agenda	Rauischholzhausen agenda for road ecology. Outstanding consideration of key research questions related to 'road ecology', and evaluation of research designs.	Roedenbeck et al. 2007

The second major distinction is between direct and indirect effects of roads and traffic. Mortality from vehicle collision is perhaps the most obvious direct effect, but non-lethal direct effects include road avoidance (Reijnen et al. 1996; Forman et al. 2002), which may be traffic dependent or independent, and traffic noise masking communication (Barber et al. 2009, 2011), which is generally traffic dependent. Roads have positive direct effects on some species, notably by creating disturbed habitat for some plants and increasing resource concentration for scavengers. Few direct effects of roads extend beyond 1 km, so roads primarily in or adjacent to parks have direct effects on park resources, but roads near a park can also exert important indirect effects. Indirect effects of roads include road avoidance or mortality modifying home ranges and migrations (Reijnen et al. 1996; Forman et al. 2002), limiting access to resources (Trombulak & Frissell 2000; Forman et al. 2003; Jaeger et al. 2005), and leading to subdivided or isolated subpopulations with limited gene flow (e.g., Gerlach & Musolf 2000; Keller & Largiadèr 2003). In general, indirect effects can extend much further from roads than direct effects.

3.1 How Far Do the Effects of Roads Extend?

A sufficient body of knowledge has accumulated to allow one to estimate broad bounds on many specific effects of roads, although these obviously differ depending on specific, local circumstances (Figure 3.1). This figure does not include restricted migration, habitat fragmentation, and other indirect effects that can extend for many kilometers from a busy road. The size of a 'road zone' will depend on the species of interest, ecosystem characteristics, season, time of day, road width, road surface, proximity to water, and traffic density. Forman et al. (2003) suggest that most road impacts occur within 1 km (0.6 mi) of roads, but effects on animal species' behaviors can extend well beyond this distance. A more quantitative meta-analysis found that the effect of roads on bird populations extends up to 1 km, and the effect on mammal populations extends out to 5 km (Benitez-Lopez et al. 2010). In the context of ecosystem-specific characteristics, this meta-

analysis found that road effects extended further in open areas than in closed forest. However, Haskell (2000) in studying continuous forest, determined macroinvertebrate soil fauna incur significant impacts up to 100 m away from relatively narrow, lightly traveled roads, illustrating the subtleties of road impacts on different species within the same general ecosystem.

3.2 Effects of Roads on Terrestrial Vertebrates

Fahrig & Rytwinski (2009) conducted a comprehensive review of literature on the effects of roads on animal abundance and evaluated the direction of effects on approximately 150 species or guilds of invertebrates, anurans, birds, and mammals (see Table 1 in Fahrig & Rytwinski 2009). From this synthesis, they developed the conceptual model in Figure 3.2. This figure effectively summarizes for terrestrial vertebrates major direct vs. indirect effects of roads, influences of roads vs. traffic, and distinctions between species that either avoid or are attracted to roads.

The most obvious direct effect of roads on vertebrates and other animal species is lethal vehicle collisions (Fahrig et al. 1995). Forman & Alexander (1998) report an estimate of one million vertebrates killed each day by vehicle collisions in the United States. Mortality is greater for more vagile species, nocturnal species, and species attracted to roads (e.g., reptiles for warmth or scavengers for food). Species with complementary habitat requirements, like amphibians that breed in ponds and feed in upland habitats, are especially vulnerable to mortality on roads between required habitat patches (Pope et al. 2000). Road-related deaths can have substantial effects on wildlife populations, particularly for smaller organisms and very large carnivores with low population densities and large home ranges. For example, in studying four amphibian species in Denmark, Hels & Buchwald (2001) found that the probability of mortality ranged from 0.34-0.61 when crossing a low to moderately traveled road (3200 vehicles/day) and from 0.89-0.98 when crossing a busy road (>15,000 vehicles/day). In their study area, about 10% of the adult populations of these species were killed

Figure 3.1. Some reasonable estimates of the size of a 'road zone'. From Forman & Alexander (1998).

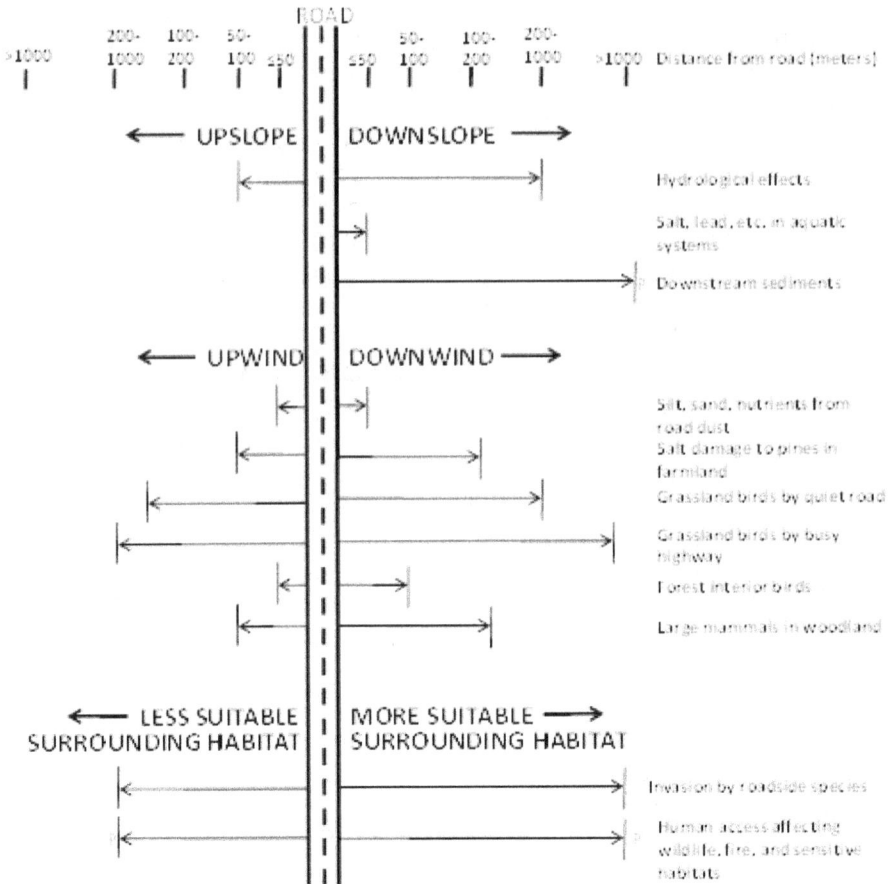

annually by traffic. Where grizzly bears are protected from hunting as in Banff and Yoho National Parks (Alberta, Canada), as much as 100% of known adult grizzly bear mortalities occurred within 500 m of roads or 200 m of high use trails (Benn & Herrero 2002). For grizzly bears in Yellowstone National Park, the effects of roads and associated development are disproportionately high on adult females and sub-adults, resulting in higher mortality and lower productivity for these age classes (Mattson et al. 1987). Before mitigation measures, ~ 9% of the Florida panther population was killed each year in vehicle collisions (Forman et al. 2003).

Habitat degradation due to the direct effects of roads is conceptualized as the product of the population impact times the road effect zone times the number of roads in the habitat. This type of impact can convert an area from favorable habitat with positive population growth acting as a source population into marginal habitat with negative population growth acting as a sink habitat. Cumula-

tive impacts of localized direct effects are reductions in habitat area and quality, which affect both population density (carrying capacity) and the ability of individuals to slowly percolate through the road impacted area (e.g., eating and wandering as opposed to rapid dispersal movement). The magnitude of the cumulative effects is conceptualized as the product of the direct effect of roads times the road effect zone times the road density.

Indirect effects of roads can be at least as large as direct effects (Kociolek et al. 2011). Indirect effects can extend much further from roads, affecting a larger fraction of the landscape and impacting park resources over greater distances. Perhaps the most important indirect effect of roads on park resources is via habitat degradation and fragmentation. Roads have also been indirectly associated with increased incidence of fire ignitions (Cardille et al. 2001; DellaSala & Frost 2001; Brown et al. 2004) and higher probability of large fires in the upper

Figure 3.2. Conceptual model of species' characteristics, attributes of roads and traffic, and the consequences on mortality and abundance. (-), (+), and (+/-) are negative, positive, and neutral, respectively. Effects are mortality (mort), habitat loss/increase (hab), and release from predation (pred). Figure and modified caption from Fahrig & Rytwinski (2009).

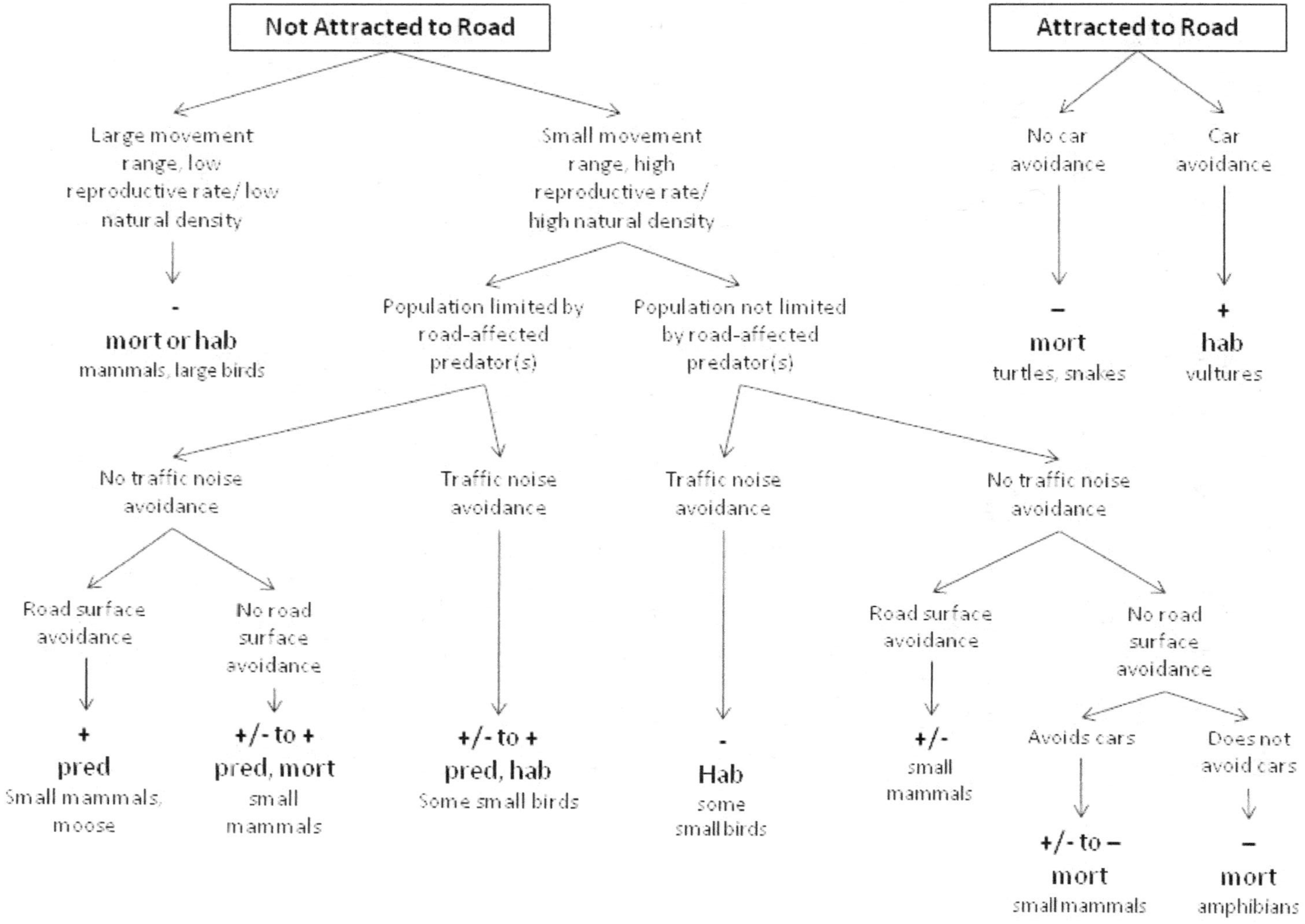

Midwest (Cardille et al. 2001; but see Dickson et al. 2006 for an example in the desert southwest where fire occurrence was higher in areas with lower road density). Additionally, roads are indirectly associated with increased occurrence of invasive species (Trombulak & Frissell 2000). Wildlife may experience increased legal hunting pressure and poaching (Trombulak & Frissell 2000) and chronic disturbance from human activity such as recreation (Thurber et al. 1994; Reijnen et al. 1996). More recent studies have identified other indirect species-specific effects, such as impacts of road salt runoff on amphibians (Karraker et al. 2008).

Road noise can have important effects on wildlife, generally affecting physiological or behavioral responses. Even on sparsely traveled roads, the noise from a passing vehicle is a potential disturbance. For example, a radio telemetry study of elk in relation to all-terrain vehicles documented responses at distances in excess of 1 km (Preisler et al. 2006); responses were more likely when animals were closer to a forest road. On roads with heavy traffic, chronic noise exposure can degrade auditory awareness by masking sounds that would otherwise be heard. Masking can inhibit perception and recognition of intentional and adventitious sounds, and can affect a variety of social and ecological processes (Barber et al. 2009, 2011). If noise is a primary inhibitory factor, then increased traffic will be problematic, even if road networks do not proliferate.

Many species of large mammals and birds behaviorally avoid roads (Forman et al. 2003), including black bears (Brody & Pelton 1989; Beringer et al. 1990; Kasworm & Manley 1990), grizzly bears (Kasworm & Manley 1990), wolves (Whittington et al. 2005), mule deer and elk (Rost & Bailey 1979). It is not always clear whether the avoidance is due to avoiding noise per se, avoiding humans and traffic (and thus additional mortality), or both. Meanwhile, other species are attracted to roads, such as reptiles attracted to warm pavement (Andrews et al. 2008) and moose and other mammals attracted to salts (Laurian et al. 2008). Roads can have positive effects on some species. Scavengers such as ravens, vultures, and coyotes are subsidized by roadkill, which is an increasing function of road traffic. Caribou use of roads during migration (Banfield 1974) occurs when there is no traffic on the roads.

Like the other measures described in this report, the effects of roads are frequently confounded with other attributes, such as the loss or fragmentation of habitats. Eigenbrod et al. (2008) proposed the use of 'accessible habitat' as a means to decouple the effects of total habitat area, road density, and the area of habitat most available to organisms. By explicitly accounting for the location of roads with respect to habitat areas around ponds, Eigenbrod et al. (2008) found 'accessible habitat' better predicted anuran species richness than total habitat area or distance to a road. For their study, Eigenbrod et al. (2008) defined accessible habitat as the forested area within 1,000 m of a pond that could be accessed without crossing a major road.

3.3 Effects of Roads on Vegetation
Roads and traffic affect vegetation and plant species in three major ways. First, roads and road margins provide open, disturbed habitat. Such high light disturbed areas are prime locations for establishment of non-native or invasive species, notably kudzu (*Pueraria thunbergiana*) in the Southeast and purple loosestrife (*Lythrium salicaria*) in the Northeast (Forman et al. 2003). In landscapes altered by fire suppression, road margins can provide habitat for disturbance-requiring native species such as wiregrass (*Aristida beyrichiana*). Road margins as refuges for native plant species (usually grassland species) is better documented in Europe than in North America (Tikka et al. 2000; Jantunen et al. 2006). In arid lands, water runoff from paved roads can support increased abundance and biomass of native as well as exotic species adjacent to roads (Johnson et al. 1975; Brooks & Lair 2005). These habitat effects rarely extend beyond tens of meters from the roads; some tests of road effects compare plots in the road margin to paired plots as close as 50 m from the road (e.g., Gelbard & Belnap 2003). While patches of some invasive species along roads eventually spread away from roads into undisturbed

areas in arid lands (Brooks & Lair 2005), invasive species along roads rarely penetrate beyond 100 m into intact forests.

Second, roads provide conduits for dispersal or colonization by invasive plant species. Frenkel's (1970) extensive survey found that the roadside vegetation in Northern California was dominated by non-native species. The early locations of *Bromus* species in the western United States follow the locations of roads (Johnson et al. 1975; Hunter 1991; Salo 2005), and many invasive species in arid areas are primarily distributed along roads (Gelbard & Belnap 2003). It is plausible to ascribe the prevalence of invasive plant species along roads to a synergistic effect of propagule pressure plus disturbance that leads to many invasive species at higher density along roads. However, efforts to quantify ongoing propagule pressure for invasive species along roads have largely failed (Harrison et al. 2002). Therefore, while introduction of propagules may be an infrequent but important event, the greater effect on invasive species may be the existence of long, linear patches of suitable disturbed habitat.

Third, dust from traffic can impact vegetation near the road. Dust particles can reduce stomatal conductance and raise leaf temperatures, metals and salts in road dust can be toxic (reviewed by Farmer 1993). Walker & Everett (1987) and Auerbach et al. (1997) found substantial impacts of dust from dirt and gravel roads on tundra and wetlands vegetation in Alaska, including an additional pathway of dust leading to earlier snow-melt. Lichens and mosses may be especially vulnerable to both particulate dust (Farmer 1993) and air pollution from busy roads (Sujetovienė 2010).

3.4 Effects of Roads on Aquatic Resources

Wheeler et al. (2005) review the effects of roads on rivers and streams. They distinguish the effects of road construction, road presence, and urbanization driven by road access. Jones et al. (2000) distinguish effects of roads directly on streams (e.g., where roads cross or follow streams) from effects of roads on upland patches or watersheds that are then drained by the stream network.

The major short term effects of road construction are sedimentation due to earth moving and possible temporary alteration of flow to allow construction of culverts and bridges. These effects tend to be especially localized, with their impact on aquatic resources a function of the number of intersections between the road and streams. Once highways are constructed, paved or even compacted roads act as impermeable surfaces, increasing the flashiness of storm flows to some extent. Roads also receive hydrocarbons and heavy metals that can contaminate runoff into streams and wetlands: tires contain zinc, brake pads contain copper, and other vehicle components give off other metals as they wear. These contaminants may be quickly transported via ditches, which are often constructed to intentionally divert road water runoff to the nearest stream. The amount of contaminants should increase linearly with traffic volume, rather than act as fixed attributes of roads. In cold areas, salts or other de-icing compounds are another contaminant from roads washed into streams. The impacts of these contaminants are usually greater than the impact on hydrology (Wheeler et al. 2005). The magnitudes of both are functions of the proximity of roads to streams and ponds, and so are located where roads cross or parallel streams and ponds or have roadside drainage ditches directly connecting to the aquatic resource, and diminish with distance downstream.

3.5 Road Metrics Related to Park Resource Condition

NPScape road metrics are derived from readily available spatial road maps and include road density, distance from roads and – by extension – roadless area. Road density, traffic-weighted road density, and distance from nearest road are perhaps the most common and intuitive road metrics (Forman et al. 2003). Together, these metrics provided by NPScape can be used to explore a number of important questions related to the direct vs. indirect effects of roads, as well as the effects of roads vs. traffic.

3.5.1 Road Density

Road density, reported by NPScape as total road length in km per km^2, is a common and convenient overall measure of the amount of road in an area (Forman et al. 2003). In certain instances, refined estimates of road density based on other road types (e.g., primary and secondary roads vs. rural, 4WD roads) may provide additional insights. This metric summarizes the integrated or cumulative effects of multiple roads, where the effects of each road extend substantial distances. Both the general degradation of habitat and the impediments to dispersal discussed above are examples of such effects. Importantly, road density is scale dependent as it must be estimated for a given area or pixel size. One's choice of denominator should be based on the resource being evaluated. For example, with a wide-ranging species it would minimally be important to measure road density at scales typical of the average home range size. But if connectivity within the range is thought to be compromised, then it would also be important to consider road densities within pixels across the range as these might highlight major barriers to dispersal.

Three park examples illustrating road density are shown in Figure 3.3. Crater Lake National Park is surrounded to the west and

east by relatively high road densities, yet to the north and south by relatively low road densities. Meanwhile, Saguaro National Park – comprised of two units separated by the city of Tucson – exhibits much greater road density in and around the west unit (Tucson Mountain District) as compared to the east unit (Rincon Mountain District). Lastly, while Santa Monica Mountains National Recreation Area has relatively high road densities within its boundaries, these values are low compared to road densities in surrounding areas. Such considerations of road density inside vs. outside park boundaries, as well as directionally with respect to the park, can provide important insights into connectivity by highlighting corridors or areas where road density is relatively low compared to the surrounding landscape (see below).

3.5.2 Weighted road density as proxy for traffic

No consistent and comprehensive information on traffic density is available at the national level. Most states and counties collect traffic data for federal, state, and county highways, but the data are inconsistent in form and coverage among states. However, the source data for roads includes a road type attribute distinguishing interstate

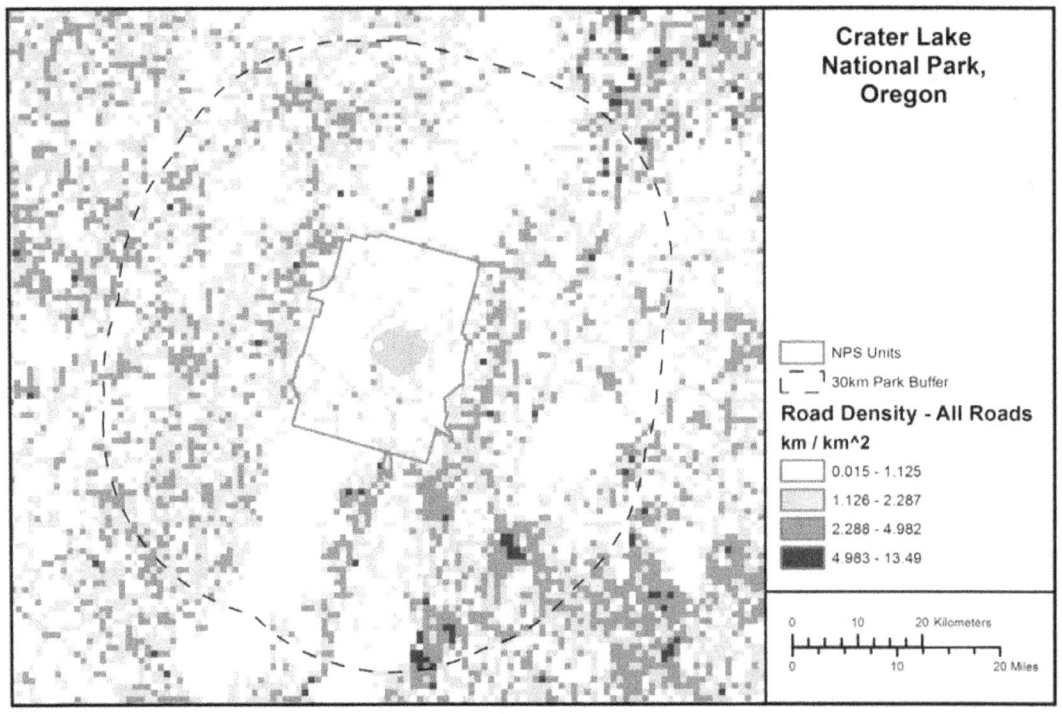

Figure 3.3. NPScape estimates of road density for Crater Lake National Park, Saguaro National Park, and Santa Monica Mountains National Recreation Area. White areas report pixels where road density is zero.

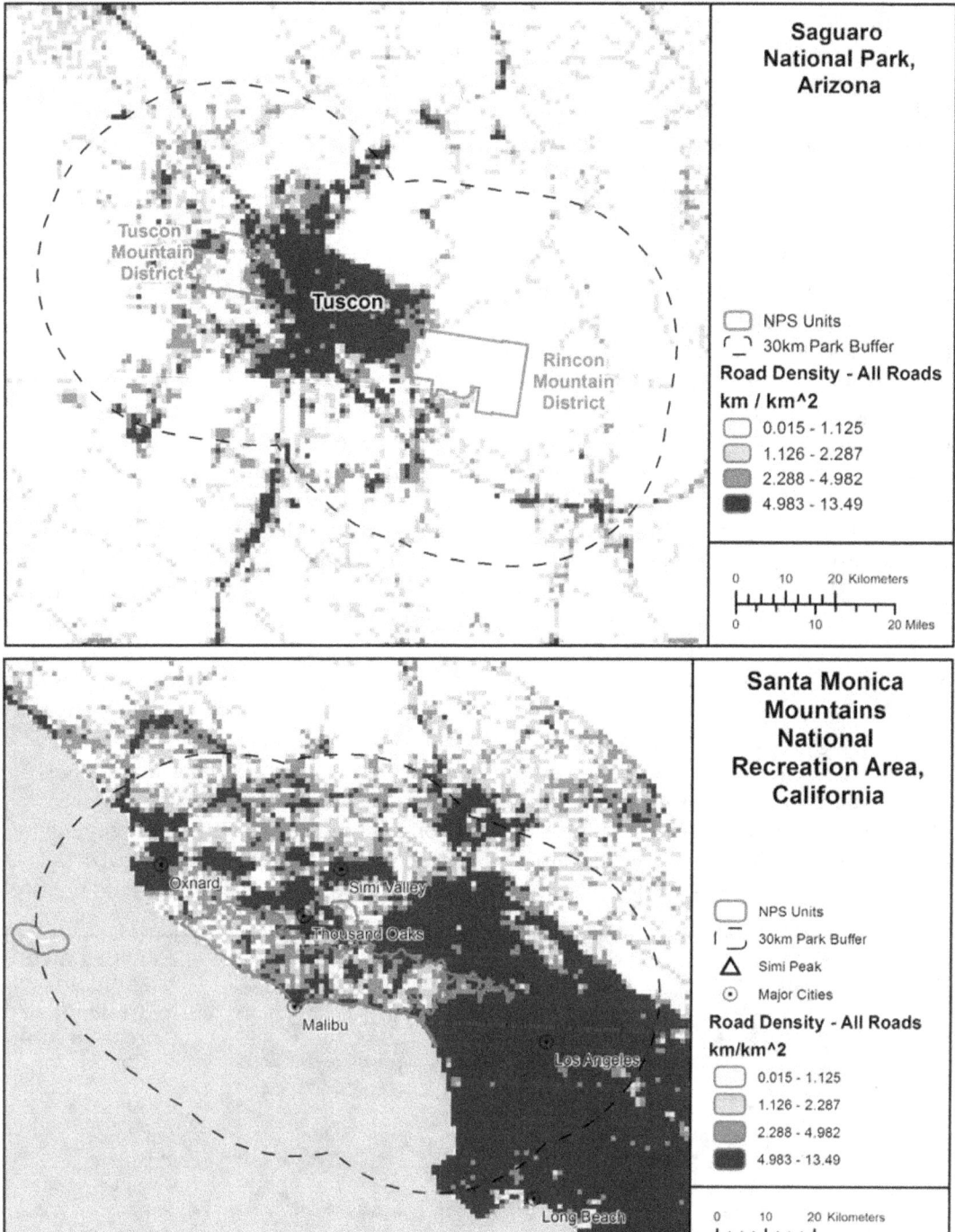

Figure 3.3.
(continued) NPScape
estimates of road
density for Crater
Lake National Park,
Saguaro National
Park, and Santa
Monica Mountains
National Recreation
Area. White areas
report pixels where
road density is zero.

highways, major roads (e.g., federal and state highways), and all other roads. These broad classes can be used as proxies for road traffic, with larger roads having higher traffic levels in any given area. As a rough approximation, the NPScape weighted road density metric weights major roads 3 times higher than minor roads and surface streets, and divided interstate highways 10 times higher (i.e., 5 times higher for each direction of lanes). Comparisons of weighted vs. un-weighted road density for a unit like Santa Monica Mountains National Recreation Area reveal areas where characteristically high levels of traffic volume exert prominent effects on road density (Figure 3.4).

3.5.3 Distance from roads as buffered roadless areas

Distance from road, measured by NPScape as the Euclidean distance (m) between any pixel on the landscape and the nearest road, is useful for considerations of 'road zones' (Figure 3.1, Exhibit 3.1) and patch size distributions of roadless area. The latter may also be considered a form of landscape pattern metric (pattern metrics described in greater detail in Chapter 2). Both distance from road and roadless area metrics are important for assessing such dynamics as road avoidance, population viability, and mortality. Roadless area patches may be calculated using distance from road maps and simple raster calculator expressions (e.g., select all grid cells that are greater than 500 m from a major road).

Park examples of distance from road and roadless area patch size distributions (> 500 m from road) are shown in Figure 3.5. Crater Lake National Park encompasses relatively large roadless area patches, but is also embedded in north-south chain of even larger roadless areas. The Rincon Mountain District of Saguaro National Park is part of a large roadless area that is adjacent to other large roadless areas, while the Tucson

Mountain District is comparably isolated and comprised of relatively small patches. Santa Monica Mountains National Recreation Area has many small roadless areas that are in close proximity (< 30 km) to larger patches to the north. As with road density, these patch size distributions relate to connectivity by illustrating potential stepping-stone routes of resource movement both within the park and through the surrounding landscape.

3.5.4 Road metrics for inferring the physical connectedness of remaining natural areas

In all three park examples (Figures 3.3 and 3.5), the roadless area and road density maps combined provide insights into the potential connectedness of natural landscapes, as revealed by areas or corridors with low road density and large patches of roadless area. For Crater Lake National Park, the physical connectedness of low road density areas and large roadless area patches is clearly greatest to the north and south, which is especially noteworthy in the context of species' tendencies to move latitudinally in response to ongoing climate change. In the case of Saguaro National Park, the physical connectedness of roadless and low road density

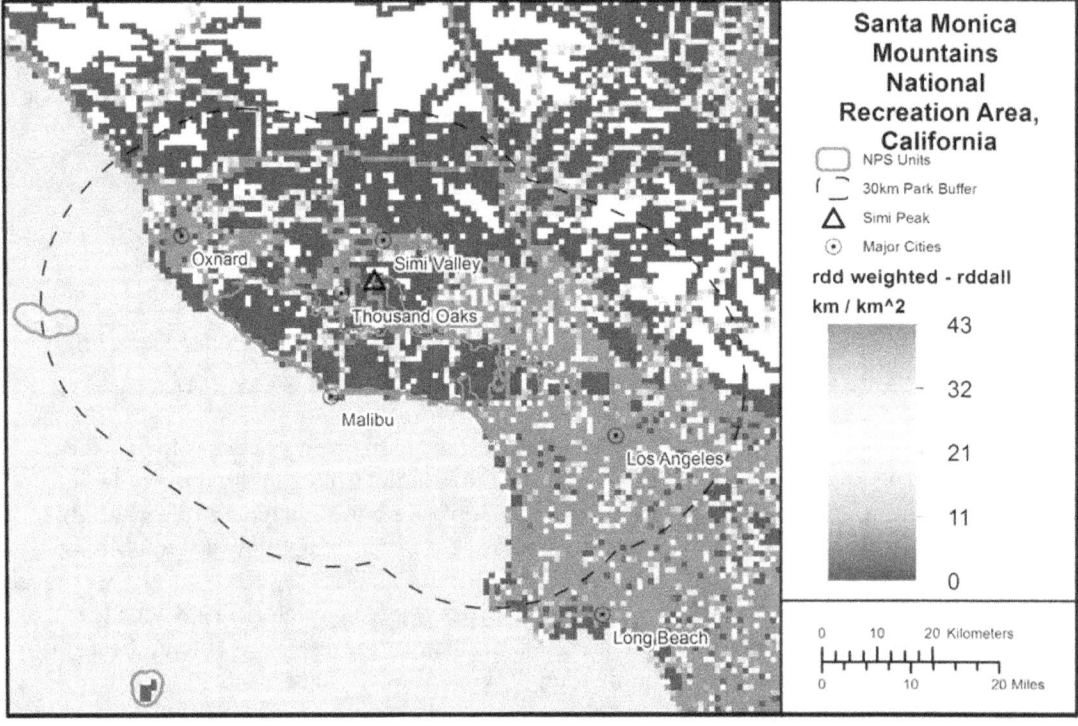

Figure 3.4. NPScape estimates of weighted road density minus un-weighted road density for Santa Monica Mountains National Recreation Area, showing areas where road density is especially influenced by major roads (interstates and highways). White areas report pixels where road density is zero.

Exhibit 3.1. North Shore Road of Great Smoky Mountains National Park – The Road to Nowhere.

In 1943, the Tennessee Valley Authority (TVA) built Fontana Dam, flooding North Carolina Route 288 and effectively cutting off access to residents of 44,000 acres of private land between the new Fontana Lake and the existing park boundary. Under a 1943 agreement, TVA purchased the 44,000 acres, which were added to the park, and DOI originally agreed to build the road along the new north shore of the lake. In 2010, the 67 year old controversy over building the 34 mile long road through pristine parkland was resolved: Plans were halted after results of an environmental impact study and negotiations to preserve land and provide financial compensation to the county.

Using the NPScape road metrics SOP as a guide, NPScape and the Appalachian Highlands I&M Network added the proposed North Shore Road to the existing ESRI streets geodatabase. The updated geodatabase was then used as an input to the NPScape road metrics toolbox to recompute the distance from road metric. As evident from the output (top map) and topographic inset (black rectangle in top map, referencing bottom map), the new road would have created 'road zone effects' in several park catchments.

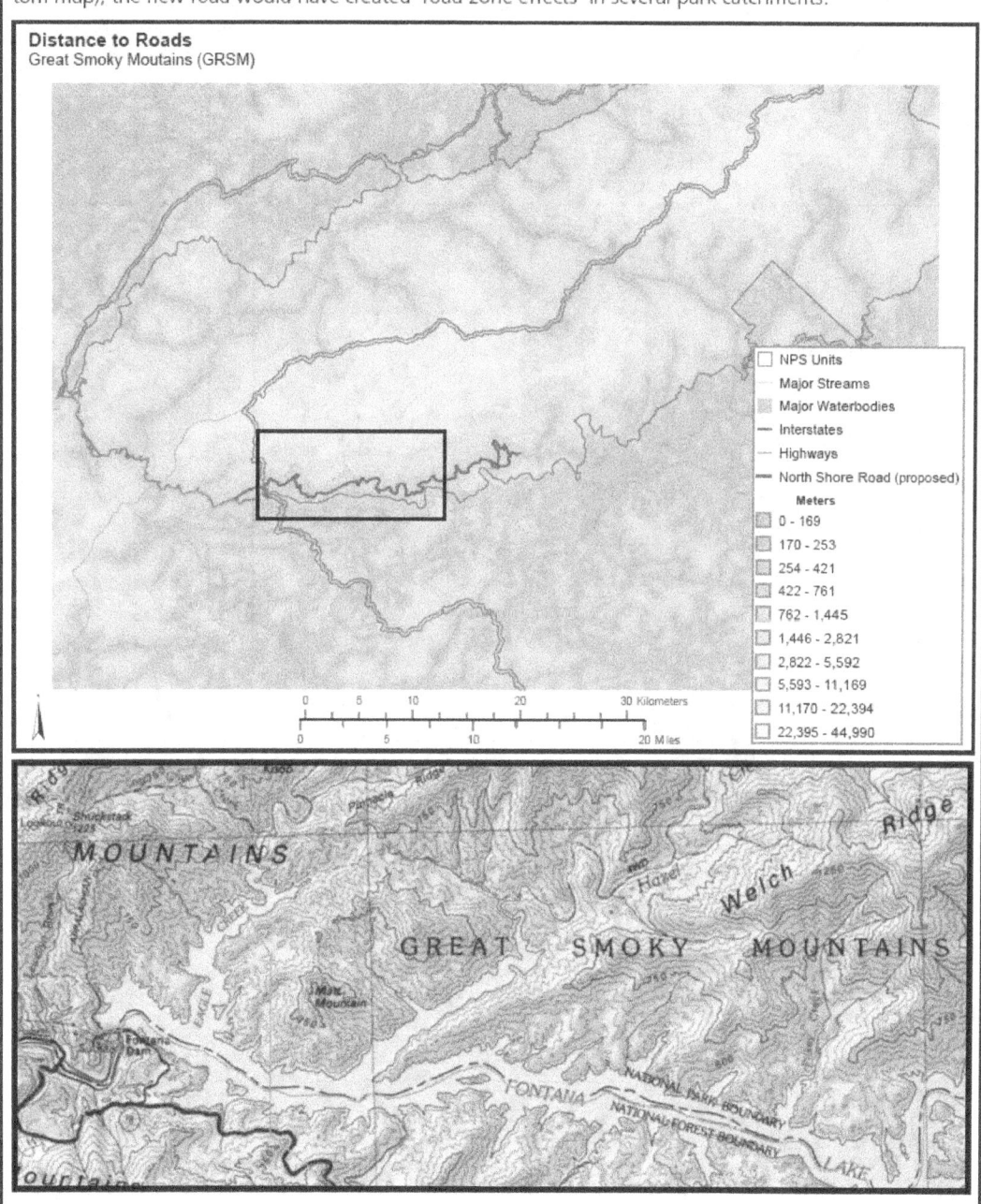

Distance to Roads
Great Smoky Moutains (GRSM)

	Legend
☐	NPS Units
	Major Streams
▨	Major Waterbodies
—	Interstates
⋯	Highways
—	North Shore Road (proposed)
	Meters
	0 - 169
	170 - 253
	254 - 421
	422 - 761
	762 - 1,445
	1,446 - 2,821
	2,822 - 5,592
	5,593 - 11,169
	11,170 - 22,394
	22,395 - 44,990

Figure 3.5. NPScape estimates of distance from road (top map) and corresponding patch size distributions of roadless area, > 500 m from all roads (bottom map), for Crater Lake National Park, Saguaro National Park, and Santa Monica Mountains National Recreation Area. In the bottom map, white areas are less than 500 m from a road.

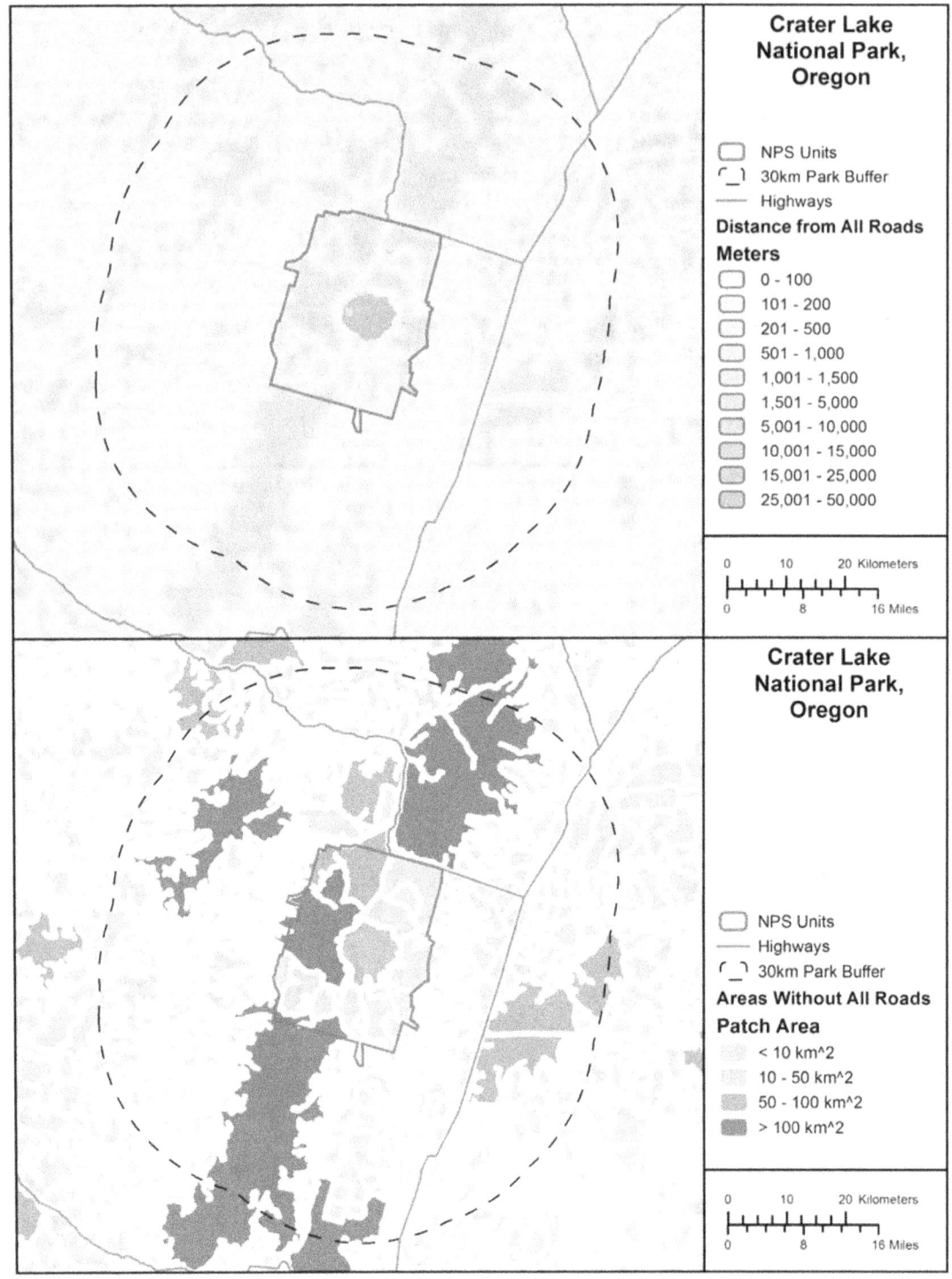

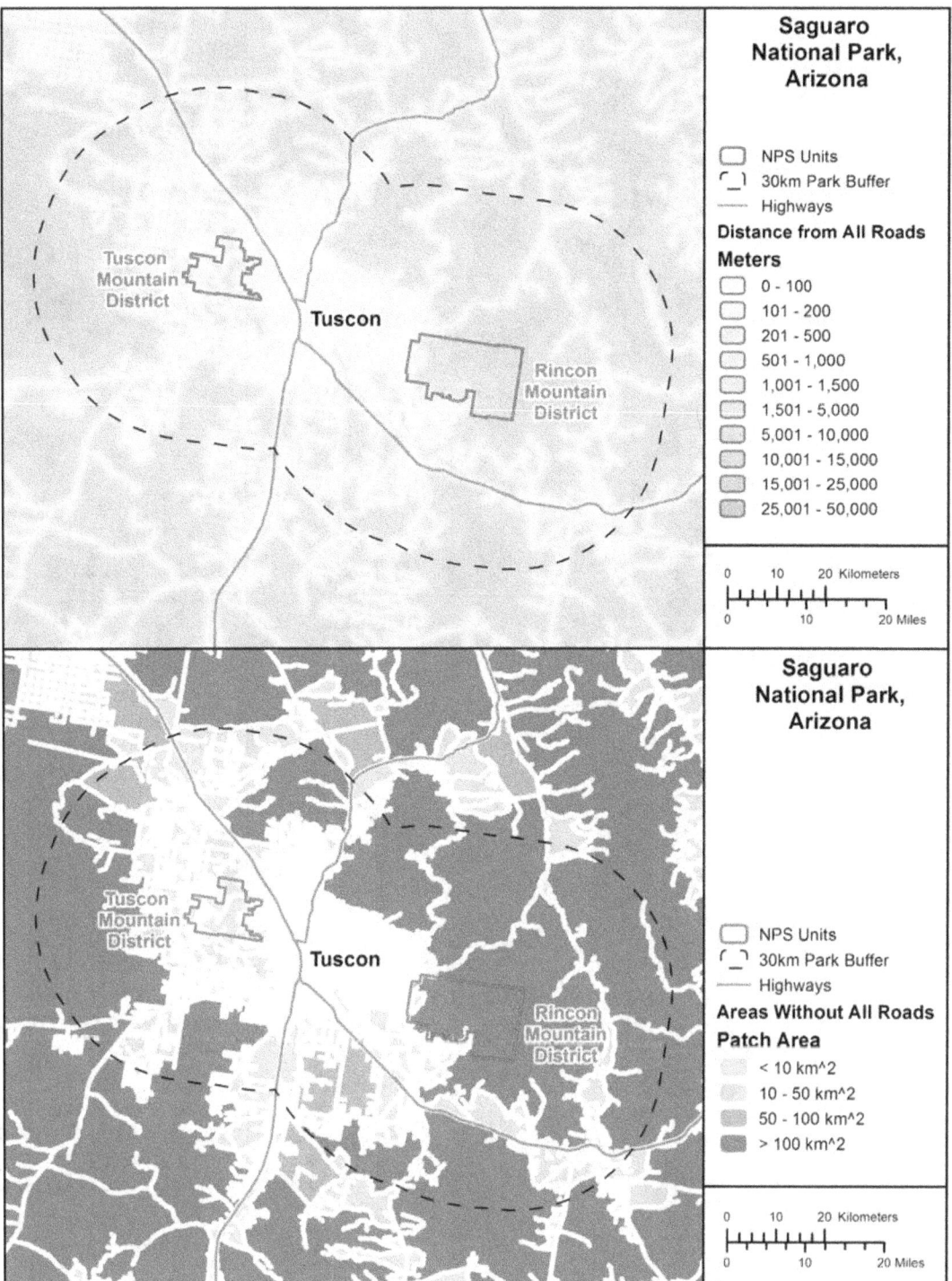

Figure 3.5 (continued). NPScape estimates of distance from road (top map) and corresponding patch size distributions of roadless area, > 500 m from all roads (bottom map), for Crater Lake National Park, Saguaro National Park, and Santa Monica Mountains National Recreation Area. In the bottom map, white areas are less than 500 m from a road.

areas is considerably greater for the Rincon Mountain District, especially throughout areas of the Madrean Archipelago (Sky Islands) to the north and east. However, it is also important to note that the two units may be connected over longer distances to the north and south though arcs of roadless areas surrounding the city of Tucson, as well as possibly for more urban-adaptable species through Tucson via washes that are eliminated by the 500 m roadless area buffer. Finally, due to high road densities and a relatively small patch size distribution of roadless areas, Santa Monica Mountains National Recreation Area is likely most connected to areas to the north towards Simi Peak via a few narrow corridors with lower road density and small patches or roadless area.

Figure 3.5 (continued).
NPScape estimates of distance from road (top map) and corresponding patch size distributions of roadless area, > 500 m from all roads (bottom map), for Crater Lake National Park, Saguaro National Park, and Santa Monica Mountains National Recreation Area. In the bottom map, white areas are less than 500 m from a road.

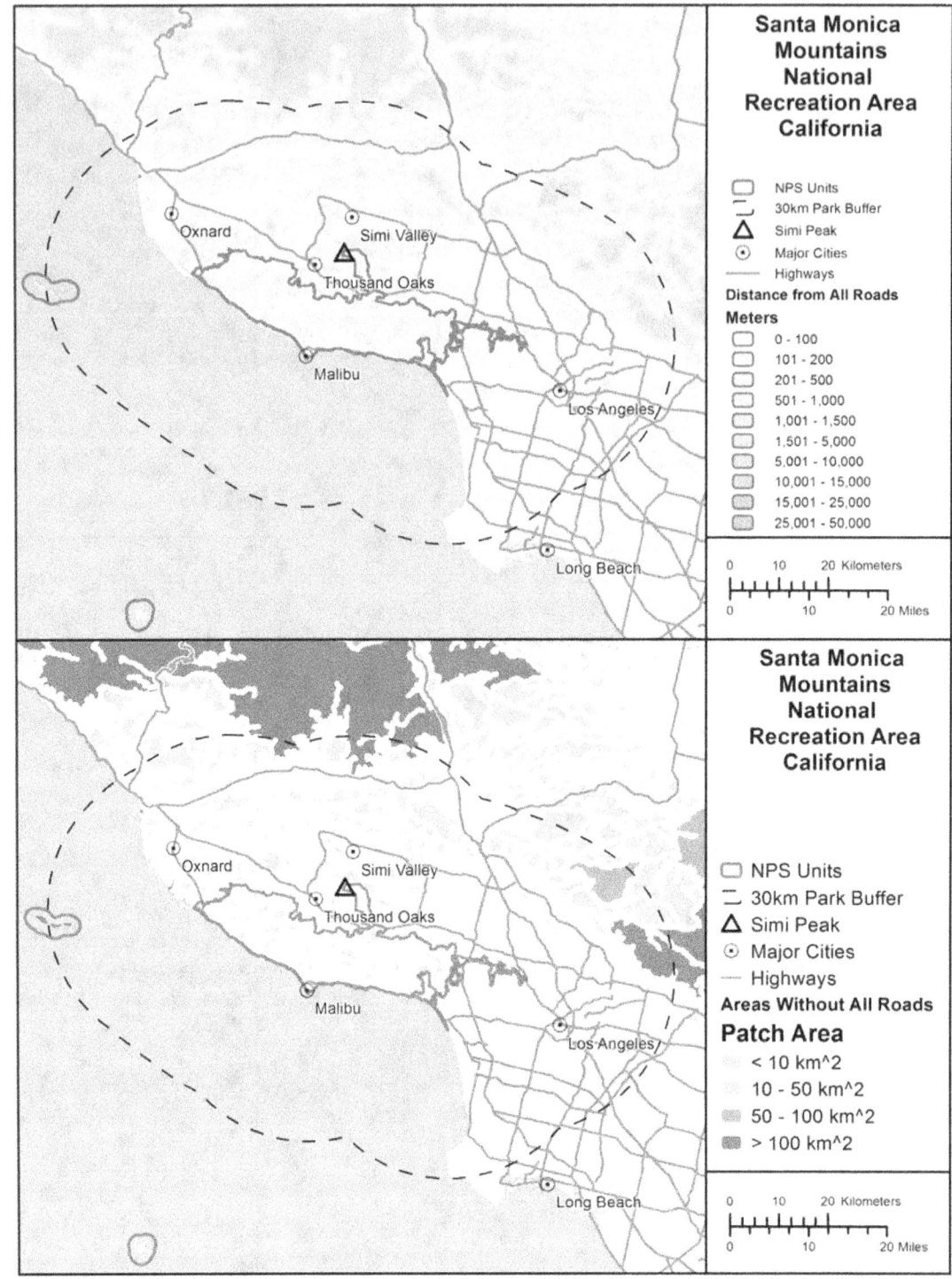

In all such cases, of additional interest is whether and how such road-based measures of connectivity relate to other measures derived from land cover and landscape pattern (Chapter 2) and protected areas (Chapter 5). We anticipate including more integrated, multivariate analyses of connectivity in a future NPScape report.

4. Human Population and Housing around Parks

Anthropogenic impacts on park resources may originate directly from the behaviors of humans, or indirectly from the roads, houses, landscaping, and other infrastructure used to support humans. Although the extent of impact is often difficult to measure, data on human population characteristics (e.g., population change, economic status, and housing density) usually provide information that is a direct indication of the magnitude of anthropogenic impacts to lands adjacent to parks. Cultural, political, and socioeconomic factors all contribute to land use decisions (Naveh 1995; Nassauer 2005; With 2005) and are widely used indicators of landscape quality or threats to biodiversity (Cincotta et al. 2000; Nassauer 2005). Because human land uses tend to expand over time (Wade et al. 2003), and we can make projections into the future, these data provide a window into potential threats to park resources.

4.1 Population, Settlement, and Housing Effects on Terrestrial Biodiversity

High human population density has been shown to adversely affect the persistence of habitats and species (Kerr & Currie 1995; Woodroffe 2000; Parks & Harcourt 2002; Luck 2007). In an assessment of the Lower 48, Svancara et al. (2009) found that counties near parks had higher population densities and experienced a greater change in population between 1990 and 2000 than distant counties. They suggested that, even with more intact landscapes surrounding parks, species in these areas may be at greater risk. Counties near parks also had significantly higher per capita income than distant counties (Svancara et al. 2009). While economic activity has been shown to impact biodiversity (Naidoo & Adamowicz 2001; McKinney 2002), there is debate whether increasing per capita income fuels land conversion (Sisk et al. 1994) or is necessary to solve environmental problems (Beckerman 1992).

Increasing human population results in development, and that development often leads to more development, with more land being converted to expand transportation networks, build schools, and accommodate businesses, which in turn may create a demand for still more housing (Heinz Center 2008b). Conversion of natural landscapes to agriculture, suburban, and urban landscapes is generally permanent (Heinz Center 2008b) and this loss of habitat is the primary cause of biodiversity declines (Wilcove et al. 1998). Thus, there is great concern about the rate of development of rural landscapes around parks (Hansen et al. 2005; Wade & Theobald 2009; Radeloff et al. 2010). For example, growth in low-density, exurban areas (1 home/0.4-16.2 ha [0.99-40 ac], Brown et al. 2005) has been shown to have numerous biological impacts (Hansen et al. 2002, 2005) and is increasingly recognized as a primary driver of ecological processes and threat to biodiversity (McKinney 2002; Miller & Hobbs 2002). In the Greater Yellowstone Ecosystem, exurban development has occurred disproportionately in low elevation, riparian areas (Exhibit 1.1) and is predicted to result in up to 40% habitat conversion by 2020 (Gude et al. 2007).

Human settlements can alter ecosystems and affect biodiversity by replacing habitat with structures and non-habitat cover types, fragmenting habitat, provisioning of food and water, increasing disturbance by people and their animals (dogs, cats, horses, etc.), altering vegetation types, and increasing light and noise. Settlements, as measured by housing density, generally result in simultaneous changes that all affect native biodiversity, and most studies are thus unable to isolate and identify the unique effect of a single factor. While these confounding effects are of scientific interest, the important questions for resource managers are more likely to focus on the cumulative effects of developments in or near protected areas, and how these alter species, ecosystem functions, or other important values (e.g., viewshed, dark sky, natural sounds, water quality).

Many studies have examined changes in species abundance or community composition along gradients from natural to rural to urban densities of human settlement. McDonnell & Hahs (2008) provide a recent synthesis of more than 200 studies and Table 4.1 summarizes effects of settlements on birds, mammals, and plants. Despite a very large number of studies, there are surprisingly few that provide clear quantitative data on housing density or the percentage of land converted for human habitation. Nonetheless, the following (sometimes obvious) conclusions can be drawn from this literature.

- Native species are often intolerant of settlements. Many studies show that certain species are highly sensitive to settlements, and the abundance of these species decline. For example, in lowland riparian areas of Colorado, bird species richness declined with increasing urbanization nearby (Miller et al. 2003). Riparian tree and shrub species richness also declined, along with ground and shrub cover, and corresponding increases in tree density and canopy closure. Results like this illustrate the often complex indirect effects that human settlement can have on native species. Meanwhile, human commensal species like crows and magpies are generally more abundant in settlements, and others like the cowbird can be correlated with human habitation when critical resources like parasite hosts happen to be co-distributed (Exhibit 1.1).

- The effects of settlements on species can extend a long distance. The extent of effects varies with species (Table 4.1) and with the magnitude and kinds of disturbance associated with housing. In some areas, the impacts of domestic predators (e.g., dogs, cats) are sufficiently strong to drive species in nearby habitat to extinction. Crooks & Soulé (1999) documented the reduced density or extirpation of a large predator (coyote) with development, and the subsequent increase in abundance of mesopredators (e.g., domestic cats, foxes.). The high abundance of small predators led to the extinction of scrub-nesting birds. In this case, the impacts of even dispersed housing can extend a long distance.

- Settlements can act as 'oases'. Especially in arid areas, settlements may provide enhanced sources of water, food (via bird feeders), and habitat for nests or breeding. Bock et al. (2008) observed an 'oasis' effect of settlements compared to other areas, but noted the effect disappeared within settled areas – i.e., within settled areas, bird species richness was negatively correlated with housing density. These effects are not limited to deserts (Maestas et al. 2003), and they appear to be scale-dependent (Pautasso 2007).

4.2 Population and Housing Effects on Watershed Condition

Human population per se within a watershed has a limited direct effect on downstream aquatic resources. Human waste can increase nutrients in streams, with the nutrient flux proportional to the population size. It is not clear whether this effect is greater in very small watersheds, where population density can reach high levels, or in large watersheds, where nutrient inputs can be aggregated over a large area. In small watersheds in rural areas, nutrient inputs from human waste can be substantial due to poorly sited septic systems, as the effect decreases with distance from the stream and increases with belowground connection to the hydraulic flow. Whitman Mission NHS is one such park that is fed by a small upstream watershed with relatively high total population and extensive rural housing development (Figure 4.1). Historically, water quality in Whitman Mission NHS suffered as a result of wastewater discharges (National Park Service 2000). However, most areas with high population densities often have some form of municipal waste water treatment, which removes the majority of nutrients before dumping effluent into watercourses. Given current water quality regulations, population growth in upstream watersheds should have minimal direct effect on aquatic nutrient levels.

Population has important indirect effects on water quality via housing density and road traffic, both of which should be highly correlated with local population size. Because of the paucity of comprehensive road traffic

Table 4.1. Selected studies of the effects of human settlements on plants and vertebrates.

Taxa	Area	Result or conclusion	Reference
Birds	California foothills	Compared suburban, exurban (4-16 ha (9.9-39.5 ac)/house), and natural areas. Results varied between guilds of ground/shrub nesters, temperate migrants, and species found only in large natural patches. There were clear effects at all housing densities.	Merelender et al. 2009
Birds	Chesapeake Bay	Examined 28 watersheds. A single-variable model with % developed land was ≥ 13 times more likely than more complex models to fit an index of waterbird community integrity.	DeLuca et al. 2008
Birds	Colorado front range	Compared ranches, dispersed housing (avg 16 ha/house), and nature preserves. Human-commensal species (e.g., ravens, blackbirds, starling) had highest densities near houses; ground and shrub-nesting species most abundant on ranches or reserves or both.	Maestas et al. 2003
Birds	Colorado oak-shrubland	At rural houses, compared densities at 30, 180, & 330 m from houses and undisturbed area, and at two densities of houses. Effects differed between human-sensitive and tolerant guilds, and clearly present to more than 180 m, but most densities did not differ between low and high density housing.	Odell & Knight 2001
Birds	Colorado, riparian	Settlement intensity best explained variance in community composition, especially building density within 1.5 km. Found that (especially) ground-feeding species were intolerant of areas with high-use trails.	Miller et al. 2003
Birds	New York: Hudson Valley	Sampled 72 sites along gradients of development, fragment size, and perimeter/area ratio. All species declined at the percent developed within 150 m increased.	De Wan et al. 2009
Birds	Rhode Island	Disturbance intolerant species predominated below 12% residential development and 3% impervious surface, whereas tolerant species predominated above these levels.	Lussier et al. 2006
Birds	Arizona - SE	Overall, low density housing generally increased the number and diversity of birds, but most effect was at very low housing density. Some species negatively affected; grazing effect minor compared to housing.	Bock et al. 2008
Birds	Arizona - Tucson	Housing density had strongest effect on native bird abundance. Study sites were in urban and suburban areas.	Germaine et al. 1998
Mammals: medium-sized	Colorado oak-shrubland	At rural houses, compared densities at 30, 180, & 330 m from houses and undisturbed area, and at two densities of houses. Cats and dogs observed closer to houses; foxes and coyotes farther away and in undisturbed areas.	Odell & Knight 2001
Mammals: predators	Colorado front range	Compared ranches, dispersed housing (avg 1 house/16 ha), and nature preserves. Domestic dogs and cats almost exclusively near houses. Coyotes most commonly seen on ranches.	Maestas et al. 2003
Mammals: rodents	Arizona - SE	Exurban development had no or virtually no effect on rodent communities in grassland, mesquite, and savanna habitats. Grazing did affect rodents.	Bock et al. 2006
Plants	Colorado front range	Compared ranches, dispersed housing (avg 1 house/16 ha), and nature preserves. Ranches had highest diversity of native plants and lowest cover of invasive species.	Maestas et al. 2003
Plants: vascular, and vertebrates	Worldwide	At large scales, a positive correlation between population density and species richness; at small scales, a negative correlation. Break in scales at a ~ 1 km study grain size.	Pautasso 2007
Macro-invertebrates, benthic	Chesapeake Bay	98% probability of change-point (impediment) at 20% development in 14-digit HUC; at 2% development, 60% probability of change-point, and 77% probability at 10% developed. Extensive study examined forested and grassland watersheds; biotic indices, etc. Considerable variation in responses across sites.	Bilkovic et al. 2006

Figure 4.1. Total population in the year 2000 (top map) and housing density in the year 2000 (bottom map) for Whitman Mission National Historic Site and its upstream watershed. Whitman Mission is located just downstream from Walla Walla, WA, while upper reaches of the watershed are dominated by rural development. Historic wastewater discharges from these sources are believed to have negatively impacted water quality inside the park.

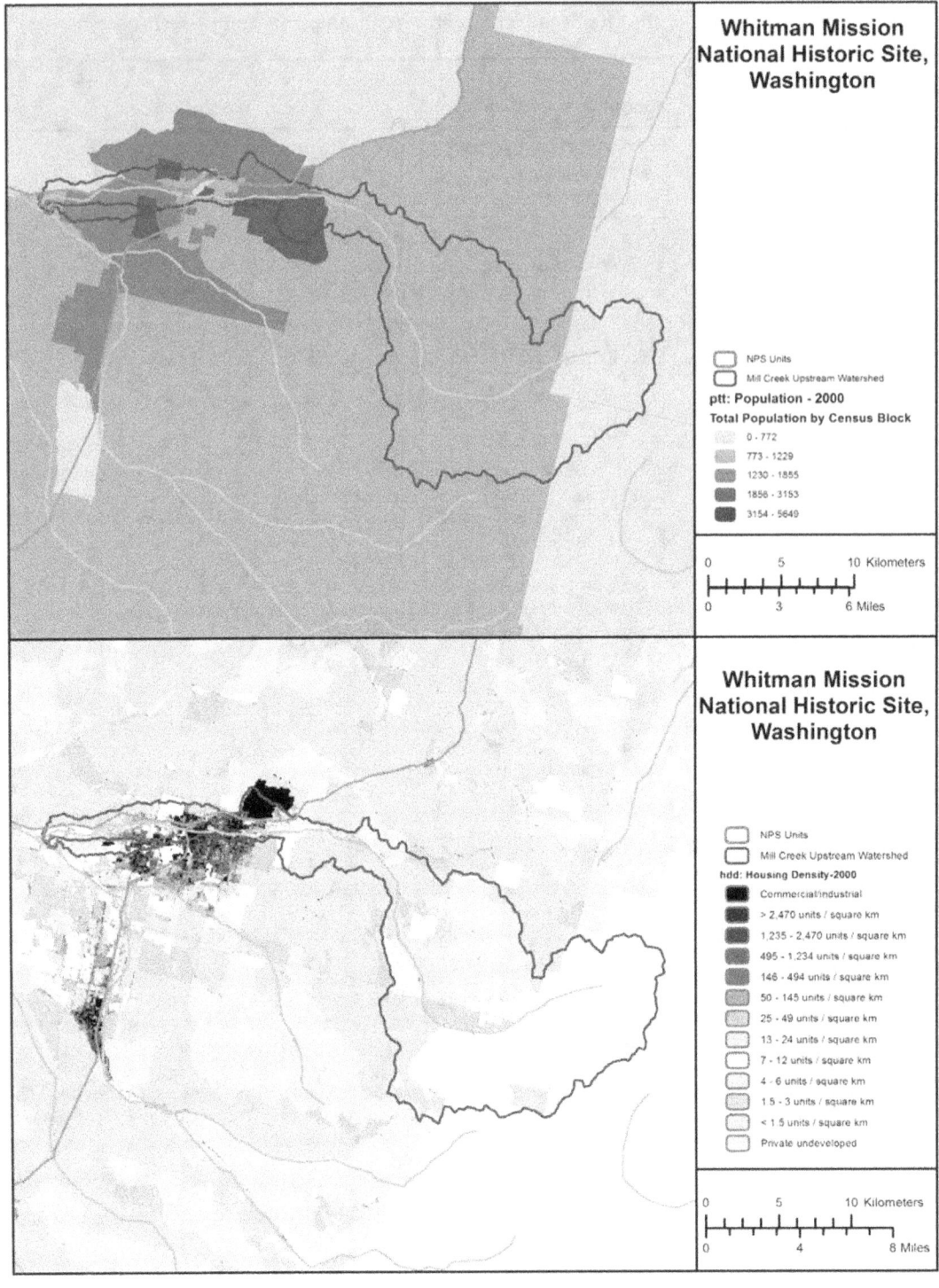

data, temporal change in population size may be the best available surrogate for change in traffic volume (road effects detailed in Chapter 3). For example, at Buffalo NR, total population and density within a 2-hr travel time AOA have more than doubled since the year 1950, and are further expected to increase by about another 25% by the year 2030. Such temporal analyses of popula-

tion for informative AOAs can be used to reconstruct or approximate changes in road metrics (e.g., road density).

Housing density within a watershed can influence aquatic resources while houses and infrastructure are constructed, and chronically thereafter via changes in infiltration rates, land cover conversion, and transport of contaminants. Housing construction disturbs the soil surface and may increase sedimentation in streams. The degree to which sediment is actually added to waterways is a function of distance from the construction to the nearest stream, the erodibility of the soil, the use of management practices such as sediment fences, and precipitation or other sources of water that result in runoff. Landscaping around dwellings typically stabilizes the soil and makes sediment runoff a transient effect. Maintenance of lawns and other landscaping can contribute to direct effects of housing on nutrient enrichment and contaminant pollution of streams. Lot sizes and prevalent types of landscaping affect the magnitude of this effect: typical suburban lawns receive large inputs of fertilizers, pesticides, and herbicides. Again, regional variation is great enough to preclude generalizations. The only empirical studies are for small urban watersheds and in the context of local-scale water quality mitigation. No quantitative data exist for the effects of landscaping in exurban housing.

4.3 Development and Hydrology

While the general relationship between development and increased flashiness of runoff is robust, few data are available to understand changes in this relationship at a specific site. In one of the few detailed site-based studies of landscape effects on hydrology, Olivera & DeFee (2007) analyzed changes in hydrologic flow parameters, parcel-level development status, and impervious surfaces estimated from parcel size and development type, from 1949-2000 in a small (223 km²)

urbanizing watershed in southeastern Texas. Developed area increased from 10% in 1950 to 30% in 1970 and 75% in 2000; estimated impervious surfaces increased from approximately 4% in 1950 to 10% in 1970 and 31% in 2000.

The increases prior to the early 1970s were primarily a result of development of new patches in the watershed; subsequent development was primarily infill, expanding and connecting earlier patches. Cumulative annual runoff and annual peak flow increased over both periods, but more rapidly after breakpoints around 1972 for cumulative runoff and 1968 for peak flow. Both annual precipitation and the percentage of developed area were significant predictors of cumulative runoff and peak flow. Overall, the model coefficients for predicting peak flow did not change across the 52 years. However, the model coefficient for the effect of the percentage of developed area on cumulative annual runoff was best fit as a non-significant relationship prior to the breakpoint in 1972, and a significant positive effect after 1972. Olivera & DeFee (2007) suggest that cumulative runoff in the urbanizing watershed was unaffected by development until a threshold was reached, and then increased significantly with further development.

4.4 NPScape Housing and Population Metrics

The general pros and cons of NPScape housing and population metrics are summarized in Table 4.2. NPScape population metrics are based on historical US Census Bureau data

Table 4.2. Summary of major pros and cons of NPScape population and housing metrics.

Metric	Pros	Cons
Population total and density	Suitable for regular monitoring (every 10 years) and a time series surrogate for the effects of road traffic; density controls for the effects of different sized census block-groups in recent decades (1990, 2000, 2010).	Long time series information (1790-2030) only available at a relatively coarse spatial resolution (by county) and thus only suited to certain AOAs.
Housing density	Suitable for regular monitoring (every 10 years); captures important indirect effects of humans resulting from development and habitation.	Estimates are derived from data-driven models that - in future projections - may not reflect real growth if assumptions underlying the socioeconomic forecasts do not hold.

Figure 4.2. Historic and contemporary changes in human population density by county for counties intersecting the 30 km AOA of Buffalo National River. In time series plots around the map, population density on the y-axis is reported as the number of people per km². Vertical line is 1972, the year Buffalo was established as a park unit. Note common peak in population density about 1900, subsequent decline to about 1950, and variable growth.

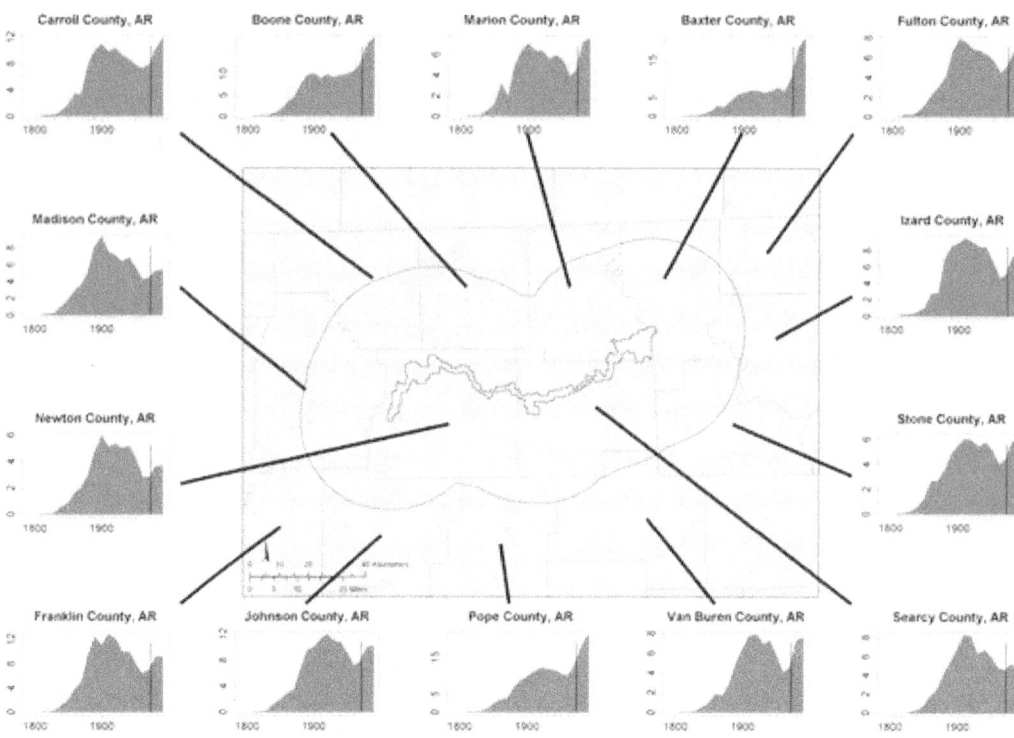

and projections from state offices (Waisanen & Bliss 2002). Metrics include total population and population density from 1790 and projected to at least 2030. Spatial resolution differs, but is no broader than the county level, and in recent decades (1990, 2000, 2010) is delivered at the level of the census block-group with area-weighted corrections for water bodies and protected areas. As described above for roads, NPScape population metrics are especially useful for considering long-term trends over relatively large AOAs (typically ≥ 30 km buffer around park). For example, the counties within 30 km of Buffalo NR all experienced population booms through the 19th century, peaking in about the year 1900, then declining to 1950 (Figure 4.2). Buffalo NR was established in the year 1972, and since that year 50% of the surrounding counties have experienced new population booms that either match or exceed those from the late 19th century.

Similarly, in another example that links to housing below, areas around Saguaro National Park have experienced and are expected to continue to experience population booms. Saguaro is located in Pima County, which has the largest total population of the four counties surrounding the park, and

based on state census projections is expected to increase about 75% by the year 2030 (Figure 4.3). Immediately to the north, Pinal County is expected to more than quadruple by the year 2030 as development continues around Phoenix and Tucson. Meanwhile, Graham and Cochise Counties to the east support relatively small human populations that will continue to grow at a more modest rate. Population trends like these are valuable for understanding and evaluating connections between a park and the broader landscape. NPScape will continue to update the population metrics as new source data are made available by decade from the US Census Bureau.

For reasons detailed in the first part of this chapter, NPScape population metrics per se are often difficult to directly relate to particular resources like biodiversity and water and air quality. The effects of human population on park resources are also challenging to disentangle from the effects of other human landscape drivers like roads and housing. NPScape housing density metrics provide a useful time series complement to the population metrics. However, it is important to note that our understanding of the quantitative effects of a particular density of houses is

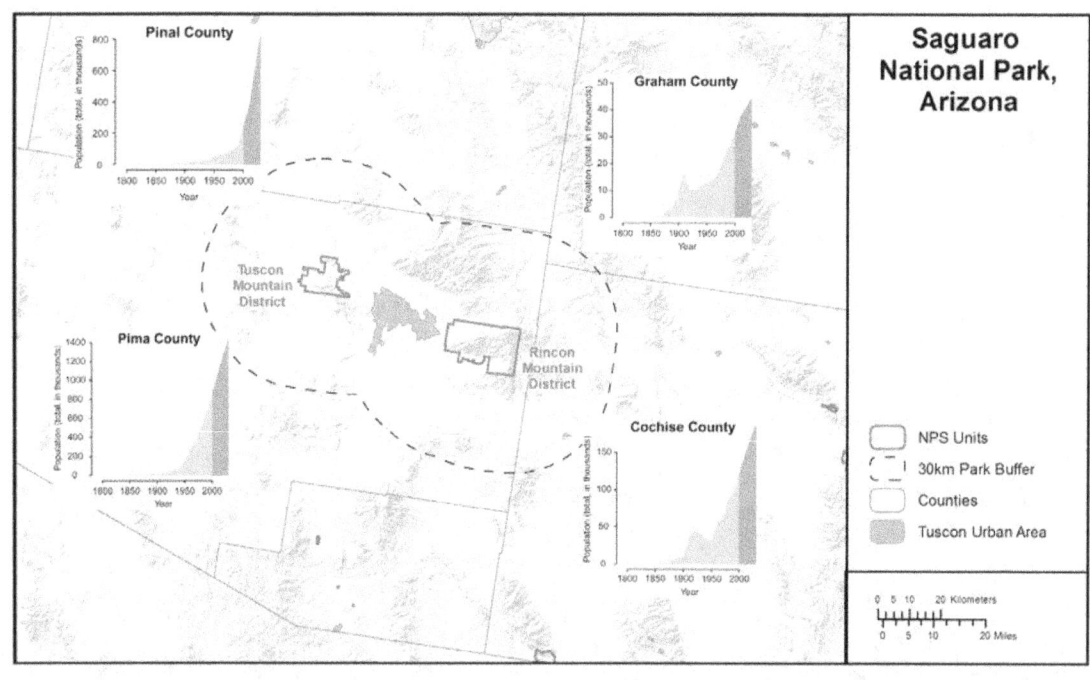

Figure 4.3. Historic, contemporary, and future changes in total human population by county for counties intersecting the 30 km AOA of Saguaro National Park. Saguaro was established as a park unit in 1933 and is comprised of two separate districts: Tucson Mountain District and Rincon Mountain District. In time series plots, blue trajectories show changes through 2000 based on Waisanen & Bliss (2002), while peach trajectories report state projections through 2030.

still limited, in part because the actual effect of one or more dwellings varies depending on the intensity of landscaping, geographical position and location, and other features like whether the landowner has pets. While NPScape land cover data identify urban centers and other built-up areas, exurban development – the low-density housing so prevalent near many parks – is much more difficult to identify and describe. It is this low-density development that has exploded in recent decades (Brown et al. 2005; Theobald 2005; Wittemyer et al. 2008; Wade & Theobald 2009; Radeloff et al. 2010) and that has a disproportionate effect on fragmentation of natural areas (Irwin & Bockstael 2007). Theobald (2004) reviewed approaches to describing population and housing density for ecological purposes, but did not provide specific recommendations for categorizing density measures.

NPScape housing density metrics are based on the Spatially Explicit Regional Growth Model (SERGoM, v3; Theobald 2005). An alternative source of housing density data is available through SILVIS (http://silvis.forest.wisc.edu/old/Library/HousingData.php); NPScape is still evaluating whether and how to extend its analytical methods and tools to consider this data input (Exhibit 4.1).

Housing density usually is strongly correlated with other factors, including population density, road density, and developed impervious surfaces (Theobald et al. 2009). Nonetheless, housing density may be a better indicator of environmental impacts than population density alone because it accounts for declining household size and second-home ownership (Liu et al. 2003; Radeloff et al. 2001, 2005). NPScape housing density data are categorized into 11 non-uniform classes (Figure 4.1, bottom map). These categories follow Theobald (2005) and the non-uniform ranges permit a much finer delineation of areas of low-density housing than is common for non-ecological studies. Theobald (2005) defines development as rural (0-0.0618 units/ha), exurban (0.0618-1.47 units/ha), suburban (1.47-10.0 unit/ha), and urban (> 10.0 units/ha). A visualization of what these categories can look like 'on-the-ground' is provided for two areas of the US with contrasting cover types (Exhibits 4.1 and 4.2); many additional examples are provided in Campoli & MacLean (2007).

In many instances it is useful to be able to compare trends in housing density across two or multiple AOAs. Such comparisons allow parks to efficiently visualize and interpret how housing densities change at different spatiotemporal scales. For example,

Exhibit 4.1. Overview of major differences between SERGoM and SILVIS housing data.

Both SERGoM and SILVIS are spatial models of housing density that are parameterized using data from the US Census. They are run for the same spatial extent (CONUS) and include estimates of past, present, and projected future housing densities. However, they also differ in some important ways.

SERGoM is a raster based model, gridded at 100 m; SILVIS is a vector-based model run for partial census block-groups. An effect of differing spatial resolutions is that SILVIS averages densities over sometimes rather large polygons, whereas SERGoM attempts to capture more fine-scale variation. This effect is evident in the example for Saguaro National Park (left maps), where immediately to the south of the western Tucson Mountain District, SERGoM captures a large county park (in green) that is split and obscured in SILVIS.

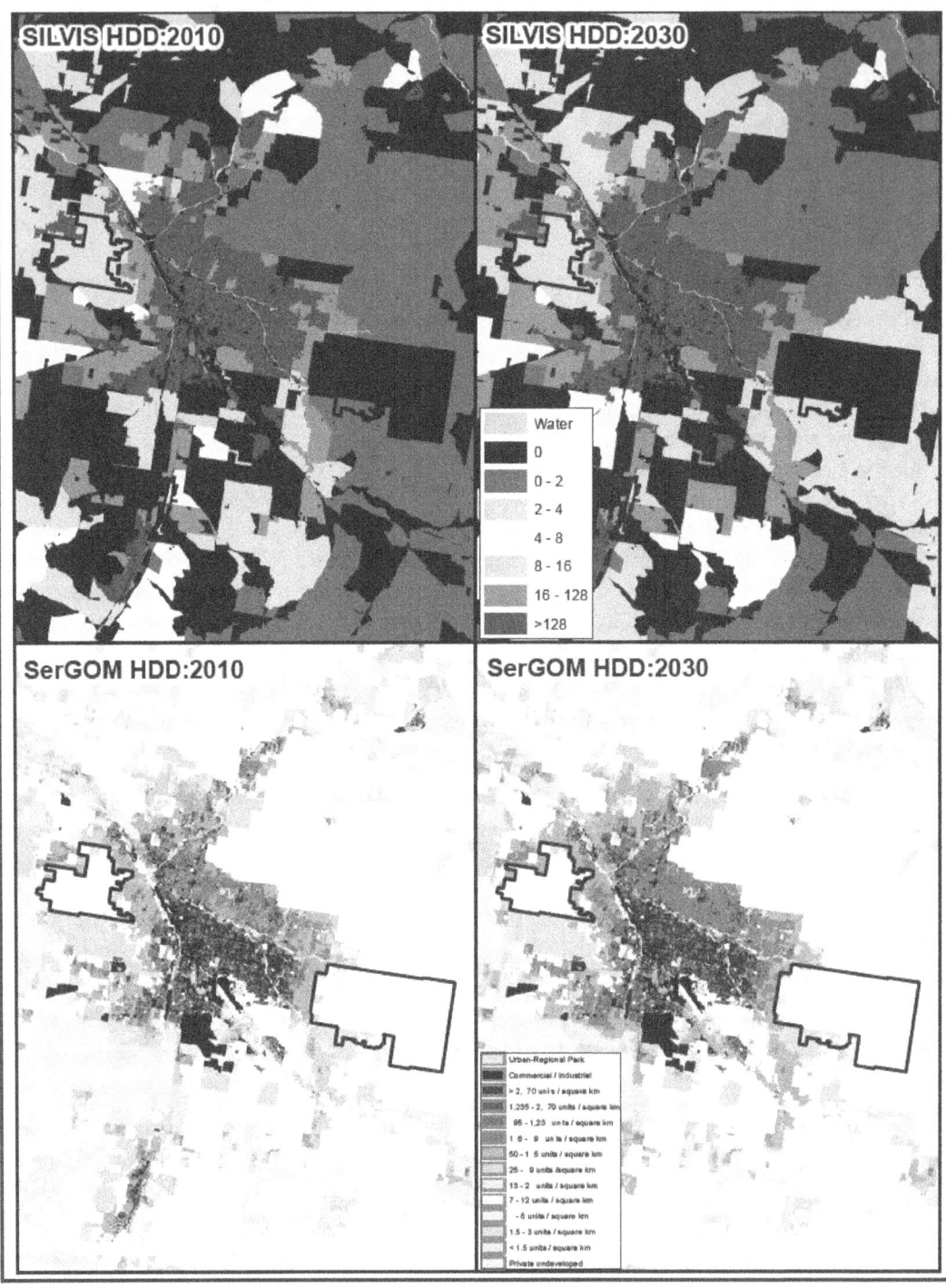

Exhibit 4.1. (continued) Overview of major differences between SERGoM and SILVIS housing data.

Such an example also illustrates another important difference: SERGoM includes two non-density map classes that are absent from SILVIS (urban-regional park, and commercial/industrial).

Because both SERGoM and SILVIS rely on input data from the Census, it is also important to recognize that they share several of the same pitfalls. In the example for San Juan Island National Historic Park (right maps), housing densities are not predicted to change because population forecasts were simply not available for inclusion in either housing model.

Note: units on both SILVIS and SERGoM maps are the number of housing units per km².

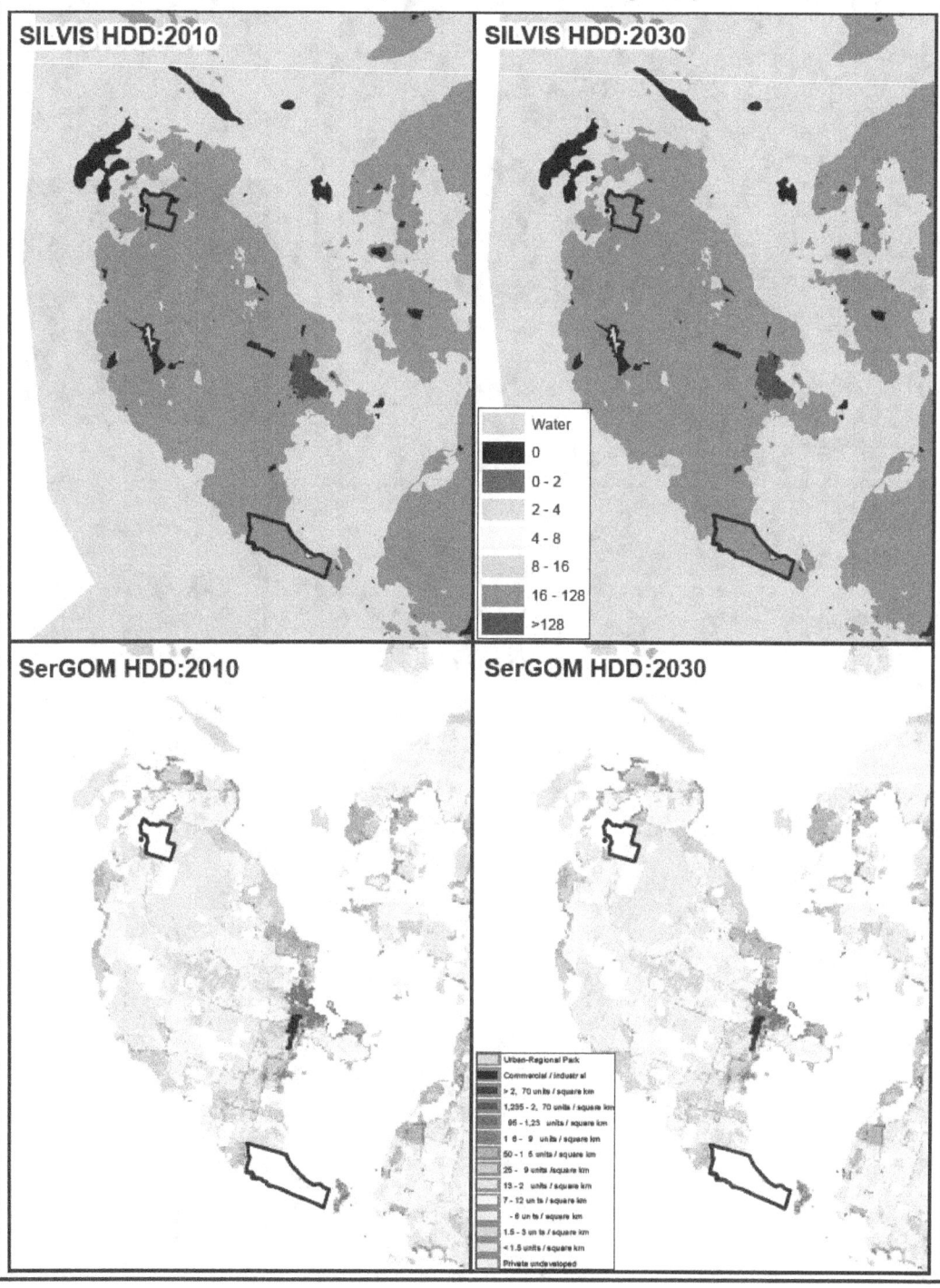

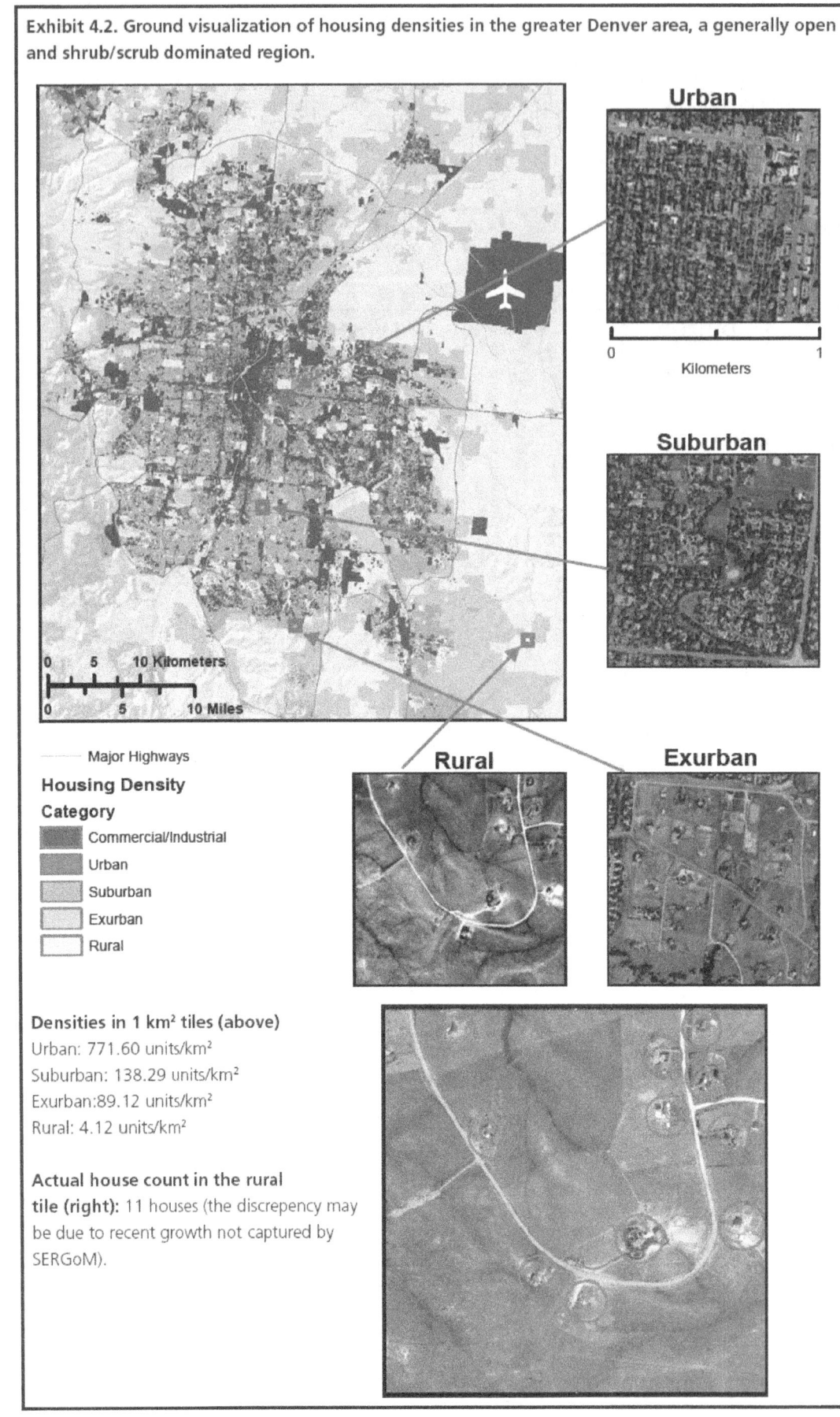

Exhibit 4.2. Ground visualization of housing densities in the greater Denver area, a generally open and shrub/scrub dominated region.

Urban

0 Kilometers 1

Suburban

Major Highways

Housing Density Category

Commercial/Industrial
Urban
Suburban
Exurban
Rural

Rural

Exurban

Densities in 1 km² tiles (above)
Urban: 771.60 units/km²
Suburban: 138.29 units/km²
Exurban: 89.12 units/km²
Rural: 4.12 units/km²

Actual house count in the rural tile (right): 11 houses (the discrepency may be due to recent growth not captured by SERGoM).

Exhibit 4.3. Ground visualization of housing densities in the greater Atlanta area, an area dominated by forest land cover.

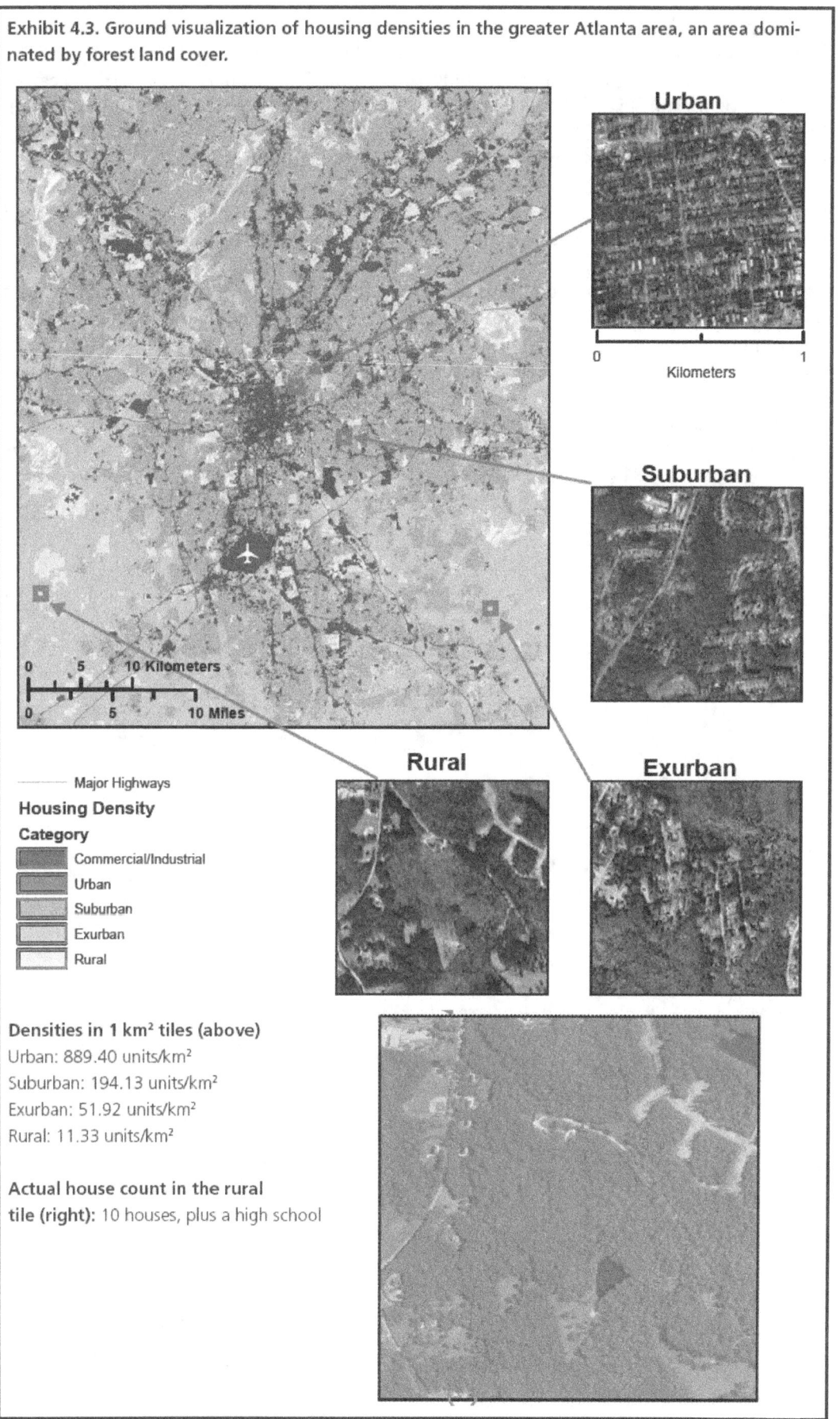

Urban

0 ———— Kilometers ———— 1

Suburban

Rural

Exurban

—— Major Highways
Housing Density
Category
- Commercial/Industrial
- Urban
- Suburban
- Exurban
- Rural

0   5   10 Kilometers
0   5   10 Miles

Densities in 1 km² tiles (above)
Urban: 889.40 units/km²
Suburban: 194.13 units/km²
Exurban: 51.92 units/km²
Rural: 11.33 units/km²

Actual house count in the rural tile (right): 10 houses, plus a high school

Saguaro National Park is comprised of East (Rincon Mountain District) and West (Tucson Mountain District) units separated by the city of Tucson (Figure 4.3). The most direct effects of housing are likely to biodiversity and manifest through human and pet encroachment originating from households immediately adjacent to the park (within 3 km). Meanwhile, housing occurring within the 30 km AOA can also exert effects on biodiversity through local recreational visitation and use of the park, and it can affect other important resources such as the viewshed, soundscape, and wilderness character. Past and future housing density trajectories for these two AOAs are notably distinct (Figure 4.4). While in the 30 km AOA Saguaro is just now entering a period of rapid suburban growth, within the 3 km AOA the park has already experienced this transition from exurban to suburban as a consequence of being on the periphery of the city. We can further split the 3 km AOA results out by unit (west vs. east) and see that most of this new suburban growth is attributed to development around the western Tucson Mountain District (Figure 4.4), which shares few borders with protected areas (Figure 4.5). Whether such changes create net negative problems for park resources is an open question. On the one hand, increases in housing density are anticipated to negatively impact at least some resources throughout portions of the park. However, in an urbanizing park like Saguaro opportunities also exist to mitigate the direct and indirect effects of housing through park interpretation, education and outreach.

Figure 4.4. Past and projected future changes in housing density for four AOAs encompassing Saguaro National Park: park plus 3 km buffer (top left), park plus 30 km buffer (top right), western Tucson Mountain District (TMD) plus 3 km buffer, and eastern Rincon Mountain District (RMD) plus 3 km buffer. Housing density classes may be further summarized according to rural (private undeveloped and housing densities up through 6 units/ km²), exurban (7-145 units/ km²), suburban (146-1,234 units/ km²), and urban (> 1,235 units/ km²). Note how the amount of housing development differs dramatically by AOA, and also how AOAs are experiencing exurban to suburban transitions at different times.

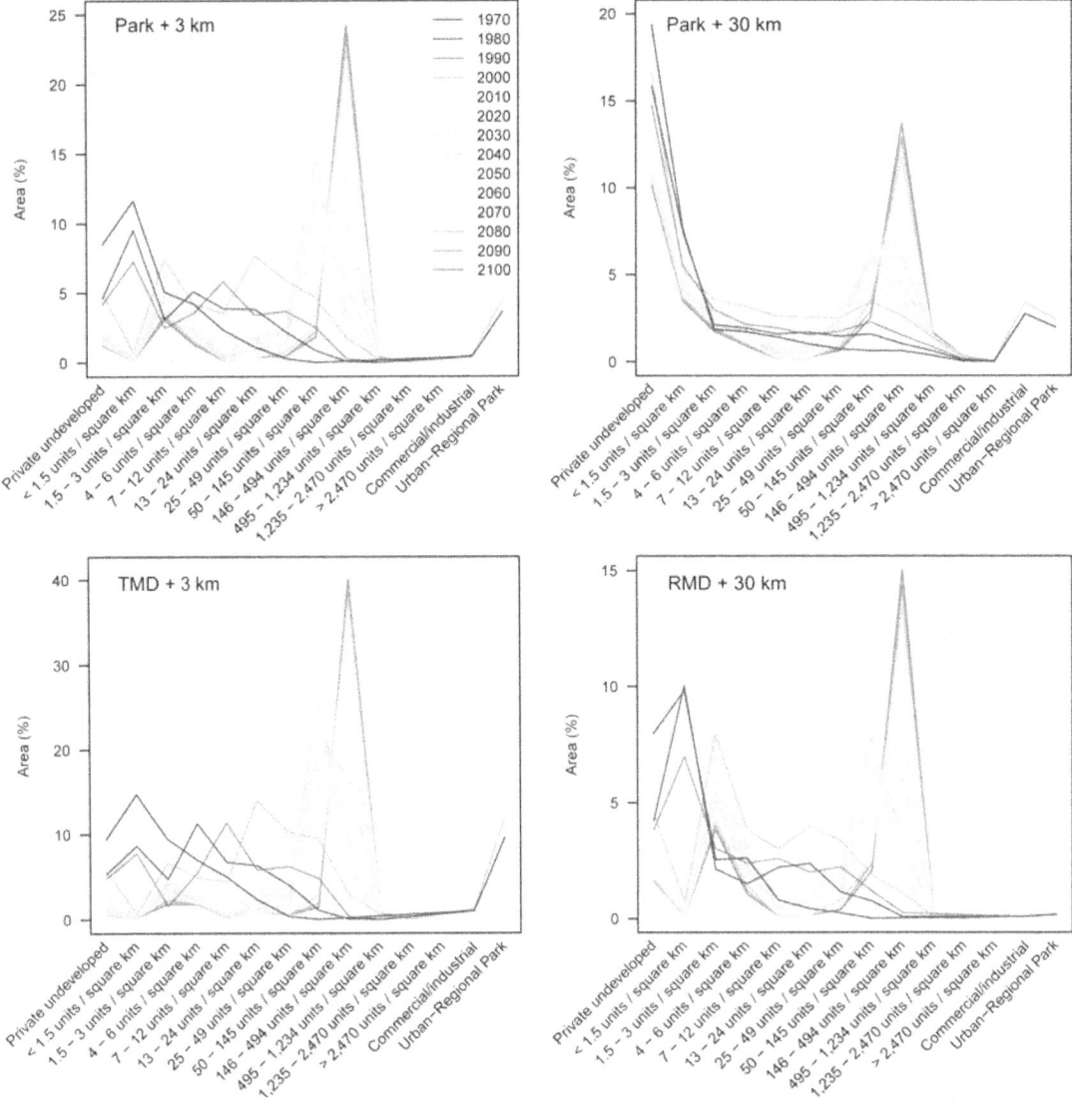

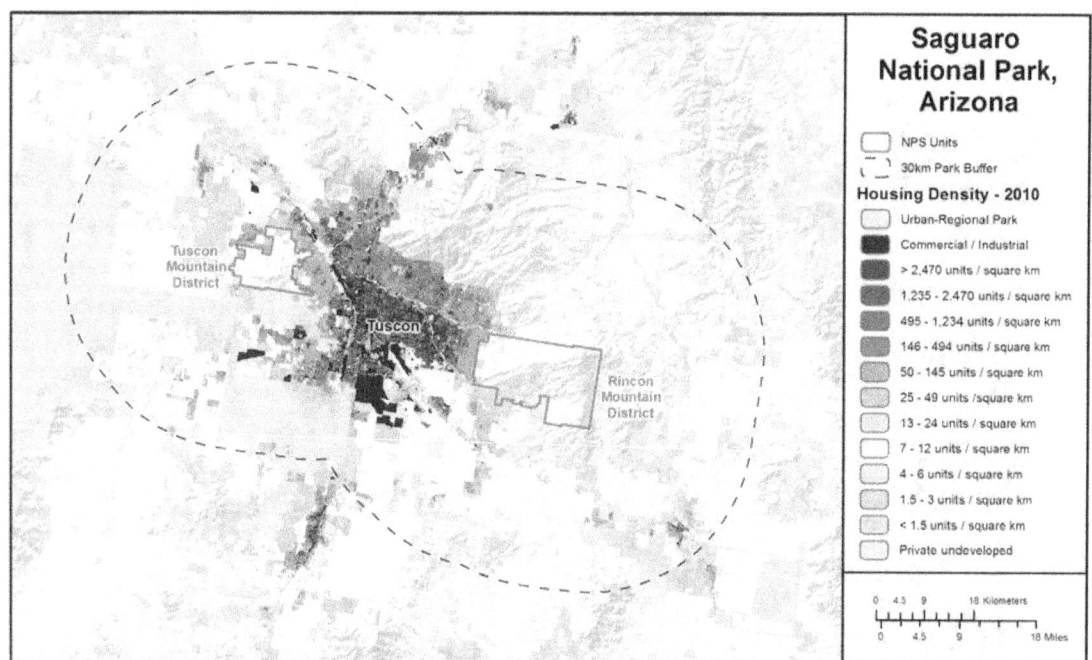

Housing density can be a major factor in more complex indices of the intensity and impact of land use, but multivariate or other transformation methods are still rapidly changing and difficult to apply in a monitoring scheme. In these indices, it will generally be more useful to estimate the amount or proportion of a landscape that has been physically or functionally modified. Ideally, ecologists will have access to region or land-use specific functions to convert readily available data on housing density to these more ecologically-relevant metrics. Leinwand et al. (2010) have attempted to do this using high-resolution data for Colorado. The study advances two metrics for assessing land use impacts: HM_c, or the amount of modified land cover, and HM_{fd} – the amount of functionally modified wildlife habitat. In the Southern Rocky Mountain ecoregion of Colorado, Leinwand et al. (2010) measured HM_c at 8% and HM_{fd} at 13%. While agriculture accounted for most HM_c, exurban growth in close proximity to public lands exerted a prominent effect on HM_{fd}. Combined, these metrics provide a way to interpret and understand how particular forms of land cover change and land use relate functionally to resources dependent on a landscape. Although Leinwand et al. (2010) developed the metrics based on high-resolution land use data collected from aerial

photographs, the general concepts underlying the metrics may be extended in certain instances to work with NPScape data.

Finally, this chapter concludes with an example of how NPScape population and housing metrics may be used in conjunction with other human-associated metrics to evaluate extrinsic challenges to park resources. Along with road traffic and agricultural activities, human population and development (including industry) are important external causes or sources for air pollution in parks. Their combined effects on air basin condition and air quality are complex for a multitude of reasons. Air basins are not always clearly identifiable on a map, and even when mapped the linkages to particular parks are not always known. Furthermore, air pollutants affecting particular parks can originate from multiple sources operating at different spatiotemporal scales. Nevertheless, certain geographies are sufficiently well studied and described to at least qualitatively evaluate these relationships.

One such example is Sequoia and Kings Canyon National Parks, which along with most of southern California suffer from problems related to air quality (Panek et al. 2012). Located within the San Joaquin Valley air basin, Sequoia-Kings is im-

Figure 4.6. Generalized diagram showing major air flow patterns in the San Joaquin Valley air basin located in the southern Central Valley of California (top); map obtained from: http://science. nature.nps.gov/im/ units/sien/AirPollution. cfm. An example of an air pollutant being captured by the Fresno eddy, ammonia (NH3, higher concentrations in red), which originates from the intensive use of agricultural fertilizers (bottom); map derived from observations provided by the CNES-EUMETSAT Infrared Atmospheric Sounding Interferometer (IASI) instrument onboard EUMETSAT's Metop satellite: http:// www.eumetsat.int/ Home/Main/News/ Features/713666.

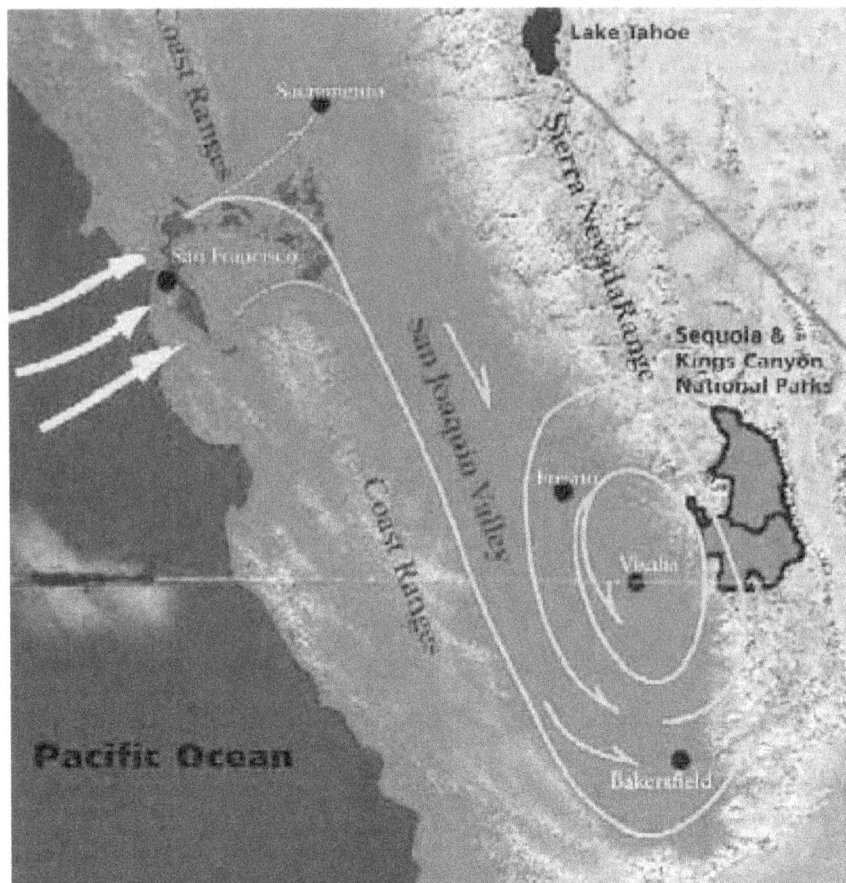

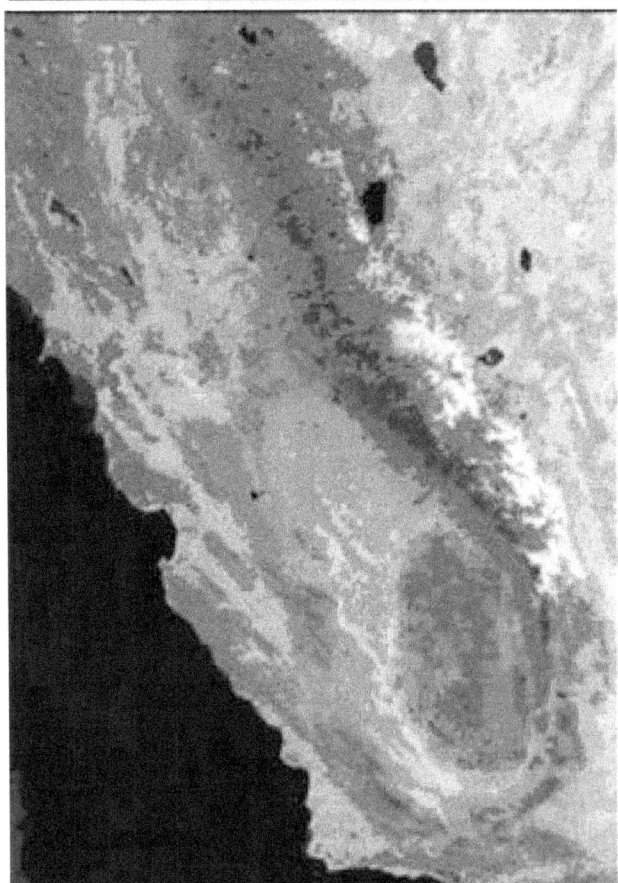

pacted by air pollutants that accumulate throughout the air basin and are subsequently carried up into the parks by the Fresno eddy (Figure 4.6). Major pollutants affecting Sequoia-Kings air quality include ozone, wet and dry nitrogen deposition, wet and dry sulfur deposition, and fine and coarse particulates related to human health and visibility (Panek et al. 2012). Primary local sources of air pollutants in the air basin include multiple large urban areas with industrial activity, major roads that receive especially high traffic volumes (I-5 and CA 99), and extensive agriculture. Eight counties encompassing the San Joaquin Valley air basin support about 9% of California's population (Figure 4.7) and contribute 14% of total statewide air emissions (Alexis et al. 1999). We expect total population in the air basin to increase 88% by the year 2030 (Figure 4.7) and – through the 21st Century – areas characterized now by exurban housing density are expected to become more suburban (Figure 4.8). The San Joaquin Valley air basin has for many decades been dominated by agriculture, with orchards generally to the east and row crops generally to the west (Figure 4.9). The road network servicing local populations and other communities beyond is both extensive and marked by relatively high road densities (Figure 4.10). While these results do not constitute a formal attribution study of air pollutants, they do provide Sequoia-Kings with a general picture of where four major air pollutant sources tend to originate within the air basin, and how two are expected to change in the near future. Such analyses may be easily repeated for other parks using NPScape metrics, and even in the absence of a detailed knowledge of the AOA are useful for understanding major human drivers of landscape change.

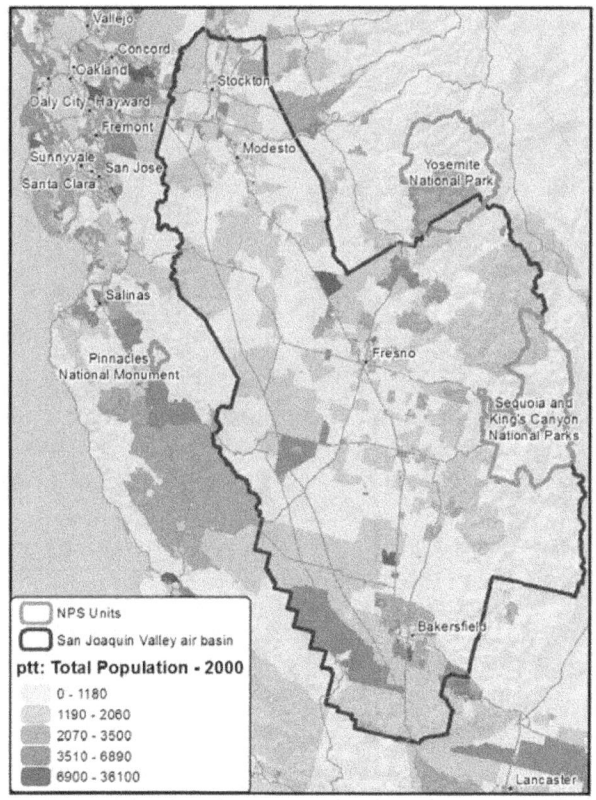

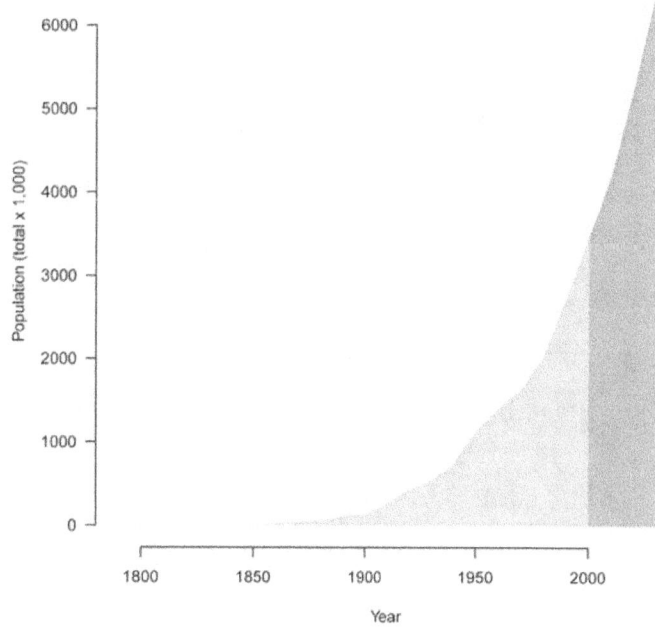

Figure 4.7. Map of total human population in the year 2000 by census block-group and time series of total population by decade (1800-2030) for the eight counties encompassing the San Joaquin Valley air basin.

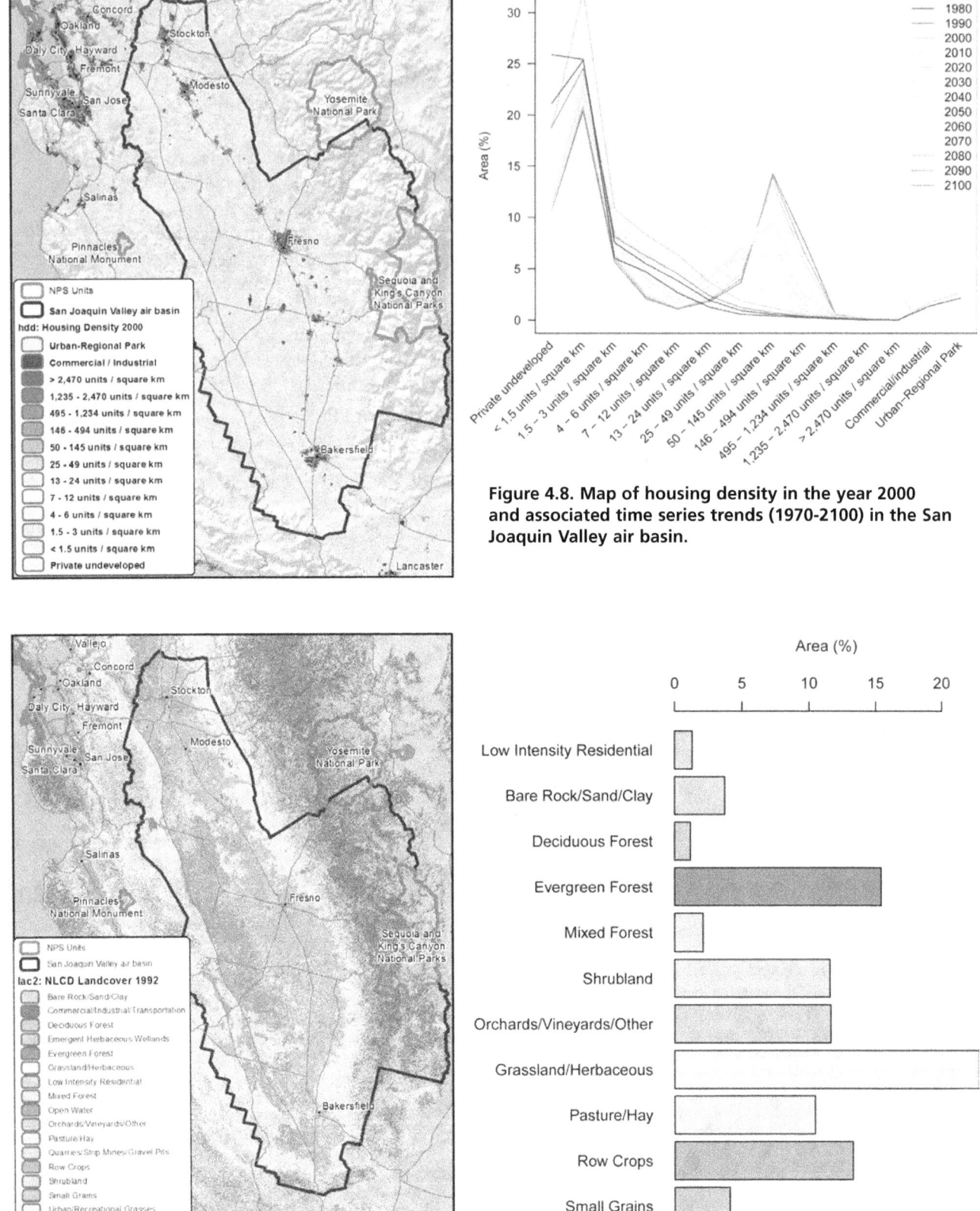

Figure 4.8. Map of housing density in the year 2000 and associated time series trends (1970-2100) in the San Joaquin Valley air basin.

Figure 4.9. Map of land cover in the year 1992 and corresponding percentage area for the more common cover classes (> 1% of AOA) in the San Joaquin Valley air basin.

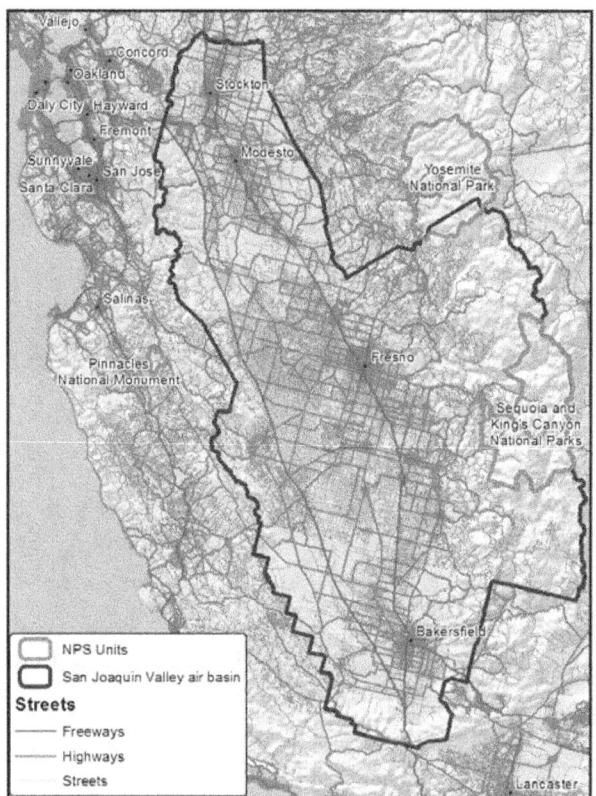

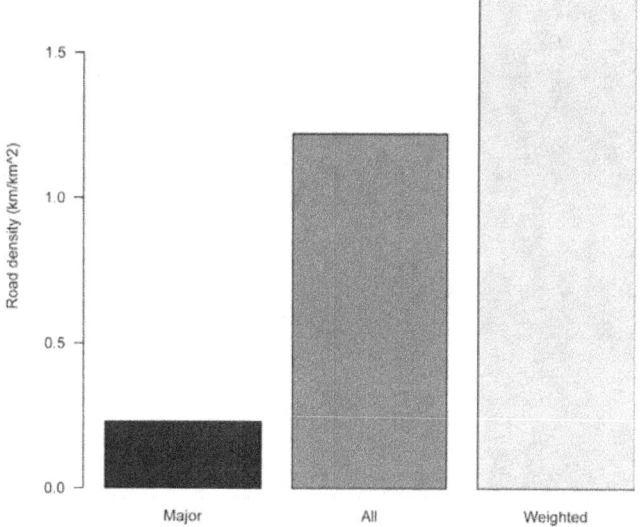

Figure 4.10. Map of road network through the San Joaquin Valley air basin and plot of road density by road class: major (freeways, highways), all (major plus streets), and weighted (all roads with highways weighted by a factor of 3 and freeways by a factor of 5 x 2 for divided lanes, or a total factor of 10).

5. Evaluating Resource Protection and Risk

The traditional response to preserving biodiversity has been the creation or expansion of protected areas. Yet the conservation status or stewardship of land surrounding these protected areas often dictates and directs potential changes in land use that can have profound impacts on park resources (US General Accounting Office 1994; Hansen et al. 2005). Impacts – positive or negative – can be categorized by changes in the effective size of reserves, in ecological flows, in the size of critical habitat, and in the amount of exposure to humans (Hansen & DeFries 2007). Within each category, Hansen & DeFries (2007) distinguish the types of mechanisms that drive change, such as species area effects, trophic structure, migration habitats outside parks, and hunting and poaching. A common feature of these drivers is that they are known, or at least strongly postulated, to be directly related to land use intensification.

Knowing the condition and changes of land stewardship and resulting land use near and adjacent to parks is important for assessing current threats and impacts and for evaluating how the situation around parks might change in the future. For example, broad-scale patterns of habitat conversion (e.g., to urban or agriculture) and protection (stewardship) have been used to estimate conservation risk and help identify areas that were at greatest risk both nationally (Svancara et al. 2009) and globally (Hoekstra et al. 2005). Combined with patterns of potential threats (e.g., roads, development), assessments of the level of resource protection have also helped identify areas at risk and refine conservation strategies on a statewide basis (Theobald 2003).

5.1 Defining What Is Protected

Although protected areas occur in nearly every country across the globe, they are by no means equal. Even within the United States, protected areas are managed by many different entities for a wide variety of purposes. Defining what is, or is not, a protected area is no trivial task. For nearly 80 years, the International Union for Conservation of Nature (IUCN) and the World Commission

of Protected Areas (WCPA) have discussed, defined, and revised such definitions. In the latest revision (Dudley 2008), a protected area is defined as, "A clearly defined geographical space, recognized, dedicated and managed, through legal or other effective means, to achieve the long-term conservation of nature with associated ecosystem services and cultural values." The IUCN further categorizes protected areas based on management intent (see Dudley 2008) and many countries, including the United States, have similar programs (e.g., US Gap Analysis Program) to further refine and define what is protected.

5.1.1 US Geological Survey, Gap Analysis Program, Protected Areas Database of the US

In the United States, the USGS Gap Analysis Program (GAP) is responsible for assessing the conservation status of biodiversity with the laudable goal of "keeping common species common." As such, GAP has been the primary developer of land stewardship and protected areas information and has compiled the Protected Areas Database of the United States (PAD-US) with significant contributions from the Bureau of Land Management, the National Park Service, the US Forest Service, and The Nature Conservancy. Originally published in 2009, PAD-US is the authoritative data source for the US contribution to the World Database on Protected Areas (see below) and the most recent version of PAD-US (Version 1.2, April 2011) reflects a great deal of review by NPS and others.

In GAP, land stewardship combines attributes of ownership, management, and a measure of intent to maintain biodiversity. The term 'stewardship' is used in place of 'ownership' in recognition that legal ownership of a land area does not necessarily equate to the entity charged with managing the resource, and that the mix of ownership and management entities is complex and can change rapidly. At the same time, it is necessary to distinguish between stewardship and management status in that a single land steward, such as a national forest, may contain several degrees of management for biodiversity (Scott et al. 1993; Jennings 2000).

GAP currently uses a scale of 1 to 4 to denote the relative degree of management committed to maintaining biodiversity in each land unit. A status of 1 denotes a permanent commitment to biodiversity protection while status 4 represents areas with no known restrictions. In assigning conservation status, the gap analysis process follows two guiding principles: first, prescribed management, not land ownership, is the primary determinant in assigning status and second, while data are imperfect and all land is subject to changes in both ownership and management, the intent of a land steward as evidenced by legal and institutional factors can be used to assign status. The status rank criteria include:

- Permanence of protection from conversion of natural land cover to unnatural (e.g., human-induced barren, arrested succession, cultivated exotic-dominated, developed).

- Relative amount of the land unit managed for natural cover, with 5% allowance for anthropogenic land cover.

- Inclusiveness of management (e.g., single feature or species versus all biota).

- Type of management (e.g., suppresses or allows natural disturbance) and degree that it is mandated through legal and institutional arrangements.

Using the above criteria, the four biodiversity management status ranks can generally be defined as follows (after Scott et al. 1993; Crist et al. 1996; National Gap Analysis Program 2011):

Status 1: An area having permanent protection from conversion of natural land cover and a mandated management plan in operation to maintain a natural state within which disturbance events (of natural type, frequency, intensity, and legacy) are allowed to proceed without interference or are mimicked through management.

Status 2: An area having permanent protection from conversion of natural land cover and a mandated management plan in operation to maintain a primarily natural state, but which may receive uses or management practices that degrade the quality of existing natural communities, including suppression of natural disturbance.

Status 3: An area having permanent protection from conversion of natural land cover for the majority of the area, but subject to extractive uses of either a broad, low-intensity type (e.g., logging) or localized, intense type (e.g., mining). It also confers protection to federally listed endangered and threatened species throughout the area.

Status 4: There are no known public or private institutional mandates or legally recognized easements or deed restrictions held by the managing entity to prevent conversion of natural habitat types to anthropogenic habitat types. The area generally allows conversion to unnatural land cover throughout.

Typically, protected lands are those considered to have permanent protection from conversion of natural land cover and a mandated management plan in operation to maintain a primarily natural state (i.e., GAP status 1 and 2) while 'multiple-use' lands, such as most areas managed by BLM or USFS, are considered status 3. National Park Service lands are typically categorized as status 1 or 2, though some cultural parks are status 3. NPScape metrics of conservation status followed this approach and identified all status 1 and 2 lands as 'protected' (e.g., Figure 5.1).

5.1.2 United Nations Environment Program – International Union for Conservation of Nature, World Database on Protected Areas

The World Database on Protected Areas (WDPA) is the result of the joint efforts of the United Nations Environment Program (UNEP) World Conservation Monitoring Center and the IUCN World Commission on Protected Areas. It is the most comprehensive global spatial dataset on marine and terrestrial protected areas available and

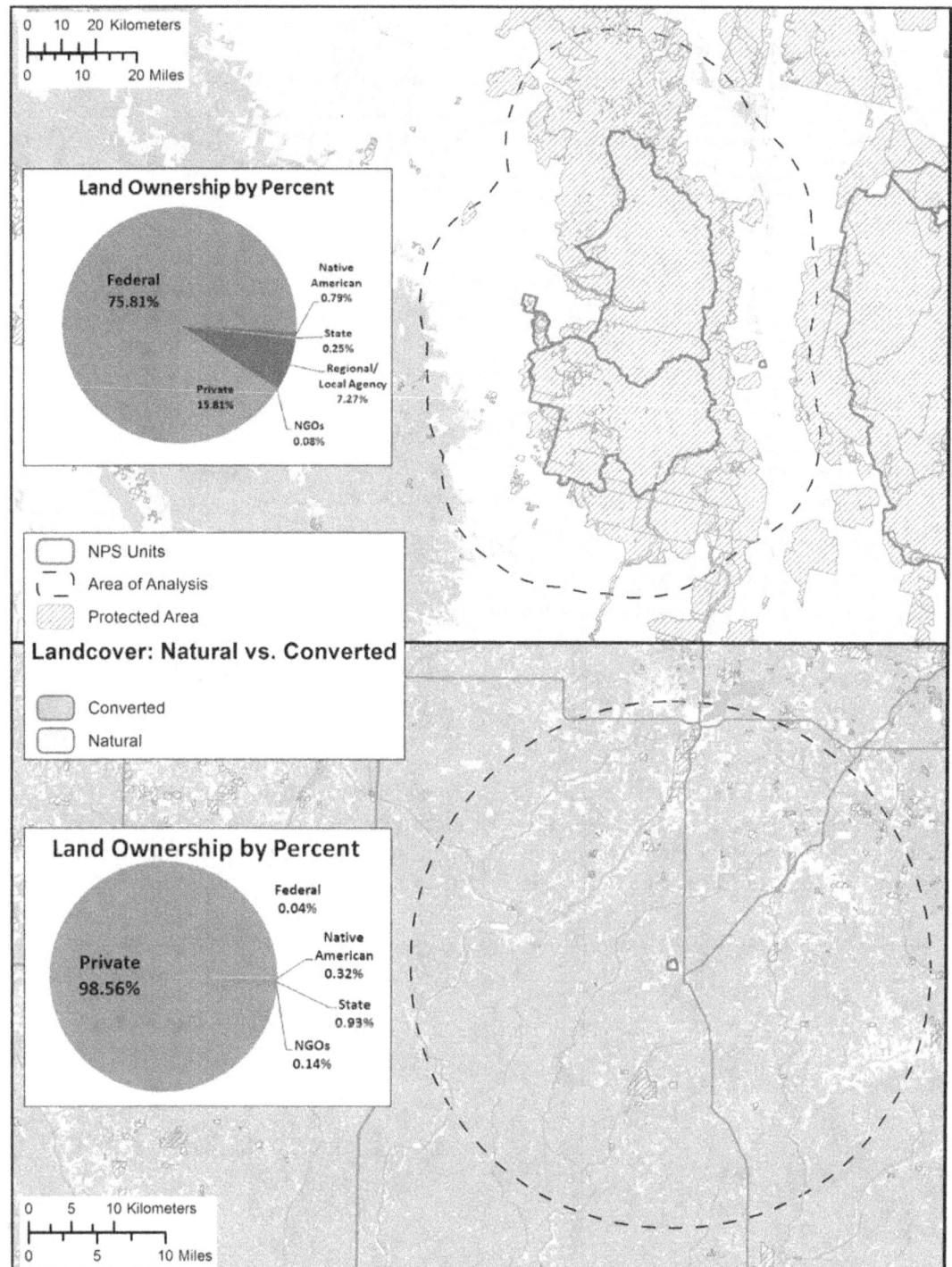

Figure 5.1. Conservation status of lands surrounding Sequoia and Kings Canyon National Parks (top) and Pipestone National Monument (bottom) as identified by the Protected Areas Database of the United States, version 1.2. NPScape metrics of conservation status identify all GAP status 1 and 2 lands as 'protected'.

provides a mechanism for NPScape to assess conservation status of land surrounding transboundary and/or near-boundary parks ranging from Mexico to the Arctic plus the outlying Pacific and Caribbean islands. All features within the WDPA dataset fall into at least one of the six IUCN categories of management intent (Dudley 2008) and are considered 'protected' (United Nations Statistics Division 2010). Across North America, this includes 8% of terrestrial area in Canada, 11% in Mexico, and 15% in the US.

For example, high in the Rocky Mountains where Montana, British Columbia, and Alberta intersect, the Waterton-Glacier International Peace Park encompasses Glacier National Park and Waterton Lakes National

Park and forms the heart of the Crown of the Continent ecosystem (Figure 5.2). This area is crucial for maintaining biodiversity in the region and assessing the conservation status in the region can aid in collaborative efforts to coordinate conservation activities. Using the WDPA, we find that 38% of the ecosystem is encompassed by over 100 protected areas, predominantly under federal or provincial authority.

5.1.3 National Oceanic and Atmospheric Administration, National Marine Protected Areas Center, Marine Protected Areas

Over the last several years, marine protected areas (MPAs) have been increasingly recognized as an important management and conservation tool to alleviate impacts from offshore development, overfishing, climate change, and other natural events (e.g., Dugan & Davis 1993; Murray et al. 1999; Nuclear Regulatory Commission 2001; Halpern 2003). Only since 2000, however, when a National System of Marine Protected Areas was developed by Presidential Executive Order (13158), has comprehensive planning, coordination, and support of the areas occurred. The Executive Order defines an MPA as "any area of the marine environment that has been reserved by federal, state, territorial, tribal or local laws or regulations to provide lasting protection for part or all of the natural and cultural resources therein." Further, the framework for the National System of MPAs in the US outlines system goals, MPA eligibility criteria and nomination procedures, process and mechanisms for improving coordination, and mechanisms for monitoring, evaluating, and reporting (National Oceanic and Atmospheric Administration 2008). Currently 297 MPAs in the US are members of the national system and exist under the authority of federal, state, territorial, tribal and local laws and regulations (National Oceanic and Atmospheric Administration 2011).

Although 4% of US waters are covered by MPAs, less than 1% are in no-take areas where extraction or significant destruction of natural or cultural resources are prohibited (National Oceanic and Atmospheric Administration 2011). Therefore, using the MPA dataset provides NPScape users an opportunity to gain insight into the current management and protection status of the marine environment surrounding parks of interest. For example, both Cape Hatteras and Cape Lookout National Seashores in the

Figure 5.2. Protected areas in and around the Crown of the Continent ecosystem based on the 2010 World Database on Protected Areas.

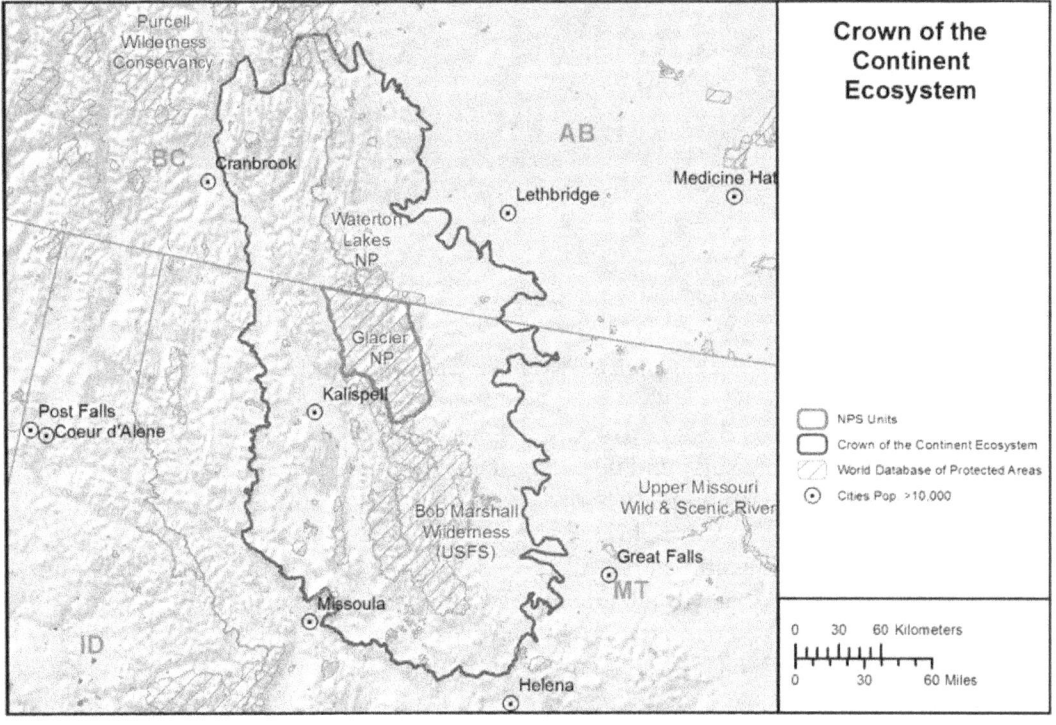

Pamlico Sound Outer Banks Marine Ecoregion (Figure 5.3) have been nominated as MPAs. Managers in these parks could use NPScape tools and the MPA dataset to discover that, while current MPAs encompass much of the ecoregion, they differ greatly in the primary conservation focus, ecological scale of conservation targets, year-round constancy, and fishery restrictions. Of the 42 MPAs (eligible or member status) within a 10 km buffer of this ecoregion, 64% were established primarily to conserve the natural heritage of the site, 57% are focused on ecosystem level protection, and 79% offer year-round protection – though those offering year-round protection cover only 37% of the ecoregion. Commercial and/or recreational fishing is prohibited in 11 (26%) of these areas and restricted in another 20 (48%). One challenge to note when dealing with the MPA dataset is that many of the MPAs overlap each other. Those depicted in Figure 5.3 represent the most conservative management at that particular site.

5.2 Measuring and Monitoring Conservation Status

NPScape metrics used for measuring and monitoring conservation status are derived from the currently available land ownership and management maps discussed above. The choice of which dataset to use depends primarily on the extent of interest. Given that PAD-US is the authoritative dataset for the US, it should be used as the primary source for any assessments of conservation status within the country. However, when evaluating marine or coastal parks the MPA data should be consulted and, when addressing border parks, the WDPA should be considered. NPScape uses all three datasets to calculate metrics, including the percentage of area protected, the percentage in broad ownership categories (e.g., federal, state, tribal, etc.), and a combined index, the Conservation Risk Index (Hoekstra et al. 2005). While NPScape analyses of these proportions are typically illustrated for the park plus a surrounding 30 km buffer, NPScape methods (SOPs and ArcGIS Toolboxes, http://science.nature.nps.gov/im/monitor/npscape/methods.cfm) can be used to assess conservation status of any area of interest

around parks (or other managed area), such as watersheds, viewsheds, migration routes, or any other ecologically relevant region.

5.2.1 Percent Protected

For terrestrial parks, NPScape calculated the percent protected as the area of land defined as 'protected' (i.e., in GAP status 1 and 2) divided by the total area of land. Open water may or may not be included in the total, depending on the management status and jurisdiction of the water, which is often not actively owned or managed by any one entity. Various combinations of the measurement can be used to gain insights into the protection status of different species and habitat types, as is done with GAP analysis (see Scott et al. 1993; Jennings 2000).

The percentage of land area protected provides an indication of conservation status and offers insight into potential threats (e.g., how much land is available for conversion and where it is located in relation to the park boundary) as well as opportunities (e.g., connectivity and networking of protected areas). For the majority of parks, < 20% of the surrounding local landscape (30 km buffer) is protected (Figure 5.4). Those parks with > 50% protection in the surrounding landscapes occur in Alaska and the western US. This suggests that – given expected rates of habitat loss and associated species loss (see Chapter 2) – many species and communities may be at risk. However, many of these parks, particularly those in the western US, still have significant amounts (≥ 60%) of natural land cover in surrounding landscapes (Figure 2.9), indicating potential opportunities for collaborative conservation partnerships.

For example, Sequoia and Kings Canyon National Parks in the southern Sierra Nevada range encompass approximately 12% of the land in the planning area for the Southern Sierra Partnership, a diverse array of landowners and managers working collaboratively to identify conservation challenges and opportunities related to climate change adaptation by focusing especially on biodiversity and ecosystem services and the network of protected areas needed to ensure future

Figure 5.3. Marine Protected Areas (MPAs) within 10 km of the Pamlico Sound Outer Banks Marine Ecoregion (dashed black outline) surrounding Cape Hatteras National Seashore and Cape Lookout National Seashore (red outline), illustrating four major categories of protected status: primary conservation focus (top left), ecological scale (top right), constancy (bottom left), and fishery restrictions (bottom right). MPAs often overlap – the most conservative restrictions are shown.

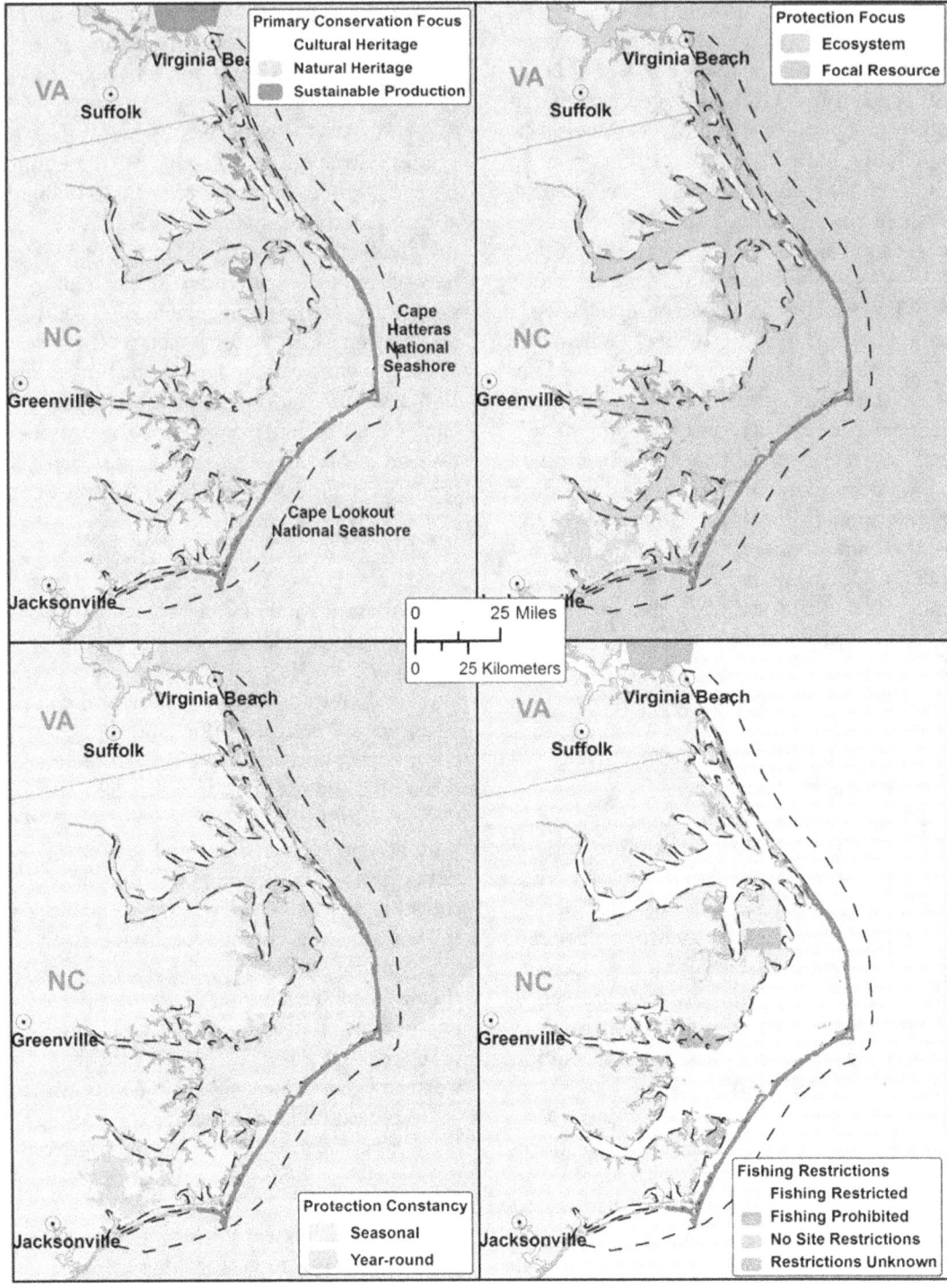

resilience of these natural resources (Southern Sierra Partnership 2010). More than 30 other protected areas occur within the 30 km local landscape of these two national parks, protecting 52% of the local landscape (Figure 5.1, top). Contrast this situation with that faced by Pipestone National Monument in southwest Minnesota where 37 protected areas within 30 km of the national monu-

ment protect only 1.3% of the landscape (Figure 5.1, bottom).

5.2.2 Percent Owned
The cornerstone of effective land conservation is partnerships ensuring all landowners and managers are represented, generating public support, and leveraging dollars. For NPS lands isolated from other protected

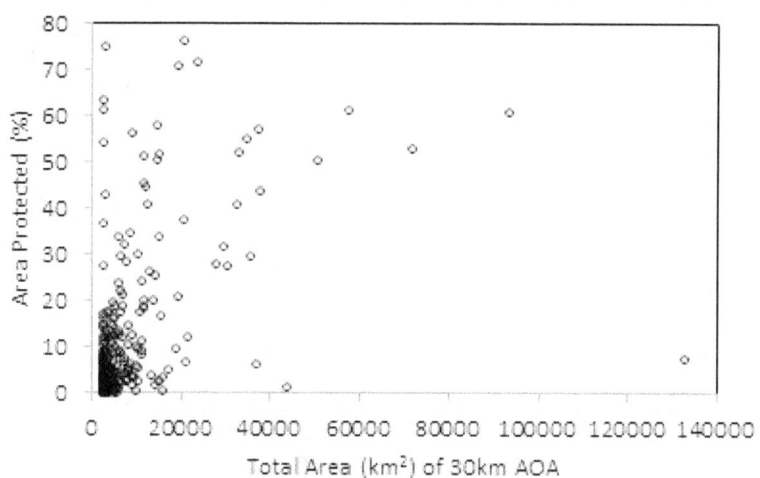

Figure 5.4. Percent of area protected in landscapes within 30 km of park boundaries, as a function of size, based on all NPScape parks encompassed by the Protected Areas Database for the United States, version 1.2. The large park AOA in the lower right is the Appalachian National Scenic Trail.

areas, ensuring compatible management of surrounding lands means facilitating connectivity of natural habitats and easing the way for species to move in response to climate change. In some cases, compatible management may only require changes in current management strategies, such as parks like Sequoia and Kings Canyon National Parks where over 75% of the surrounding lands are owned and managed by another federal agency (Figure 5.1, top). More commonly, however, are situations like Pipestone National Monument where such partnerships will need to incorporate an even broader group of owners and managers, predominantly in the private sector (Figure 5.1, bottom).

5.2.3 Multivariate Indices
By combining layers into multivariate indices, one can often gain more insight than by univariate analyses alone. Several such indices have been developed to assess current conservation risk, project future risk, and/or prioritize conservation efforts (e.g., Dinerstein & Wikramanayake 1993; Hoekstra et al. 2005; Lee & Jetz 2008; Walker et al. 2008). Some of these are straightforward and easily calculated, while others are more involved and require significant analysis.

The Conservation Risk Index (CRI) proposed by Hoekstra et al. (2005) is one such

simple index designed to measure whether particular land units (e.g., states, counties) protect their natural environments on the same scale as those they convert (i.e., change to urban or agriculture). Measured as the ratio of the percentage area converted to the percentage of area protected, the CRI is most easily interpreted as for every acre (hectare) converted, x acres (hectares) are protected. For example, 47% of the lands surrounding Mammoth Cave National Park, Kentucky, have been converted with only 4% protected (based on the 2001 NLCD and PAD-US Version 1.2) resulting in a CRI of 11 (see Svancara et al. 2009 for county-based comparisons). So, for every 47 acres that have been converted within 30 km of the park, only 4 acres have been protected. In contrast, lands outside of Craters of the Moon National Monument and Preserve in Idaho are 17% converted and 20% protected, resulting in a CRI of 0.8. In this area, land has been protected at roughly the same rate that it was converted. (Figure 5.5).

Hoekstra et al. (2005) further classify areas with >20% conversion and CRI > 2 as 'vulnerable,' those with >40% conversion and CRI > 10 as 'endangered' and those with > 50% conversion and CRI > 24 as 'critically endangered.' Combining this information with the percentage of urban area and human population change can help identify potential conservation and educational opportunities (see Svancara et al. 2009). Various modifications can also be calculated to assess the potential risks from agriculture (e.g., percentage agriculture to percentage protected) and urban (e.g., percentage urban to percentage protected) separately. Similarly, depending on the question being

Figure 5.5. NPScape map layers used to estimate the Conservation Risk Index for lands surrounding Craters of the Moon National Monument (top) and Mammoth Cave National Park (bottom).

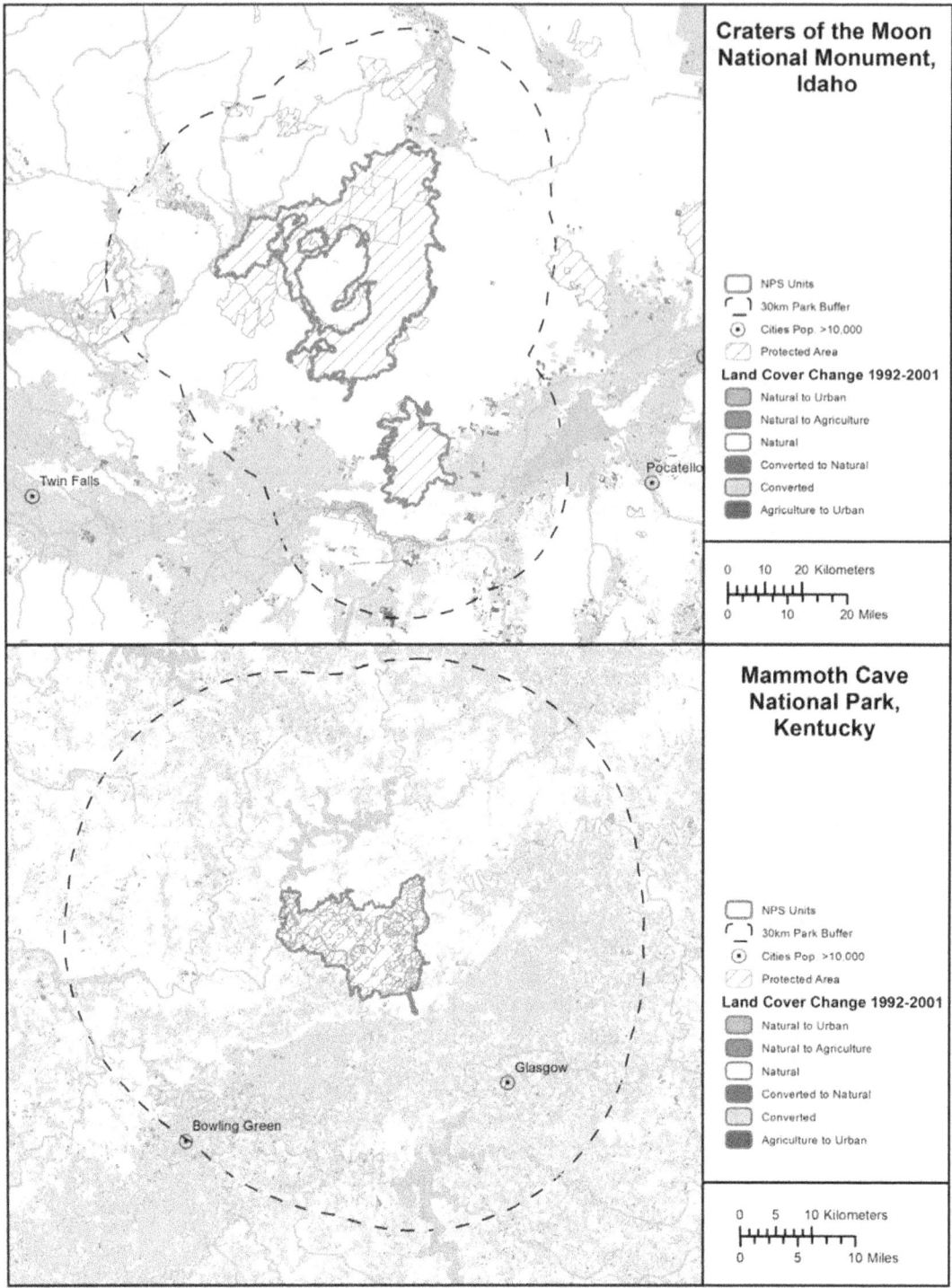

addressed, multiple-use lands (GAP status 3) can be assessed separately from those traditionally considered protected (GAP status 1 and 2; Exhibit 5.1).

5.3 How Much Protection Is Enough?

How much of a particular area or habitat needs to be conserved in order to ensure the long-term protection of biodiversity? This question has spawned endless debate in the literature as many have sought to establish quantitative targets or goals for conservation. Generic a priori targets of 10 and 12% protected land are often seen as conservation goals for political entities, such as the World Commission on Environment and Development (WCED) and the IUCN, while values

Exhibit 5.1. An illustration of how dramatically lands may vary in their conservation value, as measured by different GAP status codes.

Many parks are classified as GAP status code 1 or 2, but they can be surrounded by lands that vary dramatically in protected area status. This example illustrates two juxtapositions around Yellowstone National Park. The top photo is taken from Highway 191, entering West Yellowstone from the North (looking south). The hills beyond are Targhee National Forest. The bottom photo is taken just south of West Yellowstone and illustrates timber management on Targhee National Forest on the west border of Yellowstone National Park (green line); image date Aug 27, 2009. West Yellowstone is assigned a GAP status code of 4 (no known mandate for protection), while the Targhee National Forest has a GAP status code of 3 (permanent protection, but subject to extractive uses like timber harvest). Yellowstone National Park receives a GAP status code of 1 (Permanent commitment to protect biodiversity).

based on scientific evidence are nearly three times as high (Svancara et al. 2005). Although the arbitrary goals of 10 and 12% were considered bold when first proposed (Soulé & Sanjavan 1998), they are now often deemed inadequate (Rodrigues & Gaston 2001; Wright et al. 2001; Solomon et al. 2003).

In Chapter 2, we discussed the relationship between habitat loss and species loss (i.e., the species-area curve, Williams 1943) and the implication of critical thresholds. Applying this concept to conservation status suggests that at a 10% target level of habitat protection, 50% of species could be lost. However, as we stated earlier, species vary widely in their space requirements based on factors such as threat, natural or induced rarity, and genetic heterogeneity. Even for a single species, the area required to maintain minimally viable populations may differ greatly from that required for ecologically or evolutionarily viable populations (Peery et al. 2003; Soulé et al. 2005). A wide range of protection level (10-60%) of suitable habitat has been suggested as necessary to sustain long-term populations of area-sensitive and rare species (Andrén 1994; Enviornmental Law Institute 2003). After extensive review of the literature, Groves (2003) suggests that protection of 30-40% of any given community or ecosystem type is likely to conserve an average of 80-90% of species.

While no single percentage of protected area can be used to ensure protection or maintenance of biodiversity (Lindenmayer & Franklin 2002; Groves 2003; Svancara et al. 2005), setting quantitative conservation targets such as 10, 30, or 50% can have utility. Conservation targets provide a means for guiding and evaluating conservation plans, measuring success, and bringing together partnerships (Groves 2003; Pressey et al. 2003). Such targets, however, need to be informed by conservation planning processes based on the biological needs of species, communities, and ecosystems, as well as social and economic considerations, not simply arbitrary and capricious values selected a priori (Svancara et al. 2005).

6. References

Alexis, A., Gaffney, P., Garcia, C., Nystrom, M. & Rood, R. (1999) The 1999 California almanac of emissions and air quality. California Air Resources Board, Planning & Technical Support Division, Sacramento, CA.

Allan, J.D. (2004) Landscapes and riverscapes: the influence of land use on stream ecosystems. Annual Review of Ecology, Evolution, and Systematics, 35, 257–284.

Allan, J.D., Erickson, D. & Fay, J. (1997) The influence of catchment land use on stream integrity across multiple spatial scales. Freshwater Biology, 37, 149-161.

Andrén, H. (1994) Effects of habitat fragmentation on birds and mammals in landscapes with different proportions of suitable habitat: a review. Oikos, 71, 355-366.

Andrews, K.M., Gibbons, J.W. & Jochimsen, D.M. (2008) Ecological effects of roads on amphibians and reptiles: a literature review. Herpetological Conservation, 3, 121-143.

Angermeier, P.L., Wheeler, A.P. & Rosenberger, A.E. (2004) A conceptual framework for assessing impacts of roads on aquatic biota. Fisheries, 29, 19-29.

Auerbach, N.A., Walker, M.D. & Walker, D.A. (1997) Effects of roadside disturbance on substrate and vegetation properties in Arctic tundra. Ecological Applications, 7, 218-235.

Baker, W.L. & Cai, Y. (1992) The r. le programs for multiscale analysis of landscape structure using the GRASS geographical information system. Landscape Ecology, 7, 291–302.

Banfield, A.W.F. (1974) The relationship of caribou migration behavior to pipeline construction. The behavior of ungulates and its relation to management. (eds V. Geist & F. Walther), pp. 797-804. International Union for the Conservation of Nature Press, Morges, Switzerland.

Barber, J.R., Burdett, C.L., Reed, S.E., Warner, K.A., Formichella, C., Crooks, K.R., Theobald, D.M. & Fristrup, K.M. (2011) Anthropogenic noise exposure in protected natural areas: estimating the scale of ecological consequences. Landscape Ecology, 26, 1281-1295.

Barber, J.R., Crooks, K.R. & Fristrup, K.M. (2009) The costs of chronic noise exposure for terrestrial organisms. Trends in Ecology & Evolution, 25, 180-189.

Bascompte, J. & Solé, R.V. (1996) Habitat fragmentation and extinction thresholds in spatially explicit models. Journal of Animal Ecology, 65, 465–473.

Beatley, T. (2000) Preserving biodiversity. Journal of the American Planning Association, 66, 5-21.

Beckerman, W. (1992) Economic growth and the environment: whose growth? whose environment? World Development, 20, 481-496.

Bee, M. & Swanson, E. (2007) Auditory masking of anuran advertisement calls by road traffic noise. Animal Behaviour, 74, 1765-1776.

Bender, D.J., Tischendorf, L. & Fahrig, L. (2003) Using patch isolation metrics to predict animal movement in binary landscapes. Landscape Ecology, 18, 17–39.

Benitez-Lopez, A., Alkemade, R. & Verweij, P.A. (2010) The impacts of roads and other infrastructure on mammal and bird populations: A meta-analysis. Biological Conservation, 143, 1307-1316.

Benn, B. & Herrero, S. (2002) Grizzly bear mortality and human access in Banff and Yoho National Parks, 1971-98. Ursus, 13, 213–221.

Bennetts, R.E., Gross, J.E., Cahill, K., McIntyre, C., Bingham, B., Hubbard, A., Cameron, L. & Carter, S. (2007) Linking monitoring to management and planning: assessment points as a generalized approach. George Wright Forum, 64, 59-77.

Berger, J. (2007) Fear, human shields and the redistribution of prey and predators in protected areas. Biology Letters, 3, 620-623.

Beringer, J.J., Seibert, S.G. & Pelton, M.R. (1990) Incidence of road crossing by black bears on Pisgah National Forest, North Carolina. International Association of Bear Research and Management, 8, 85-92.

Betts, M.G., Forbes, G.J., Diamond, A.W. & Taylor, P.D. (2006) Independent effects of fragmentation on forest songbirds: an organism-based approach. Ecological Applications, 16, 1076-1089.

Betts, M.G., Hagar, J.C., Rivers, J.W., Alexander, J.D., McGarigal, K. & McComb, B.C. (2010) Thresholds in forest bird occurrence as a function of the amount of early-seral broadleaf forest at landscape scales. Ecological Applications, 20, 2116-2130.

Bilkovic, D.M., Roggero, M., Hershner, C.H. & Havens, K.H. (2006) Influence of land use on macrobenthic communities in nearshore estuarine habitats. Estuaries and Coasts, 29, 1185–1195.

Bissonette, J.A., Harrison, D.J., Hargis, C.D. & Chapin, T.G. (1997) Scale-sensitive properties influence marten demographics. Wildlife and landscape ecology: effects of pattern and scale. (ed J.A. Bissonette), pp. 368-385. Springer-Verlag, NY.

Bissonette, J.A. & Rosa, S.A. (2009) Road zone effects in small-mammal communities. Ecology and Society, 14, 27.

Bledsoe, B.P. & Watson, C.C. (2001) Effects of urbanization on channel instability. Journal of American Water Resources Association, 37, 255-270.

Bock, C.E., Jones, Z.F. & Bock, J.H. (2006) Rodent communities in an exurbanizing southwestern landscape (U.S.A.). Conservation Biology, 20, 1242-1250.

Bock, C.E., Jones, Z.F. & Bock, J.H. (2008) The oasis effect: response of birds to exurban development in a southwestern savanna. Ecological Applications, 18, 1093-1106.

Booth, D.B., Hartley, D. & Jackson, R. (2002) Forest cover, impervious-surface area, and the mitigation of stormwater impacts. Journal of the American Water Resources Association, 38, 835-845.

Booth, D.B. & Jackson, C.R. (1997) Urbanization of aquatic systems-degradation thresholds, stormwater detention, and the limits of mitigation. Journal of the American Water Resources Association, 22, 1-20.

Boswell, G.P., Britton, N.F. & Franks, N.R. (1998) Habitat fragmentation, percolation theory and the conservation of a keystone species. Proceedings of the Royal Society B: Biological Sciences, 265, 1921-1925.

Bourque, C.P.A. & Pomeroy, J.H. (2001) Effects of forest harvesting on summer stream temperatures in New Brunswick, Canada: an inter-catchment, multiple-year comparison. Hydrology and Earth System Sciences, 5, 599-614.

Bowers, M.A. & Dooley, J.L. (1993) Predation hazard and seed removal by small mammals: microhabitat versus patch scale effects. Oecologia, 94, 247–254.

Brody, A.J. & Pelton, M.R. (1989) Effects of roads on black bear movements in western North Carolina. Wildlife Society Bulletin, 17, 5–10.

Brooks, M.L. & Lair, B. (2005) Ecological effects of vehicular routes in a desert ecosystem. United States Geological Survey, Western Ecological Research Center, Henderson, NV.

Brown, D.G., Johnson, K.M., Loveland, T.R. & Theobald, D.M. (2005) Rural land-use trends in the conterminous United States, 1950-2000. Ecological Applications, 15, 1851–1863.

Brown, R.T., Agee, J.K. & Franklin, J.F. (2004) Forest restoration and fire: principles in the context of place. Conservation Biology, 18, 903-912.

Burkhead, N.M. & Jelks, H.L. (2001) Effects of suspended sediment on the reproductive success of the tricolor shiner, a crevice-spawning minnow. Transactions of the American Fisheries Society, 130, 959-968.

Burns, C.E., Johnston, K.M. & Schmitz, O.J. (2003) Global climate change and mammalian species diversity in U.S. national parks. Proceedings of the National Academy of Sciences of the United States of America, 100, 11474-11477.

Cain, D.H., Riitters, K.H. & Orvis, K. (1997) A multi-scale analysis of landscape statistics. Landscape Ecology, 12, 199-212.

Calabrese, J.M. & Fagan, W.F. (2004) A comparison-shopper's guide to connectivity metrics. Frontiers in Ecology and the Environment, 2, 529–536.

Campoli, J. & MacLean, A.S. (2007) Visualizing Density. Lincoln Institute of Land Policy. Cambridge, MA.

Cardille, J.A., Ventura, S.J. & Turner, M.G. (2001) Environmental and social factors influencing wildfires in the Upper Midwest, United States. Ecological Applications, 11, 111–127.

Carpenter, S.R., Caraco, N.F., Correll, D.L., Howarth, R.W., Sharpley, A.N. & Smith, V.H. (1998) Nonpoint pollution of surface waters with phosphorus and nitrogen. Ecological Applications, 8, 559–568.

Carr, L.W., Fahrig, L. & Pope, S.E. (2002) Impacts of landscape transformation by roads. Applying landscape ecology in biological conservation. (ed K.J. Gutzwiller), p. 225–243. Springer-Verlag, New York, NY.

Carter, R. & Andrews, J. (2007) Effects of roads on reptiles and amphibians. Available at http://community.middlebury.edu/~herpatlas/roads_biblio.php. Accessed 1 July 2011.

Chalfoun, A.D., Ratnaswamy, M.J. & Thompson III, F.R. (2002) Songbird nest predators in forest–pasture edge and forest interior in a fragmented landscape. Ecological Applications, 12, 858-867.

Chapin III, F.S., Torn, M.S. & Tateno, M. (1996) Principles of ecosystem sustainability. American Naturalist, 148, 1016–1037.

Chen, J., Saunders, S.C., Crow, T.R., Naiman, R.J., Brosofske, K.D., Mroz, G.D., Brookshire, B.L. & Franklin, J.F. (1999) Microclimate in forest ecosystem and landscape ecology. BioScience, 49, 288-297.

Cincotta, R.P., Wisnewski, J. & Engelman, R. (2000) Human population in the biodiversity hotspots. Nature, 404, 990-992.

Clark, W.C. (1985) Scales of climate impacts. Climatic Change, 7, 5-27.

Clements, W.H., Carlisle, D.M., Lazorchak, J.M. & Johnson, P.C. (2000) Heavy metals structure benthic communities in Colorado mountain streams. Ecological Applications, 10, 626–638.

Coggins, G.C. (1987) Protecting the wildlife resources of national parks from external threats. Land and Water Law Review, 22, 1-27.

Cole, K.L. (2010) Vegetation response to early holocene warming as an analog for current and future changes. Conservation Biology, 24, 29-37.

Coleman, J.S. & Fraser, J.D. (1989) Habitat use and home ranges of black and turkey vultures. Journal of Wildlife Management, 53, 782–792.

Collingham, Y.C. & Huntley, B. (2000) Impacts of habitat fragmentation and patch size upon migration rates. Ecological Applications, 10, 131–144.

Cooper, C.M. (1993) Biological effects of agriculturally derived surface water pollutants on aquatic systems: a review. Journal of Environmental Quality, 22, 402-408.

Crist, P., Thompson, B. & Prior-Magee, J. (1996) Land management status categorization for Gap Analysis: A potential enhancement. Gap Analysis Bulletin #5. National Biological Service, Moscow, ID.

Crooks, K.R. & Soulé, M.E. (1999) Mesopredator release and avifaunal extinctions in a fragmented system. Nature, 400, 563–566.

Cushman, S.A., Mcgarigal, K. & Neel, M.C. (2008) Parsimony in landscape metrics: strength, universality, and consistency. Ecological Indicators, 8, 691-703.

Davis, C.R. & Hansen, A.J. (2011) Trajectories in land use change around US National Parks and challenges and opportunities for management. Ecological Applications, 21, 3299-3316.

De Wan, A.A., Sullivan, P.J., Lembo, A.J., Smith, C.R., Maerz, J.C., Lassoie, J.P. & Richmond, M.E. (2009) Using occupancy models of forest breeding birds to prioritize conservation planning. Biological Conservation, 142, 982-991.

Debinski, D.M. & Holt, R.D. (2000) A survey and overview of habitat fragmentation experiments. Conservation Biology, 14, 342–355.

DellaSala, D.A. & Frost, E. (2001) An ecologically based strategy for fire and fuels management in national forest roadless areas. Fire Management Today, 61, 12-23.

Delong, M.D. & Brusven, M.A. (1998) Macroinvertebrate community structure along the longitudinal gradient of an agriculturally impacted stream. Environmental Management, 22, 445-457.

DeLuca, W.V., Studds, C.E., King, R.S. & Marra, P.P. (2008) Coastal urbanization and the integrity of estuarine waterbird communities: threshold responses and the importance of scale. Biological Conservation, 141, 2669-2678.

Dickson, B.G., Prather, J.W., Xu, Y., Hampton, H.M., Aumack, E.N. & Sisk, T.D. (2006) Mapping the probability of large fire occurrence in northern Arizona, USA. Landscape Ecology, 21, 747-761.

Didham, R.K. & Lawton, J.H. (1999) Edge structure determines the magnitude of changes in microclimate and vegetation structure in tropical forest fragments. Biotropica, 31, 17-30.

Dinerstein, E. & Wikramanayake, E.D. (1993) Beyond "hotspots": how to prioritize investments to conserve biodiversity in the Indo-Pacific Region. Conservation Biology, 7, 53-65.

Donnelly, R. & Marzluff, J.M. (2006) Relative importance of habitat quantity, structure, and spatial pattern to birds in urbanizing environments. Urban Ecosystems, 9, 99-117.

Donner, D.M., Ribic, C.A. & Probst, J.R. (2009) Male Kirtland's warblers' patch-level response to landscape structure during periods of varying population size and habitat amounts. Forest Ecology and Management, 258, 1093-1101.

Donovan, T.M., Jones, P.W., Annand, E.M. & Thompson, F.R. (1997) Variation in local-scale edge effects: mechanisms and landscape context. Ecology, 78, 2064-2075.

Drapeau, P., Leduc, A., Giroux, J.-F., Savard, J.-P.L., Bergeron, Y. & Vickery, W.L. (2000) Landscape-scale disturbances and changes in bird communities of boreal mixed-wood forests. Ecological Monographs, 70, 423-444.

Dudley, N. (2008) Guidelines for Applying Protected Area Management Categories. Gland, Switzerland, IUCN.

Dugan, J.E. & Davis, G.E. (1993) Applications of marine refugia to coastal fisheries management. Canadian Journal of Fisheries and Aquatic Science, 50, 2029-2042.

Dunning, J.B., Danielson, B.J. & Pulliam, H.R. (1992) Ecological processes that affect populations in complex landscapes. Oikos, 65, 169–175.

Ehrman, T.P. & Lamberti, G.A. (1992) Hydraulic and particulate matter retention in a 3rd-order Indiana stream. Journal of the North American Benthological Society, 11, 341-349.

Eigenbrod, F., Hecnar, S.J. & Fahrig, L. (2008) Accessible habitat: an improved measure of the effects of habitat loss and roads on wildlife populations. Landscape Ecology, 23, 159-168.

Eigenbrod, F., Hecnar, S.J. & Fahrig, L. (2009) Quantifying the road-effect zone: threshold effects of a motorway on anuran populations in Ontario, Canada. Ecology and Society, 14, 24.

Enviornmental Law Institute. (2003) Conservation thresholds for land use planners. Environmental Law Institute, Washington, DC.

Ercelawn, A. (1999) End of the road. Natural Resources Defense Council, New York, NY.

Ewers, R.M. & Didham, R.K. (2006) Confounding factors in the detection of species responses to habitat fragmentation. Biological Reviews, 81, 117-142.

Ewers, R.M. & Didham, R.K. (2007) Habitat fragmentation: panchreston or paradigm? Trends in Ecology & Evolution, 22, 511.

Fahrig, L. (1997) Relative effects of habitat loss and fragmentation on population extinction. Journal of Wildlife Management, 61, 603-610.

Fahrig, L. (1998) When does fragmentation of breeding habitat affect population survival? Ecological Modelling, 105, 273–292.

Fahrig, L. (2001) How much habitat is enough? Biological Conservation, 100, 65–74.

Fahrig, L. (2003) Effects of habitat fragmentation on biodiversity. Annual Review of Ecology, Evolution, and Systematics, 34, 487–515.

Fahrig, L., Pedlar, J.H., Pope, S.E., Taylor, P.D. & Wegner, J.F. (1995) Effect of road traffic on amphibian density. Biological Conservation, 73, 177-182.

Fahrig, L. & Rytwinski, T. (2009) Effects of roads on animal abundance: an empirical review and synthesis. Ecology and Society, 14, 21.

Fancy, S.G., Gross, J.E. & Carter, S.L. (2009) Monitoring the condition of natural resources in US national parks. Environmental Monitoring and Assessment, 151, 161-174.

Farmer, A.M. (1993) The effects of dust on vegetation-a review. Environmental Pollution, 79, 63-75.

Findlay, C.S. & Bourdages, J. (2000) Response time of wetland biodiversity to road construction on adjacent lands. Conservation Biology, 14, 86-94.

Findlay, S., Quinn, J.M., Hickey, C.W., Burrell, G. & Downes, M. (2001) Effects of land use and riparian flowpath on delivery of dissolved organic carbon to streams. Limnology and Oceanography, 46, 345-355.

Fischer, J. & Lindenmayer, D.B. (2007) Landscape modification and habitat fragmentation: a synthesis. Global Ecology and Biogeography, 16, 265-280.

Fletcher Jr., R.J., Ries, L., Battin, J. & Chalfoun, A.D. (2007) The role of habitat area and edge in fragmented landscapes: definitively distinct or inevitably intertwined? Canadian Journal of Zoology, 85, 1017-1030.

Forman, R.T.T. (1995) Land mosaics: the ecology of landscapes and regions. Cambridge University Press, NY.

Forman, R.T.T. (2000) Estimate of the area affected ecologically by the road system in the United States. Conservation Biology, 14, 31–35.

Forman, R.T.T. & Alexander, L.E. (1998) Roads and their major ecological effects. Annual Review of Ecology and Systematics, 29, 207-231.

Forman, R.T.T. & Deblinger, R.D. (2000) The ecological road-effect zone of a Massachusetts (USA) suburban highway. Conservation Biology, 14, 36–46.

Forman, R.T.T., Galli, A.E. & Leck, C.F. (1976) Forest size and avian diversity in New Jersey woodlots with some land use implications. Oecologia, 26, 1–8.

Forman, R.T.T., Reineking, B. & Hersperger, A.M. (2002) Road traffic and nearby grassland bird patterns in a suburbanizing landscape. Environmental Management, 29, 782-800.

Forman, R.T.T., Sperling, D., Bissonette, J.A., Clevenger, A.P., Cutshall, C.D. & Dale, A.H. et al. (2003) Road ecology: science and solutions. Island Press, Washington, DC.

Franklin, J.F. (1993) Preserving biodiversity: species, ecosystems, or landscapes? Ecological Applications, 3, 202–205.

Franklin, J.F. & Lindenmayer, D.B. (2009) Importance of matrix habitats in maintaining biological diversity. Proceedings of the National Academy of Sciences of the United States of America, 106, 349-350.

Frenkel, R.E. (1970) Ruderal vegetation along some California roadsides. University of California Press, Berkeley.

Frimpong, E.A., Sutton, T.M., Engel, B.A. & Simon, T.P. (2005) Spatial-scale effects on relative importance of physical habitat predictors of stream health. Environmental Management, 36, 899-917.

Fry, J.A., Coan, M.J., Homer, C.G., Meyer, D.K. & Wickham, J.D. (2009) Completion of the National Land Cover Database (NLCD) 1992–2001 Land Cover Change Retrofit product. U.S. Geological Survey Open-File Report 2008–1379, 18 p.

Galpern, P., Manseau, M. & Fall, A. (2011) Patch-based graphs of landscape connectivity: A guide to construction, analysis and application for conservation. Biological Conservation, 144, 44-55.

Gardner, R.H., Lookingbill, T.R., Townsend, P.A. & Ferrari, J.R. (2008) A new approach for rescaling land cover data. Landscape Ecology, 23, 513-526.

Gardner, R.H., Milne, B.T., Turner, M.G. & O'Neill, R.V. (1987) Neutral models for the analysis of broad-scale landscape pattern. Landscape Ecology, 1, 19-28.

Gardner, R.H. & O'Neill, R.V. (1991) Pattern, process, and predictability: the use of neutral models for landscape analysis. Quantitative methods in landscape ecology: the analysis and interpretation of landscape heterogeneity. (eds M.G. Turner & R.H. Gardner), pp. 289-307. Springer-Verlag, NY.

Gardner, R.H., O'Neill, R.V., Turner, M.G. & Dale, V.H. (1989) Quantifying scale-dependent effects of animal movement with simple percolation models. Landscape Ecology, 3, 217-227.

Gelbard, J.L. & Belnap, J. (2003) Roads as conduits for exotic plant invasions in a semiarid landscape. Conservation Biology, 17, 420-432.

Gerlach, G. & Musolf, K. (2000) Fragmentation of landscape as a cause for genetic subdivision in bank voles. Conservation Biology, 14, 1066–1074.

Germaine, S.S., Rosenstock, S.S., Schweinsburg, R.E. & Richardson, W.S. (1998) Relationships among breeding birds, habitat, and residential development in greater Tucson, Arizona. Ecological Applications, 8, 680-691.

Goetz, S.J., Jantz, P. & Jantz, C.A. (2009) Connectivity of core habitat in the Northeastern United States: parks and protected areas in a landscape context. Remote Sensing of Environment, 113, 1421-1429.

Gregory, S.V., Swanson, F.J., Mckee, W.A. & Cummins, K.W. (1991) An ecosystem perspective of riparian zones: focus on links between land and water. BioScience, 41, 540-551.

Groffman, P.M., Baron, J.S., Blett, T., Gold, A.J., Goodman, I.A., Gunderson, L.H., Levinson, B.M., Palmer, M.A., Paerl, H.W., Peterson, G.D., Poff, N.L.R., Rejeski, D.W., Reynolds, J.F., Turner, M.G., Weathers, K.C. & Wiens, J.A. (2006) Ecological thresholds: the key to successful environmental management or an important concept with no practical application? Ecosystems, 9, 1-13.

Gross, J.E., Nemani, R.R., Turner, W. & Melton, F. (2006) Remote sensing for the national parks. Park Science, 24, 30-36.

Grover, K.E. & Thompson, M.J. (1986) Factors influencing spring feeding site selection by elk in the Elkhorn Mountains, Montana. Journal of Wildlife Management, 50, 466–470.

Groves, C.G. (2003) Drafting a conservation blueprint. Island Press, Washington, DC.

Gude, P.H., Hansen, A.J. & Jones, D.A. (2007) Biodiversity consequences of alternative future land use scenarios in Greater Yellowstone. Ecological Applications, 17, 1004-1018.

Guerry, A.D. & Hunter, M.L. (2002) Amphibian distributions in a landscape of forests and agriculture: an examination of landscape composition and configuration. Conservation Biology, 16, 745-754.

Gurnell, A.M., Gregory, K.J. & Petts, G.E. (1995) The role of coarse woody debris in forest aquatic habitats: implications for management. Aquatic Conservation, 5, 143-166.

Halpern, B.S. (2003) The impact of marine reserves: do reserves work and does reserve size matter? Ecological Applications, 13, S117-S137.

Hancock, P.J. (2002) Human impacts on the stream-groundwater exchange zone. Environmental Management, 29, 763-781.

Hansen, A.J., Davis, C.R., Piekielek, N., Gross, J., Theobald, D.M., Goetz, S., Melton, F. & DeFries, R. (2011) Delineating the ecosystems containing protected areas for monitoring and management. BioScience, 61, 363-373.

Hansen, A.J. & DeFries, R. (2007) Ecological mechanisms linking protected areas to surrounding lands. Ecological Applications, 17, 974–988.

Hansen, A.J., Knight, R.L., Marzluff, J.M., Powell, S., Brown, K., Gude, P.H. & Jones, K. (2005) Effects of exurban development on biodiversity: patterns, mechanisms, and research needs. Ecological Applications, 15, 1893–1905.

Hansen, A.J., Rasker, R., Maxwell, B., Rotella, J.J., Johnson, J.D., Parmenter, A.W., Langner, U., Cohen, W.B., Lawrence, R.L. & Kraska, M.P.V. (2002) Ecological causes and consequences of demographic change in the New West. BioScience, 52, 151–162.

Hansen, A.J. & Urban, D.L. (1992) Avian response to landscape pattern: the role of species' life histories. Landscape Ecology, 7, 163-180.

Harding, J.S., Benfield, E.F., Bolstad, P.V., Helfman, G.S. & Jones, E.B.D. (1998) Stream biodiversity: the ghost of land use past. Proceedings of the National Academy of Sciences of the United States of America, 95, 14843-14847.

Harrison, S. & Bruna, E. (1999) Habitat fragmentation and large-scale conservation: what do we know for sure? Ecography, 22, 225–232.

Harrison, S., Hohn, C. & Ratay, S. (2002) Distribution of exotic plants along roads in a peninsular nature reserve. Biological Invasions, 4, 425-430.

Hartley, M.J. & Hunter Jr, M.L. (1998) A meta-analysis of forest cover, edge effects, and artificial nest predation rates. Conservation Biology, 12, 465–469.

Haskell, D.G. (2000) Effects of forest roads on macroinvertebrate soil fauna of the southern Appalachian Mountains. Conservation Biology, 14, 57–63.

Heilman Jr, G.E., Strittholt, J.R., Slosser, N.C. & DellaSala, D.A. (2002) Forest fragmentation of the conterminous United States: assessing forest intactness through road density and spatial characteristics. BioScience, 52, 411–422.

Heinz Center (H. John Heinz III Center for Science). (2008a) Landscape pattern indicators for the nation: a report from the Heinz Center's landscape pattern task group. The John Heinz III Center for Science, Economics, and the Environment), Washington, DC.

Heinz Center (H. John Heinz III Center for Science). (2008b) The state of the nation's ecosystems 2008: measuring the land, waters, and living resources of the United States. Island Press, Washington, DC.

Hels, T. & Buchwald, E. (2001) The effect of road kills on amphibian populations. Biological Conservation, 99, 331–340.

Henein, K., Wegner, J. & Merriam, G. (1998) Population effects of landscape model manipulation on two behaviourally different woodland small mammals. Oikos, 81, 168-186.

Henley, W.F., Patterson, M.A., Neves, R.J. & Lemly, A.D. (2000) Effects of sedimentation and turbidity on lotic food webs: a concise review for natural resource managers. Reviews in Fisheries Science, 8, 125-139.

Hilty, J.A., Lidicker Jr, W.Z. & Merenlender, A.M. (2006) Corridor Ecology: The Science and Practice of Linking Landscapes for Biodiversity Conservation. Island Press, Washington, DC.

Hobbs, R.J. (2005) Restoration ecology and landscape ecology. Issues and Perspectives in Landscape Ecology. (eds J. Wiens & M. Moss), pp. 217-229. Cambridge University Press.

Hoekstra, J.M., Boucher, T.M., Ricketts, T.H. & Roberts, C. (2005) Confronting a biome crisis: global disparities of habitat loss and protection. Ecology Letters, 8, 23-29.

Homer, C., Huang, C., Yang, L., Wylie, B. & Coan, M. (2004) Development of a 2001 National Landcover Database for the United States. Photogrammetric Engineering and Remote Sensing, 70, 829-840.

Howell, C.A., Dijak, W.D. & Thompson III, F.R. (2006) Landscape context and selection for forest edge by breeding brown-headed cowbirds. Landscape Ecology, 22, 273-284.

Huggett, A.J. (2005) The concept and utility of ecological thresholds in biodiversity conservation. Biological Conservation, 124, 301-310.

Hunter, R. (1991) *Bromus* invasions on the Nevada Test Site: present status of *B. rubens* and *B. tectorum* with notes on their relationship to disturbance and altitude. Western North American Naturalist, 51, 176-182.

Irwin, E.G. & Bockstael, N.E. (2007) The evolution of urban sprawl: evidence of spatial heterogeneity and increasing land fragmentation. Proceedings of the National Academy of Sciences of the United States of America, 104, 20672-20677.

Jackson, S.D. (2000) Overview of transportation impacts on wildlife movement and populations. Wildlife and highways: seeking solutions to an ecological and socio-economic dilemma. (eds T.A. Messmer & B. West), p. 7–20. The Wildlife Society.

Jaeger, J.A.G., Bowman, J., Brennan, J., Fahrig, L., Bert, D., Bouchard, J., Charbonneau, N., Frank, K., Gruber, B. & VonToschanowitz, K.T. (2005) Predicting when animal populations are at risk from roads: an interactive model of road avoidance behavior. Ecological Modelling, 185, 329-348.

Jantunen, J., Saarinen, K., Valtonen, A. & Saarnio, S. (2006) Grassland vegetation along roads differing in size and traffic density. Annales Botanici Fennici, 43, 107-117.

Jennings, M.D. (2000) Gap analysis: concepts, methods, and recent results. Landscape Ecology, 15, 5-20.

Johnson, H.B., Vasek, F.C. & Yonkers, T. (1975) Productivity, diversity and stability relationships in Mojave Desert roadside vegetation. Bulletin of the Torrey Botanical Club, 102, 106-115.

Johnson, L.B., Breneman, D.H. & Richards, C. (2003) Macroinvertebrate community structure and function associated with large wood in low gradient streams. River Research and Applications, 19, 199-218.

Johnston, V.R. (1947) Breeding birds of the forest edge in Illinois. Condor, 49, 45-53.

Jones, J.A., Swanson, F.J., Wemple, B.C. & Snyder, K.U. (2000) Effects of roads on hydrology, geomorphology, and disturbance patches in stream networks. Conservation Biology, 14, 76–85.

Karr, J.R. & Chu, E.W. (2000) Sustaining living rivers. Hydrobiologia, 423, 1-14.

Karraker, N.E., Gibbs, J.P. & Vonesh, J.R. (2008) Impacts of road deicing salt on the demography of vernal pool-breeding amphibians. Ecological Applications, 18, 724-734.

Kasworm, W.F. & Manley, T.L. (1990) Road and trail influences on grizzly bears and black bears in northwest Montana. International Association of Bear Research and Management, 8, 79-84.

Keitt, T.H., Urban, D.L. & Milne, B.T. (1997) Detecting critical scales in fragmented landscapes. Conservation Ecology, 1, 4.

Keller, I. & Largiadèr, C.R. (2003) Recent habitat fragmentation caused by major roads leads to reduction of gene flow and loss of genetic variability in ground beetles. Proceedings of the Royal Society B: Biological Sciences, 270, 417-423.

Kennedy, R.E., Townsend, P.A., Gross, J.E., Cohen, W.B., Bolstad, P.V., Wang, Y.Q. & Adams, P. (2009) Remote sensing change detection tools for natural resource managers: Understanding concepts and tradeoffs in the design of landscape monitoring projects. Remote Sensing of Environment, 113, 1382-1396.

Kerr, J.T. & Currie, D.J. (1995) Effects of human activity on global extinction risk. Conservation Biology, 9, 1528–1538.

Keymer, J.E., Marquet, P.A., Velasco-Hernández, J.X. & Levin, S.A. (2000) Extinction thresholds and metapopulation persistence in dynamic landscapes. American Naturalist, 156, 478-494.

King, A.W. & With, K.A. (2002) Dispersal success on spatially structured landscapes: when do spatial pattern and dispersal behavior really matter? Ecological Modelling, 147, 23-39.

King, R.S., Baker, M.E., Whigham, D.F., Weller, D.E., Jordan, T.E., Kazyak, P.F. & Hurd, M.K. (2005) Spatial considerations for linking watershed land cover to ecological indicators in streams. Ecological Applications, 15, 137–153.

Klein, R.D. (1979) Urbanization and stream quality impairment. Water Resources Bulletin, 15, 948-963.

Kociolek, A.V., Clevenger, A.P., St. Clair, C.C. & Proppe, D.S. (2011) Effects of road networks on bird populations. Conservation Biology, 25, 241–249.

Kolpin, D.W., Furlong, E.T., Meyer, M.T., Thurman, E.M., Zaugg, S.D., Barber, L.B. & Buxton, H.T. (2002) Pharmaceuticals, hormones, and other organic wastewater contaminants in US streams, 1999– 2000: A national reconnaissance. Environmental Science and Technology, 36, 1202-1211.

Kristan III, W.B., Lynam, A.J., Price, M.V. & Rotenberry, J.T. (2003) Alternative causes of edge-abundance relationships in birds and small mammals of California coastal sage scrub. Ecography, 26, 29-44.

Kupfer, J.A. (2006) National assessments of forest fragmentation in the US. Global Environmental Change, 16, 73-82.

Kupfer, J.A., Malanson, G.P. & Franklin, S.B. (2006) Not seeing the ocean for the islands: the mediating influence of matrix-based processes on forest fragmentation effects. Global Ecology and Biogeography, 15, 8–20.

Kurki, S., Nikula, A., Helle, P. & Lindén, H. (1998) Abundaces of red fox and pine marten in relation to composition of boreal forest landscapes. Journal of Animal Ecology, 67, 874-886.

Kuussaari, M., Bommarco, R., Heikkinen, R.K., Helm, A., Krauss, J., Lindborg, R., Ockinger, E., Pärtel, M., Pino, J., Rodà, F., Stefanescu, C., Teder, T., Zobel, M. & Steffan-Dewenter, I. (2009) Extinction debt: a challenge for biodiversity conservation. Trends in Ecology & Evolution, 24, 564-571.

Lamberson, R.H., McKelvey, R., Noon, B.R. & Voss, C. (1992) A dynamic analysis of northern spotted owl viability in a fragmented forest landscape. Conservation Biology, 6, 505–512.

Lande, R. (1987) Extinction thresholds in demographic models of territorial populations. American Naturalist, 130, 624–635.

Lande, R. (1988) Demographic models of the northern spotted owl (*Strix occidentalis caurina*). Oecologia, 75, 601–607.

Laurance, W.F., Goosem, M. & Laurance, S.G.W. (2009) Impacts of roads and linear clearings on tropical forests. Trends in Ecology & Evolution, 24, 659-669.

Laurian, C., Dussault, C., Ouellet, J.-P., Courtois, R., Poulin, M. & Breton, L. (2008) Behavior of moose relative to a road network. Journal of Wildlife Management, 72, 1550-1557.

Lawrence, D.J., Larson, E.R., Liermann, C.A.R., Mims, M.C., Pool, T.K. & Olden, J.D. (2011) National parks as protected areas for U.S. freshwater fish diversity. Conservation Letters, 4, 364-371.

Lee, T.M. & Jetz, W. (2008) Future battlegrounds for conservation under global change. Proceedings of the Royal Society B: Biological Sciences, 275, 1261-1270.

Leinwand, I.I.F., Theobald, D.M., Mitchell, J. & Knight, R.L. (2010) Landscape dynamics at the public–private interface: a case study in Colorado. Landscape and Urban Planning, 97, 182-193.

Lenat, D.R. & Crawford, J.K. (1994) Effects of land use on water quality and aquatic biota of three North Carolina Piedmont streams. Hydrobiologia, 294, 185-199.

Leopold, A. (1933) Game Management. Charles Scribner's Sons, NY.

Levin, S.A. (1981) The problem of pattern and scale in ecology. Ecology, 73, 1942-1968.

Liess, M. & Schulz, R. (1999) Linking insecticide contamination and population response in an agricultural stream. Environmental Toxicology and Chemistry, 18, 1948-1955.

Lindenmayer, D.B., Fischer, J. & Cunningham, R.B. (2005) Native vegetation cover thresholds associated with species responses. Biological Conservation, 124, 311-316.

Lindenmayer, D.B. & Franklin, J.F. (2002) Conserving forest biodiversity: a comprehensive multi-scaled approach. Island Press, Washington, DC.

Liu, J., Daily, G.C., Ehrlich, P.R. & Luck, G.W. (2003) Effects of household dynamics on resource consumption and biodiversity. Nature, 421, 530-533.

Lookingbill, T.R., Carter, S.L., Gorsira, B. & Kingdon, C. (2008) Using landscape analysis to evaluate ecological impacts of battlefield restoration. Park Science, 25, article 17.

Lookingbill, T.R., Gardner, R.H., Ferrari, J.R. & Keller, C.E. (2010) Combining a dispersal model with network theory to assess habitat connectivity. Ecological Applications, 20, 427-441.

Lowrance, R., Todd, R., Fail Jr, J., Hendrickson Jr, O., Leonard, R. & Asmussen, L. (1984) Riparian forests as nutrient filters in agricultural watersheds. BioScience, 34, 374–377.

Luck, G.W. (2007) A review of the relationships between human population density and biodiversity. Biological Reviews, 82, 607-645.

Lussier, S.M., Enser, R.W., Dasilva, S.N. & Charpentier, M. (2006) Effects of habitat disturbance from residential development on breeding bird communities in riparian corridors. Environmental Management, 38, 504-521.

Maestas, J.D., Knight, R.L. & Gilgert, W.C. (2003) Biodiversity across a rural land-use gradient. Conservation Biology, 17, 1425-1434.

Mainstone, C.P. & Parr, W. (2002) Phosphorus in rivers--ecology and management. The Science of the Total Environment, 282, 25-47.

Mann, C.C. (2005) 1491: New revelations of the Americas before Columbus. Alfred A. Knopf, NY.

Mantyka-pringle, C.S., Martin, T.G. & Rhodes, J.R. (2012) Interactions between climate and habitat loss effects on biodiversity: a systematic review and meta-analysis. Global Change Biology, 18, 1239–1252.

Maridet, L., Wasson, J.G., Philippe, M. & Amoros, C. (1995) Benthic organic matter dynamics in three streams: riparian vegetation or bed morphology control? Archiv für Hydrobiologie, 132, 415-425.

Martin, T.L., Kaushik, N.K., Trevors, J.T. & Whiteley, H.R. (1999) Review: denitrification in temperate climate riparian zones. Water, Air, & Soil Pollution, 111, 171 186.

Mattson, D.J., Knight, R.R. & Blanchard, B.M. (1987) The effects of developments and primary roads on grizzly bear habitat use in Yellowstone National Park, Wyoming. International Conference on Bear Research and Management, 7, 259-273.

Mazerolle, D.F. & Hobson, K.A. (2003) Do ovenbirds (*Seiurus aurocapillus*) avoid boreal forest edges? A spatiotemporal analysis in an agricultural landscape. Auk, 120, 152-162.

McDonnell, M.J. & Hahs, A.K. (2008) The use of gradient analysis studies in advancing our understanding of the ecology of urbanizing landscapes: current status and future directions. Landscape Ecology, 23, 1143-1155.

McGarigal, K. & Marks, B.J. (1995) FRAGSTATS. Spatial pattern analysis program for quantifying landscape structure. Version 2.0.

McIntyre, S. & Hobbs, R.J. (1999) A framework for conceptualizing human effects on landscapes and its relevance to management and research models. Conservation Biology, 13, 1282–1292.

McIntyre, S. & Hobbs, R.J. (2000) Human impacts on landscapes: matrix condition and management priorities. Nature Conservation 5: Nature Conservation in Production Environments. (eds J. Craig, D.A. Saunders & N. Mitchell), pp. 301-307. Chipping Norton, NSW, Surrey Beatty.

McKinney, M.L. (2002) Urbanization, biodiversity, and conservation. BioScience, 52, 883–890.

McLellan, B.N. & Shackleton, D.M. (1988) Grizzly bears and resource-extraction industries: effects of roads on behaviour, habitat use and demography. Journal of Applied Ecology, 25, 451-460.

Merelender, A.M., Reed, S.E. & Heise, K.L. (2009) Exurban development influences woodland bird composition. Landscape and Urban Planning, 92, 255-263.

Merriam, G. (1984) Connectivity: a fundamental ecological characteristic of landscape pattern. Proceedings First international seminar on methodology in landscape ecological research and planning. (eds J. Brandt & P. Agger), pp. 5-15. International Association for Landscape Ecology. Roskilde University.

Metzgar, L.H. & Bader, M. (1992) Large mammal predators in the northern Rockies: grizzly bears and their habitat. Northwest Environmental Journal, 8, 231-233.

Miller, J.R. & Hobbs, R.J. (2002) Conservation where people live and work. Conservation Biology, 16, 330-337.

Miller, J.R., Wiens, J.A., Hobbs, N.T. & Theobald, D.M. (2003) The effect of human settlement on bird communities in lowland riparian areas of Colorado (USA). Ecological Applications, 13, 1041-1059.

Miller, M.E. (2005) The Structure and Functioning of Dryland Ecosystems-conceptual Models to Inform Long-term Ecological Monitoring. USGS Scientific Investigations Report 2005-5197.

Monahan, W.B. & Gross, J.E. (2012) Upstream Landscape Dynamics of US National Parks with Implications for Water Quality and Watershed Management. Sustainable Natural Resources Management, Abiud Kaswamila (Ed.), InTech. ISBN: 978-953-307-670-6.

Monahan, W.B. & Hijmans, R.J. (2008) Ecophysiological constraints shape autumn migratory response to climate change in the North American field sparrow. Biology Letters, 4, 595-598.

Morley, S.A. & Karr, J.R. (2002) Assessing and restoring the health of urban streams in the Puget Sound basin. Conservation Biology, 16, 1498-1509.

Muradian, R. (2001) Ecological thresholds: a survey. Ecological Economics, 38, 7-24.

Murray, S.N., Ambrose, R.F., Bohnsack, J.A., Botsford, L.W., Carr, M.H., Davis, G.E., Dayton, P.K., Gotshall, D., Gunderson, D.R., Hixon, M.A., Lubchenco, J., Mangel, M., MacCall, A., McArdle, D.A., Ogden, J.C., Roughgarden, J., Starr, R.M., Tegner, M.J. & Yoklavich, M.M. (1999) No-take reserve networks: protection for fishery populations and marine ecosystems. Fisheries, 24, 11-25.

Naidoo, R. & Adamowicz, W.L. (2001) Effects of economic prosperity on numbers of threatened species. Conservation Biology, 15, 1021–1029.

Nassauer, J.I. (2005) Using cultural knowledge to make new landscape patterns. Issues and Perspectives in Landscape Ecology. (eds J.A. Wiens & M.R. Moss), pp. 274-280. Cambridge University Press.

National Academy of Public Administration. (2010) An Independent Review of the National Park Service's Natural Resource Stewardship and Science Directorate. National Academy of Public Administration. Available at www.napawash.org.

National Gap Analysis Program. (2011) Standards and methods manual for state data stewards. Available at http://gapanalysis.usgs.gov.

National Oceanic and Atmospheric Administration. (2008) Framework for the national system of marine protected areas of the United States of America. National Marine Protected Areas Center, NOAA, Maryland.

National Oceanic and Atmospheric Administration. (2011) The National System of MPAs: Analysis of National System Sites (March 2011). National Marine Protected Areas Center, NOAA, Maryland.

National Park Service. (1999) Natural Resource Challenge: The National Park Service's Action Plan for Preserving Natural Resources.

National Park Service. (2000) General Management Plan for Whitman Mission National Historic Site. Whitman Mission National Historic Site, Walla Walla, WA.

National Park Service. (2010) National Park Service Climate Change Response Strategy. National Park Service Climate Change Response Program, Fort Collins, Colorado.

National Park Service. (2011) A Call to Action: Preparing for a Second Century of Stewardship and Engagement. Available at http://www.nps.gov/calltoaction/.

Naugle, D.E., Johnson, R.R., Estey, M.E. & Higgins, K.F. (2001) A landscape approach to conserving wetland bird habitat in the prairie pothole region of eastern South Dakota. Wetlands, 21, 1-17.

Naveh, Z. (1995) Interactions of landscapes and cultures. Landscape and Urban Planning, 32, 43-54.

Newmark, W.D. (1986) Species-area relationship and its determinants for mammals in western North American national parks. Biological Journal of the Linnean Society, 28, 83-98.

Newmark, W.D. (1987) A land-bridge island perspective on mammalian extinctions in western North American parks. Nature, 325, 430–432.

Nickel, A.M., Danielson, B.J. & Moloney, K.A. (2003) Wooded habitat edges as refugia from microtine herbivory in tallgrass prairies. Oikos, 100, 525-533.

Niyogi, D.K., Simon, K.S. & Townsend, C.R. (2003) Breakdown of tussock grass in streams along a gradient of agricultural development in New Zealand. Freshwater Biology, 48, 1698-1708.

Noe, G.B. & Hupp, C.R. (2009) Retention of riverine sediment and nutrient loads by Coastal Plain floodplains. Ecosystems, 12, 728-746.

Noss, R.F. (1990) Indicators for monitoring biodiversity: a hierarchical approach. Conservation Biology, 4, 355-364.

Noss, R.F. (1991) A critical review of the U.S. Fish and Wildlife Service's proposal to establish a captive breeding population of Florida panthers, with emphasis on the population reestablishment issue. Report to the Fund for Animals, Washington, DC.

Noss, R.F. (1993) A conservation plan for the Oregon Coast Range: some preliminary suggestions. Natural Areas Journal, 13, 276-290.

Nuclear Regulatory Commission. (2001) Marine Protected Areas: tools for sustaining ocean ecosystems. National Academy Press, Washington, DC.

Odell, E.A. & Knight, R.L. (2001) Songbird and medium-sized mammal communities associated with exurban development in Pitkin County, Colorado. Conservation Biology, 15, 1143-1150.

Olivera, F. & DeFee, B.B. (2007) Urbanization and its effect on runoff in the whiteoak bayou watershed, Texas. Journal of the American Water Resources Association, 43, 170–182.

O'Neill, R.V., Hunsaker, C.T., Jones, K.B., Riitters, K.H., Wickham, J.D., Schwartz, P.M., Goodman, I.A., Jackson, B.L. & Baillargeon, W.S. (1997) Monitoring environmental quality at the landscape scale. BioScience, 47, 513–519.

O'Neill, R.V., Krummel, J.R., Gardner, R.H., Sugihara, G., Jackson, B., DeAngelis, D.L., Milne, B.T., Turner, M.G., Zygmunt, B., Christensen, S.W., Dale, V.H. & Graham, R.L. (1988) Indices of landscape pattern. Landscape Ecology, 1, 153-162.

Orbach, R. (1986) Dynamics of fractal networks. Science, 231, 814-819.

Osborne, L.L. & Kovacic, D.A. (1993) Riparian vegetated buffer strips in water-quality restoration and stream management. Freshwater Biology, 29, 243-58.

Ostapowicz, K., Vogt, P., Riitters, K.H., Kozak, J. & Estreguil, C. (2008) Impact of scale on morphological spatial pattern of forest. Landscape Ecology, 23, 1107-1117.

Panek, J., Saah, D. & Esperanza, A. (2012) Air Quality. Appendix in: National Park Service. 2012. A natural resource condition assessment for Sequoia and Kings Canyon national parks. Natural Resource Report NPS/SEKI/NRR-2012/XXX. Eds. J.A. Panek and C.A. Sydoriak. National Park Service, Fort Collins, CO.

Parker, M. & Mac Nally, R. (2002) Habitat loss and the habitat fragmentation threshold: an experimental evaluation of impacts on richness and total abundances using grassland invertebrates. Biological Conservation, 105, 217-229.

Parks, S.A. & Harcourt, A.H. (2002) Reserve size, local human density, and mammalian extinctions in US protected areas. Conservation Biology, 16, 800-808.

Parris, K.M. & Schneider, A. (2009) Impacts of traffic noise and traffic volume on birds of roadside habitats. Ecology and Society, 14, 29.

Paul, M.J. & Meyer, J.L. (2001) Streams in the urban landscape. Annual Review of Ecological Systems, 32, 333-365.

Pautasso, M. (2007) Scale dependence of the correlation between human population presence and vertebrate and plant species richness. Ecology Letters, 10, 16-24.

Pearson, S.M., Turner, M.G., Gardner, R.H. & O'Neill, R.V. (1996) An organism-based perspective of habitat fragmentation. Biodiversity in Managed Landscapes: Theory and Practice. pp. 77-95. Oxford University Press.

Peery, C.A., Kavanagh, K.L. & Scott, J.M. (2003) Pacific salmon: setting ecologically defensible recovery goals. BioScience, 53, 622-623.

Piekielek, N.B., Davis, C. & Hansen, A.J. (2010a) PALMS Standard Operating Procedure: Analyzing Protected-area Centered Ecosystems. Inventory and Monitoring Program, Natural Resource Program Center, National Park Service, Fort Collins, CO.

Piekielek, N.B., Davis, C. & Hansen, A.J. (2010b) PALMS Standard Operating Procedure: Estimating Protected-area Centered Ecosystems. Inventory and Monitoring Program, Natural Resource Program Center, National Park Service, Fort Collins, CO.

Poff, N.L.R. & Allan, J.D. (1995) Functional organization of stream fish assemblages in relation to hydrological variability. Ecology, 76, 606–627.

Poff, N.L.R., Bledsoe, B.P. & Cuhaciyan, C.O. (2006) Hydrologic variation with land use across the contiguous United States: Geomorphic and ecological consequences for stream ecosystems. Geomorphology, 79, 264-285.

Ponsero, A. & Joly, P. (1998) Clutch size, egg survival and migration distance in the agile frog (*Rana dalmatina*) in a floodplain. Archiv für Hydrobiologie, 142, 343–352.

Pope, S.E., Fahrig, L. & Merriam, H.G. (2000) Landscape complementation and metapopulation effects on leopard frog populations. Ecology, 81, 2498–2508.

Preisler, H.K., Ager, A.A. & Wisdom, M.J. (2006) Statistical methods for analysing responses of wildlife to human disturbance. Journal of Applied Ecology, 43, 164-172.

Pressey, R.I., Cowling, R.M. & Rouget, M. (2003) Formulating conservation targets for biodiversity pattern and process in the Cape Floristic Region, South Africa. Biological Conservation, 112, 99-127.

Prugh, L.R., Hodges, K.E., Sinclair, A.R.E. & Brashares, J.S. (2008) Effect of habitat area and isolation on fragmented animal populations. Proceedings of the National Academy of Sciences of the United States of America, 105, 20770-20775.

Quinn, J.M. (2000) Effects of pastoral development. New Zealand Stream Invertebrates: Ecology and Implications for Management. (eds K.J. Collier & M.J. Winterbourn), pp. 208-29. The New Zealand Limnological Society (NZFSS), Christchurch.

Radeloff, V.C., Hammer, R.B., Stewart, S.I., Fried, J.S., Holcomb, S.S. & McKeefry, J.F. (2005) The wildland-urban interface in the United States. Ecological Applications, 15, 799–805.

Radeloff, V.C., Hammer, R.B., Voss, P.R., Hagen, A.E., Field, D.R. & Mladenoff, D.J. (2001) Human demographic trends and landscape level forest management in the northwest Wisconsin Pine Barrens. Forest Science, 47, 229–241.

Radeloff, V.C., Stewart, S.I., Hawbaker, T.J., Gimmi, U., Pidgeon, A.M., Flather, C.H., Hammer, R.B. & Helmers, D.P. (2010) Housing growth in and near United States protected areas limits their conservation value. Proceedings of the National Academy of Sciences of the United States of America, 107, 940-945.

Radford, J.Q. & Bennett, A.F. (2007) The relative importance of landscape properties for woodland birds in agricultural environments. Journal of Applied Ecology, 44, 737-747.

Radford, J.Q., Bennett, A.F. & Cheers, G.J. (2005) Landscape-level thresholds of habitat cover for woodland-dependent birds. Biological Conservation, 124, 317-337.

Reijnen, R. & Foppen, R. (2006) Impact of road traffic on breeding bird populations. The Ecology of Transportation: Managing Mobility for the Environment. (eds J. Davenport & J.L. Davenport), pp. 255-274. Springer.

Reijnen, R., Foppen, R. & Meeuwsen, H. (1996) The effects of traffic on the density of breeding birds in Dutch agricultural grasslands. Biological Conservation, 75, 255-260.

Rempel, R. (2009) Patch Analyst. Center for Northern Forest Ecosystem Research, Ontario.

Rheindt, F.E. (2003) The impact of roads on birds: Does song frequency play a role in determining susceptibility to noise pollution? Journal fur Ornithologie, 144, 295-306.

Ries, L. & Fagan, W.F. (2003) Habitat edges as a potential ecological trap for an insect predator. Ecological Entomology, 28, 567-572.

Ries, L., Fletcher, Jr., R.J., Battin, J. & Sisk, T.D. (2004) Ecological responses to habitat edges: mechanisms, models, and variability explained. Annual Review of Ecology, Evolution, and Systematics, 35, 491-522.

Ries, L. & Sisk, T.D. (2004) A predictive model of edge effects. Ecology, 85, 2917–2926.

Riitters, K.H. (2011) Spatial patterns of land cover in the United States: a technical document supporting the Forest Service 2010 RPA Assessment. Gen. Tech. Rep. SRS-136.

Riitters, K.H., O'Neill, R.V., Hunsaker, C.T., Wickham, J., Yankee, D.H., Timmins, S.P., Jones, K.B. & Jackson, B.L. (1995) A factor analysis of landscape pattern and structure metrics. Landscape Ecology, 10, 23-39.

Riitters, K.H., O'Neill, R.V. & Jones, K.B. (1997) Assessing habitat suitability at multiple scales: A landscape-level approach. Biological Conservation, 81, 191-202.

Riitters, K.H., Vogt, P. & Soille, P. (2007) Neutral model analysis of landscape patterns from mathematical morphology. Landscape Ecology, 22, 1033-1043.

Riitters, K.H., Vogt, P., Soille, P. & Estreguil, C. (2009b) Landscape patterns from mathematical morphology on maps with contagion. Landscape Ecology, 24, 699-709.

Riitters, K.H. & Wickham, J.D. (2003) How far to the nearest road? Frontiers in Ecology and the Environment, 1, 125–129.

Riitters, K.H., Wickham, J.D., O'Neill, R.V., Jones, K.B., Smith, E.R., Coulston, J.W., Wade, T.G. & Smith, J.H. (2002) Fragmentation of continental United States forests. Ecosystems, 5, 815–822.

Riitters, K.H., Wickham, J.D. & Wade, T.G. (2009a) An indicator of forest dynamics using a shifting landscape mosaic. Ecological Indicators, 9, 107-117.

Ritchie, L.E., Betts, M.G., Forbes, G. & Vernes, K. (2009) Effects of landscape composition and configuration on northern flying squirrels in a forest mosaic. Forest Ecology and Management, 257, 1920-1929.

Rodrigues, A. & Gaston, K. (2001) How large do reserve networks need to be? Ecology Letters, 4, 602-609.

Roedenbeck, I.A., Fahrig, L., Findlay, C.S., Houlahan, J.E., Jaeger, J.A.G., Klar, N., Kramer-Schadt, S. & Grift, E.A. van der. (2007) The Rauischholzhausen agenda for road ecology. Ecology and Society, 12, 11.

Rolland, R.M. (2000) A review of chemically induced alterations in thyroid and vitamin A status from field studies of wildlife and fish. Journal of Wildlife Diseases, 36, 615-635.

Rompré, G., Robinson, W.D., Desrochers, A. & Angehr, G. (2009) Predicting declines in avian species richness under nonrandom patterns of habitat loss in a neotropical landscape. Ecological Applications, 19, 1614-1627.

Rost, G.R. & Bailey, J.A. (1979) Distribution of mule deer and elk in relation to roads. Journal of Wildlife Management, 43, 634–641.

Sabo, J.L., Sinha, T., Bowling, L.C., Schoups, G.H.W., Wallender, W.W., Campana, M.E., Cherkauer, K.A., Fuller, P.L., Graf, W.L., Hopmans, J.W., Kominoski, J.S., Taylor, C., Trimble, S.W., Webb, R.H. & Wohl, E.E. (2010) Reclaiming freshwater sustainability in the Cadillac Desert. Proceedings of the National Academy of Sciences of the United States of America, 107, 21263-21270.

Salo, L.F. (2005) Red brome (*Bromus rubens* subsp. *madritensis*) in North America: possible modes for early introductions, subsequent spread. Biological Invasions, 7, 165-180.

Saunders, S.C., Mislivets, M.R., Chen, J.Q. & Cleland, D.T. (2002) Effects of roads on landscape structure within nested ecological units of the Northern Great Lakes Region, USA. Biological Conservation, 103, 209-225.

Schueler, T.R. (1994) The importance of imperviousness. Watershed Protection Techniques, 1, 100-111.

Schulte, L.A., Mladenoff, D.J., Crow, T.R., Merrick, L.C. & Cleland, D.T. (2007) Homogenization of northern U.S. Great Lakes forests due to land use. Landscape Ecology, 22, 1089-1103.

Schulz, R. & Liess, M. (1999) A field study of the effects of agriculturally derived insecticide input on stream macroinvertebrate dynamics. Aquatic Toxicology, 46, 155-176.

Scott, J.M., Davis, F., Csuti, B., Noss, R.F., Butterfield, B., Groves, C., Anderson, H., Caicco, S., D'Erchia, F. & Edwards Jr, T.C. (1993) Gap analysis: a geographic approach to protection of biological diversity. Wildlife Monographs, 123, 3–41.

Seabloom, E.W., Dobson, A.P. & Stoms, D.M. (2002) Extinction rates under nonrandom patterns of habitat loss. Proceedings of the National Academy of Sciences of the United States of America, 99, 11229-11234.

Shandas, V. & Alberti, M. (2009) Exploring the role of vegetation fragmentation on aquatic conditions: Linking upland with riparian areas in Puget Sound lowland streams. Landscape and Urban Planning, 90, 66-75.

Sherwood, B., Cutler, D.F. & Burton, J.A. (2003) Wildlife and roads: the ecological impact. Imperial College Press, London, UK.

Sisk, T.D., Launer, A.E. & Switky, K.R. (1994) Identifying extinction threats. BioScience, 44, 592-604.

Soille, P. & Vogt, P. (2009) Morphological segmentation of binary patterns. Pattern Recognition Letters, 30, 456-459.

Solomon, M., Van Jaarsveld, A.S., Biggs, H.C. & Knight, M.H. (2003) Conservation targets for viable species assemblages? Biodiversity and Conservation, 12, 2435-2441.

Soulé, M.E., Estes, J.A., Miller, B. & Honnold, D.L. (2005) Strongly interacting species: conservation policy, management, and ethics. BioScience, 55, 168-176.

Soulé, M.E. & Sanjavan, M.A. (1998) Conservation targets: do they help? Science, 179, 2060-2061.

Southern Sierra Partnership. (2010) Climate-adapted Conservation Plan for the Southern Sierra Nevada and Tehachapi Mountains. San Francisco, CA.

Spellerberg, I.F. (1998) Ecological effects of roads and traffic: a literature review. Global Ecology and Biogeography Letters, 7, 317-333.

Stauffer, D. (1985) Introduction to percolation theory. Taylor and Francis, Philadelphia, PA.

Stauffer, J.C., Goldstein, R.M. & Newman, R.M. (2000) Relationship of wooded riparian zones and runoff potential to fish community composition in agricultural streams. Canadian Journal of Fisheries and Aquatic Sciences, 57, 307-316.

Stephenson, N.L. (1990) Climatic control of vegetation distribution: the role of the water balance. American Naturalist, 135, 649–670.

Story, M., Svancara, L.K., Curdts, T., Gross, J. & McAninch, S. (2009) A Comparison of Available National-Level Land Cover Data for National Park Applications. National Park Service, Natural Resource Program Center, Fort Collins, CO.

Stranko, S.A., Hilderbrand, R.H., Morgan II, R.P., Staley, M.W., Becker, A.J., Roseberry-Lincoln, A., Perry, E.S. & Jacobson, P.T. (2008) Brook trout declines with land cover and temperature changes in Maryland. North American Journal of Fisheries Management, 28, 1223-1232.

Suding, K.N. & Hobbs, R.J. (2009) Threshold models in restoration and conservation: a developing framework. Trends in Ecology & Evolution, 24, 271-279.

Sujetovienė, G. (2010) Road traffic pollution effects on epiphytic lichens. Ekologija, 56, 64-71.

Summerville, K.S. & Crist, T.O. (2001) Effects of experimental habitat fragmentation on patch use by butterflies and skippers (Lepidoptera). Ecology, 82, 1360–1370.

Sutherland, A.B., Meyer, J.L. & Gardiner, E.P. (2002) Effects of land cover on sediment regime and fish assemblage structure in four southern Appalachian streams. Freshwater Biology, 47, 1791-1805.

Sutherland, W.J. & Anderson, C.W. (1993) Predicting the distribution of individuals and the consequences of habitat loss: the role of prey depletion. Journal of Theoretical Biology, 160, 271-279.

Svancara, L.K. (2010) Ecological content and context of the National Park System. Ph.D. Dissertation, University of Idaho, Moscow, ID.

Svancara, L.K., Brannon, R., Scott, J.M., Groves, C.R., Noss, R.F. & Pressey, R.L. (2005) Policy-driven versus evidence-based conservation: a review of political targets and biological needs. BioScience, 55, 989–995.

Svancara, L.K., Scott, J.M., Loveland, T.R. & Pidgorna, A.B. (2009) Assessing the landscape context and conversion risk of protected areas using satellite data products. Remote Sensing of Environment, 113, 1357-1369.

Tallmon, D.A., Jules, E.S., Radke, N.J. & Mills, L.S. (2003) Of mice and men and trillium: cascading effects of forest fragmentation. Ecological Applications, 13, 1193–1203.

Taylor, P.D., Fahrig, L., Henein, K. & Merriam, G. (1993) Connectivity is a vital element of landscape structure. Oikos, 73, 43-48.

Theobald, D.M. (2003) Targeting conservation action through assessment of protection and exurban threats. Conservation Biology, 17, 1624-1637.

Theobald, D.M. (2004) Placing exurban land-use change in a human modification framework. Frontiers in Ecology and the Environment, 2, 139–144.

Theobald, D.M. (2005) Landscape patterns of exurban growth in the USA from 1980 to 2020. Ecology and Society, 10, 32.

Theobald, D.M. (2006) Exploring the functional connectivity of landscapes using landscape networks. Connectivity Conservation. (eds K.R. Crooks & M. Sanjayan), pp. 416-444. Cambridge University Press, NY.

Theobald, D.M., Crooks, K.R. & Norman, J.B. (2011) Assessing effects of land use on landscape connectivity: loss and fragmentation of western U.S. forests. Ecological Applications, 21, 2445–2458.

Theobald, D.M., Goetz, S.J., Norman, J.B. & Jantz, P. (2009) Watersheds at risk to increased impervious surface cover in the conterminous United States. Journal of Hydrologic Engineering, 14, 362.

Theobald, D.M., Reed, S.E., Fields, K. & Soulé, M. (2012) Connecting natural landscapes using a landscape permeability model to prioritize conservation activities in the United States. Conservation Letters, 5, 123–133.

Thompson III, F.R., Donovan, T.M., DeGraaf, R.M., Faaborg, J. & Robinson, S.K. (2002) A multi-scale perspective of the effects of forest fragmentation on birds in eastern forests. Studies in Avian Biology, 25, 8-19.

Thompson III, F.R., Robinson, S.K., Donovan, T.M., Faaborg, J., Whitehead, D.R. & Larsen, D.R. (2000) Biogeographic, landscape, and local factors affecting cowbird abundance and host parasitism levels. Ecology and Management of Cowbirds and their Hosts. (eds J.M.N. Smith, T.L. Cook, S.I. Rothstein, S.K. Robinson & S.G. Sealy), pp. 271-279. University of Texas Press, Austin.

Thurber, J.M., Peterson, R.O., Drummer, T.D. & Thomasma, S.A. (1994) Gray wolf response to refuge boundaries and roads in Alaska. Wildlife Society Bulletin, 22, 61–68.

Tikka, P.M., Koski, P.S., Kivelä, R.A. & Kuitunen, M.T. (2000) Can grassland plant communities be preserved on road and railway verges? Applied Vegetation Science, 3, 25-32.

Tischendorf, L., Bender, D.J. & Fahrig, L. (2003) Evaluation of patch isolation metrics in mosaic landscapes for specialist vs. generalist dispersers. Landscape Ecology, 18, 41–50.

Tischendorf, L. & Fahrig, L. (2000) On the usage and measurement of landscape connectivity. Oikos, 90, 7-19.

Townsend, P.A., Lookingbill, T.R., Kingdon, C.C. & Gardner, R.H. (2009) Spatial pattern analysis for monitoring protected areas. Remote Sensing of Environment, 113, 1410-1420.

Trombulak, S.C. & Frissell, C.A. (2000) Review of ecological effects of roads on terrestrial and aquatic communities. Conservation Biology, 14, 18–30.

Trzcinski, M.K., Fahrig, L. & Merriam, G. (1999) Independent effects of forest cover and fragmentation on the distribution of forest breeding birds. Ecological Applications, 9, 586–593.

Turner, M.G. (1989) Landscape ecology: the effect of pattern on process. Annual Review of Ecology and Systematics, 20, 171-197.

Turner, M.G. (2005) Landscape ecology: what is the state of the science? Annual Review of Ecology, Evolution, and Systematics, 36, 319-344.

Turner, M.G. & Gardner, R.H. (1991) Quantitative methods in landscape ecology: an introduction. Quantitative Methods in Landscape Ecology. pp. 3-14. Springer-Verlag New York, NY.

Turner, W., Spector, S., Gardiner, N., Fladeland, M., Sterling, E. & Steininger, M. (2003) Remote sensing for biodiversity science and conservation. Trends in Ecology & Evolution, 18, 306-314.

Umetsu, F., Metzger, J.P. & Pardini, R. (2008) Importance of estimating matrix quality for modeling species distribution in complex tropical landscapes: a test with Atlantic forest small mammals. Ecography, 31, 359-370.

United Nations Statistics Division. (2010) Millennium Development Goals Indicators. United Nations.

US Army Corps of Engineers. (2010) National Inventory of Dams. http://nid.usace.army.mil.

US Fish and Wildlife Service. (2005) Final Critical Habitat for the California Tiger Salamander (*Ambystoma californiense*) - Central Population. US Fish and Wildlife Service, Sacramento, CA.

US Fish and Wildlife Service. (2010a) LCC Information Bulletin #1: Form and Function. Office of the Science Advisor, US Fish and Wildlife Service.

US Fish and Wildlife Service. (2010b) LCC Information Bulletin #2: Developing the National Geographic Framework. Office of the Science Advisor, US Fish and Wildlife Service.

US General Accounting Office. (1994) Activities outside park borders have caused damage to resources and will likely cause more. US Government Printing Office, GAO/RCED-94-59.

Utz, R.M., Hilderbrand, R.H. & Boward, D.M. (2009) Identifying regional differences in threshold responses of aquatic invertebrates to land cover gradients. Ecological Indicators, 9, 556-567.

Van Buskirk, J. (2005) Local and landscape influence on amphibian occurrence and abundance. Ecology, 86, 1936-1947.

Vergara, P.M. (2011) Matrix-dependent corridor effectiveness and the abundance of forest birds in fragmented landscapes. Landscape Ecology, 26, 1085-1096.

Vogelmann, J.E., Howard, S.M., Yang, L., Larson, C.R., Wylie, B.K. & Van Driel, J.N. (2001) Completion of the 1990's National Land Cover Data Set for the conterminous United States. Photogrammetric Engineering and Remote Sensing, 67, 650-662.

Vogt, P., Ferrari, J.R., Lookingbill, T.R., Gardner, R.H., Riitters, K.H. & Ostapowicz, K. (2009) Mapping functional connectivity. Ecological Indicators, 9, 64-71.

Vogt, P., Riitters, K.H., Estreguil, C., Kozak, J., Wade, T.G. & Wickham, J.D. (2007a) Mapping spatial patterns with morphological image processing. Landscape Ecology, 22, 171-177.

Vogt, P., Riitters, K.H. & Iwanowski, M. (2007b) Mapping landscape corridors. Ecological Indicators, 7, 481-488.

Vranckx, G., Jacquemyn, H., Muys, B. & Honnay, O. (2012) Meta-analysis of susceptibility of woody plants to loss of genetic diversity through habitat fragmentation. Conservation Biology, 26, 228–237.

Wade, A.A. & Theobald, D.M. (2009) Residential development encroachment on US protected areas. Conservation Biology, 24, 151-161.

Wade, T.G., Riitters, K.H., Wickham, J.D. & Jones, K.B. (2003) Distribution and causes of global forest fragmentation. Conservation Ecology, 7, 7.

Waisanen, P.J. & Bliss, N.B. (2002) Changes in population and agricultural land in conterminous United States counties, 1790-1997. Global Biogeochemical Cycles, 16, 84-91.

Walker, D.A. & Everett, K.R. (1987) Road dust and its environmental impact on Alaskan taiga and tundra. Arctic and Alpine Research, 19, 479-489.

Walker, S., Price, R. & Stephens, R.T.T. (2008) An index of risk as a measure of biodiversity conservation achieved through land reform. Conservation Biology, 22, 48-59.

Walser, C.A. & Bart, H.L. (1999) Influence of agriculture on in-stream habitat and fish community structure in Piedmont watersheds of the Chattahoochee River System. Ecology of Freshwater Fish, 8, 237-246.

Walsh, C.J., Sharpe, A.K., Breen, P.F. & Sonneman, J.A. (2001) Effects of urbanization on streams of the Melbourne region, Victoria, Australia. I. Benthic macroinvertebrate communities. Freshwater Biology, 46, 535-551.

Wang, L., Lyons, J., Kanehl, P. & Bannerman, R. (2001) Impacts of urbanization on stream habitat and fish across multiple spatial scales. Environmental Management, 28, 255–266.

Ward Jr, J.P., Gutierrez, R.J. & Noon, B.R. (1998) Habitat selection by Northern Spotted Owls: the consequences of prey selection and distribution. Condor, 100, 79-92.

Ward, J.V. & Stanford, J.A. (1979) The Ecology of Regulated Streams. Plenum Press, New York.

Watt, A.S. (1947) Pattern and process in the plant community. Journal of Ecology, 35, 1-22.

Wheeler, A.P., Angermeier, P.L. & Rosenberger, A.E. (2005) Impacts of new highways and subsequent landscape urbanization on stream habitat and biota. Reviews in Fisheries Science, 13, 141–164.

Whittaker, R.H. (1967) Gradient analysis of vegetation. Biological Reviews, 42, 207-264.

Whittington, J., St. Clair, C.C. & Mercer, G. (2005) Spatial responses of wolves to roads and trails in mountain valleys. Ecological Applications, 15, 543-553.

Wickham, J.D., Riitters, K.H., Wade, T.G. & Coulston, J.W. (2007) Temporal change in forest fragmentation at multiple scales. Landscape Ecology, 22, 481-489.

Wiens, J.A. (1989) Spatial scaling in ecology. Functional Ecology, 3, 385-397.

Wiens, J.A., Rotenberry, J.T. & Van Horne, B. (1987) Habitat occupancy patterns of North American shrubsteppe birds: the effects of spatial scale. Oikos, 48, 132-147.

Wiens, J.A., Schooley, R.L. & Weeks Jr, R.D. (1997) Patchy landscapes and animal movements: do beetles percolate? Oikos, 78, 257–264.

Wiersma, Y.F., Nudds, T.D. & Rivard, D.H. (2004) Models to distinguish effects of landscape patterns and human population pressures associated with species loss in Canadian national parks. Landscape Ecology, 19, 773-786.

Wilcove, D.S., Rothstein, D., Dubow, J., Phillips, A. & Losos, E. (1998) Quantifying threats to imperiled species in the United States. BioScience, 48, 607-615.

Williams, C.B. (1943) Area and number of species. Nature, 152, 264-267.

With, K.A. (2005) Landscape conservation: a new paradigm for the conservation of biodiversity. Issues and Perspectives in Landscape Ecology. (eds J.A. Wiens & M.R. Moss), pp. 238-247. Cambridge University Press.

With, K.A. & Crist, T.O. (1995) Critical thresholds in species' responses to landscape structure. Ecology, 76, 2446–2459.

With, K.A. & King, A.W. (1999) Extinction thresholds for species in fractal landscapes. Conservation Biology, 13, 314–326.

With, K.A., Pavuk, D.M., Worchuck, J.L., Oates, R.K. & Fisher, J.L. (2002) Threshold effects of landscape structure on biological control in agroecosystems. Ecological Applications, 12, 52–65.

Wittemyer, G., Elsen, P., Bean, W.T., Burton, A.C.O. & Brashares, J.S. (2008) Accelerated human population growth at protected area edges. Science, 321, 123-126.

Wood, P.J. & Armitage, P.D. (1997) Biological effects of fine sediment in the lotic environment. Environmental Management, 21, 203-217.

Woodroffe, R. (2000) Predators and people: using human densities to interpret declines of large carnivores. Animal Conservation, 3, 165-173.

Woodward, D.F., Goldstein, J.N., Farag, A.M. & Brumbaugh, W.G. (1997) Cutthroat trout avoidance of metals and conditions characteristic of a mining waste site: Coeur d'Alene River, Idaho. Transactions of the American Fisheries Society, 126, 699-706.

Wright, R.G., Scott, J.M., Mann, S. & Murray, M. (2001) Identifying unprotected and potentially at risk plant communities in the western USA. Biological Conservation, 98, 97-106.

Zabel, C.J., McKelvey, K. & Ward Jr, J.P. (1995) Influence of primary prey on home-range size and habitat-use patterns of northern spotted owls (*Strix occidentalis caurina*). Canadian Journal of Zoology, 73, 433-439.

NPS 909/114195, May 2012